the JEWISH APPROACH to REPAIRING the WORLD (TIKKUN OLAM)

A Brief Introduction for CHRISTIANS

RABBI ELLIOT N. DORFF, PhD
WITH REVEREND CORY WILLSON

For People of All Faiths, All Backgrounds

JEWISH LIGHTS Publishing

Woodstock, Vermont

The Jewish Approach to Repairing the World (Tikkun Olam):
A Brief Introduction for Christians

2008 Quality Paperback Edition, First Printing
© 2008 by Rabbi Elliot N. Dorff

Library of Congress Cataloging-in-Publication Data
Dorff, Elliot N.
The Jewish approach to repairing the world (*tikkun olam*) : a brief introduction for Christians / Rabbi Elliot N. Dorff ; with Cory Willson.
p. cm.
Includes bibliographical references and index.
ISBN-13: 978-1-58023-349-1 (quality pbk.)
ISBN-10: 1-58023-349-X (quality pbk.)
1. Jewish ethics. 2. Jewish way of life. 3. Jewish families—Conduct of life. 4. Judaism—Relations—Christianity. 5. Christianity and other religions—Judaism. I. Willson, Cory. II. Title.
BJ1285.2.D668 2008
296.3'6—dc22
2008025719

Manufactured in the United States of America
Cover Design: Melanie Robinson

For People of All Faiths, All Backgrounds
Published by Jewish Lights Publishing
A Division of LongHill Partners, Inc.
Sunset Farm Offices, Route 4, P.O. Box 237
Woodstock, VT 05091
Tel: (802) 457-4000   Fax: (802) 457-4004
www.jewishlights.com

In honor of Richard Mouw,

president of Fuller Theological Seminary,
professor of philosophy at Fuller,
intelligently committed Dutch Reformed Christian,
active creator and participant in interfaith efforts of
    understanding and cooperation,
top-notch philosopher, wonderful friend,
a mensch who fixes the world each and every day,
a blessing to us all.

—∿—

Our Rabbis taught: [What blessing does one say] ... when one sees those of the nations of the world who are wise and learned? "[Praised are You, Lord our God, Sovereign of the universe], who has given of His wisdom to flesh and blood."

Babylonian Talmud, Berakhot 58a

CONTENTS

Preface   vii

Acknowledgments   x

Introduction   xiii

Part One: Repairing the World (*Tikkun Olam*) in Theory

  1. The Meaning and Significance of *Tikkun Olam*   3

  2. Why Should I Care? The Example of Caring
    for the Poor   11

Part Two: *Tikkun Olam* in Practice: Individuals and Society

  3. The Power of Words   61

  4. The Ministry of Presence   102

Part Three: *Tikkun Olam* in Practice: Families

  5. Duties of Spouses to Each Other   127

  6. Children's Duties to Their Parents   142

  7. Parents' Duties to Their Children   162

Part Four: Envisioning a World Shaped by *Tikkun Olam*

  8. Elements of the Traditional Jewish Vision
    of the Ideal World   181

Notes   197

Glossary   217

Suggestions for Further Reading   227

PREFACE

Tikkun olam—repairing the world. Quite a task! Yet this is precisely the goal that the Jewish tradition sets for our lives. This gives us a mission and thereby lends meaning to our lives. It also imposes a heavy burden on each of us every day. We may certainly take time to enjoy ourselves, our families, our work, and our play, but throughout our lives we must dedicate at least part of our time, energy, and resources to improving the lot of others.

Jews understand this almost instinctively. Surveys show that Jews feel in their bones that they have a duty as Jews to make this a better world, that this is the essence of what it means to be a Jew.

This book describes the roots in Jewish beliefs and laws of Judaism's commitment to improve the world. It explores *why* Judaism would have us engage in such activities, reasons that include but go far beyond a general humanitarian feeling or the hope that if you help others, others will in turn help you. It also describes *how* the Jewish tradition would have us seek to repair the world in some key ways.

The book is divided into four parts. Part One addresses the underlying theory of repairing the world (*tikkun olam*). Chapter 1 describes how the meaning of the term has developed over time and indicates related terms and concepts that Judaism has used for thousands of years to describe the duties we now identify as acts of *tikkun olam*. It also cites sources to demonstrate the great significance that classical Judaism ascribes to such activities. Chapter 2 then explores why any person, and why any Jew in particular, should care about the lot of someone else, using alleviating the circumstances of the poor as its example. It first addresses why we should be wary of helping the poor and then suggests reasons to nevertheless offer aid, the proper limits of such support, the duties of the poor, and the modes of assistance we should offer.

Part Two explores the theory and practice of Jewish *tikkun olam* in our social interactions. Chapter 3 deals with language—how we should speak to others and what we should avoid saying. Chapter 4 addresses our duties to assist others in their times of need and joy, such as providing health care to the sick, including the emotional support we must offer the ill by visiting them. This kind of communal support also extends to helping couples celebrate their weddings and families to mourn the loss of a loved one. Attending to the emotional needs of people in these situations constitutes a form of *tikkun olam*.

Part Three addresses *tikkun olam* within families. Chapter 5 considers the duties of spouses to each other, Chapter 6 describes Judaism's specification of filial duties, and Chapter 7 delineates Judaism's understanding of parental duties. In each case, the chapter cites traditional sources, but it also takes into account how modern society has evolved and explores how that might affect how we use traditional materials in approaching a given issue in our day.

Finally, Part Four describes Judaism's vision of the ideal world, the one toward which we should strive to repair our world. It includes some elements that are undoubtedly common to many religions' ideals—for example, peace and prosperity—but also some specifically Jewish components, such as ingathering of Jews living in other countries to Israel and spreading of knowledge of Torah to everyone.

A Guide to the Text

For the Hebrew Bible translations throughout this book, I use the *Tanakh: The Holy Scriptures* (Philadelphia: Jewish Publication Society, 1985). For the New Testament translations, I use the New Revised Standard Version.

I refer to the sages whose interpretations of the Hebrew Bible and discussions of the Oral Torah—that is, the traditions transmitted orally and in action from one generation to another—as the Rabbis with a capital R. These sages lived between the fifth century BCE (Before the Common Era) and the sixth century CE (Common Era). (The years of BCE = BC, and CE = AD, but Jews do not refer to these years with reference to Christ or "Our Lord," meaning Jesus, but instead use the religiously more neutral designations). The most important works that were produced in this period are (1) the Mishnah, the first collection of oral traditions, edited by Rabbi Judah, president of the Sanhedrin, in approximately 200 CE; (2) the Jerusalem (or Western, or Palestinian) Talmud, edited c. 400 CE; and (3) the Babylonian Talmud, edited c. 500 CE, both of which record continued discussions of the Bible and the Mishnah by the Rabbis in those two locales in the years after 200 CE until they were edited; and (4) the Midrash, consisting of rabbinic interpretations and expansions of both the legal and non-legal sections of the Bible. The largest work of Midrash is *Midrash Rabbah*, which consists of the Rabbis' interpretations of each of the books of the Torah (the Pentateuch, the Five Books of Moses) and some of the other biblical books read in the synagogue. They are designated as, for example, *Genesis Rabbah*, "the expanded, or great, Genesis." The two major codes of Jewish law are Maimonides's *Mishneh Torah* (1180 CE) and Joseph Karo's *Shulhan Arukh* (1565 CE). References to the Mishnah begin with "M."; to the Jerusalem Talmud with "J."; to the Babylonian Talmud with "B." ; to the *Mishneh Torah* with "M.T."; and to the *Shulhan Arukh* with "S.A."

ACKNOWLEDGMENTS

There are many people I would like to thank for helping me make this book possible. Stuart M. Matlins, publisher of Jewish Lights, first suggested that I write *The Way Into* Tikkun Olam *(Repairing the World)* for the Jewish community and then this version for Christian readers, with comparative Christian materials and ideas. It has been a true work of love and, I hope, useful too, so I want to thank him for conceiving the idea of *The Way Into …* series and for asking me to contribute to it. Emily Wichland, vice president of editorial and production, applied her considerable editorial talents to my manuscript, making it better than the one I created, and I thank her sincerely for that. I would also like to thank all the talented people at Jewish Lights for their help in publishing and marketing this book.

Father Michael Wakefield, my co-chair in the Los Angeles Priest–Rabbi Dialogue and a good friend, lent me some of his books so that I could include the Catholic view of the topics I treat in this volume. I thank him for that, for the immense amount he has taught me in the Dialogue, and for his friendship. I also want to thank the love of my life, my wife Marlynn, for her support in joining me in many acts of *tikkun olam* and for her patience in allowing me to spend the time necessary to write about it. I am grateful to her and, indeed, God for the incredible blessings of our children and grandchildren—Tammy and her son Zachary Ethan; Michael and Tanya and their daughter Zoe Elliana; Havi and Adam and their daughters Noa Yarden and Ayden Chaya; and Jonathan and Mara and their children Amiel Shalom and Shira Rose. As I mention in this book, and as my children have heard me say ad nauseum, children are one of the greatest blessings of life, an integral part of God's promise to Abraham long ago, so I hope that many more grandchildren are on the way!

I would especially like to acknowledge Cory Willson, a graduate student at Fuller Theological Seminary in Pasadena, California, who collected relevant Christian sources for me from his own Evangelical tradition as well as mainline Protestant and Catholic documents. Catholics have a magisterium, so what constitutes official Catholic beliefs is fairly easy to ascertain, but I had no idea how to identify the significant writers and writings within the Protestant world. He did a masterful job of locating such sources for me, making it possible for me and the readers of this book to see some Christian thought that sometimes resembles and sometimes differs from the Jewish materials I have collected, thus illuminating both traditions. In my own name and in that of all our readers, then, I thank you, Cory, for enlightening us in such an effective and significant way.

I have dedicated this book to Richard Mouw, president of Fuller Theological Seminary and a professor of philosophy there. He was so interested in this project that he found the funds to pay Cory for his work on this book, for which I want to thank him publicly. But my decision to honor Richard Mouw in this way has far deeper roots than that. I first met Richard when we each accompanied our students to Intersem, an annual gathering since 1973 of those studying for the rabbinate, ministry, and priesthood at seminaries in Southern California for two days at a camp in Malibu. Our philosophical and religious interests immediately made us friends. We also

bonded around our common recognition that interfaith discussions are not only critically important in this multifaith
world of ours but also always illuminate a person's own faith
and make issues more tractable. In the last decade or so,
Richard has involved me in several projects at Fuller, and I in
turn have invited him to the American Jewish University (for-
merly the University of Judaism) in Southern California to
speak and to engage in dialogues with me before our community. Frankly, we have each sought and found recurring opportunities to interact for personal reasons as well as professional
ones, for we love to reconnect and stretch each other's minds
and hearts yet again. A prolific and insightful writer, Richard
has brought his keen mind, his philosophical acumen, his religious convictions, and his immense and broad learning to the
analysis of many contemporary issues, always making them
much clearer than they were before he wrote about them.
Much to his surprise, I think, he has also turned out to be an
amazingly effective fundraiser and administrator in his position
as president. When he was first appointed to that position, a
reporter from the *Los Angeles Times* told me that she was writing a full-page article about him and that all the people she had
contacted up to that point had said very positive but also very
serious things about him, so she wanted something funny. I
told her that Richard Mouw laughs too much to be a committed Calvinist! She must have told him what I said because
the article then quotes him as responding, "Rabbi Dorff clearly
does not understand the Christian doctrine of grace!" A wonderful friend and a terrific sparring partner, Richard manages
to fix the world each and every day in many, many ways. He is
a true model of what we Jews call a mensch, a human being of
real character—indeed, a model for us all. It is both a pleasure
and a privilege to know him.

—Rabbi Elliot N. Dorff

INTRODUCTION

Modern Jews often think of repairing the world—*tikkun olam*—as a core commitment of Judaism. In fact, a 1988 poll by the *Los Angeles Times*[1] showed that half of all American Jews listed a commitment to social equality as the most important factor in their Jewish identity, while only 17 percent cited religious observance and another 17 percent cited support for Israel. A 2000 study conducted by Steven M. Cohen and Leonard Fein similarly found that social equality topped the list by far: 47 percent said that "a commitment to social equality" was the most important factor in their Jewish identity, 24 percent said "religious observance," 13 percent said support for Israel, and 16 percent said "other."[2] Finally, a poll conducted by the American Jewish Committee in 2003 asked 1,008 Jews to choose the quality most important to their Jewish identity; 41 percent said "being part of the Jewish people," 21 percent said "commitment to social justice," and 13 percent chose "religious observance."[3]

Those deeply committed to Judaism may find these results disturbing, for they indicate that Jews are mistaking the fruit for the tree. After all, in classical Jewish sources, Judaism's commitment to social equality stems from its more fundamental convictions regarding God, covenant, and *mitzvot* (sacred commandments). Thus Jews should not only include those elements in their Jewish identity but also see them as central.

This pattern, though, is apparently not as new as some might suppose. Hundreds of years ago the Rabbis of the Midrash[4] described their own Jewish community in very similar terms:

> "I sleep, but my heart wakes" (Song of Songs 5:2). The congregation of Israel said to the Holy One: "I sleep" in neglect of ritual precepts, but "my heart wakes" for the practice of loving-kindness.
> —*Shir Ha-Shirim Rabbah* 5:2, par. 1

That should provide at least some comfort to contemporary Jewish religious leaders!

Moreover, the large percentage of Jews who singled out social justice as the most critical factor in their Jewish commitment were not wrong in identifying concern for helping others as an important Jewish conviction. The Torah (the Five Books of Moses, Judaism's central sacred text consisting of Genesis, Exodus, Leviticus, Numbers, and Deuteronomy) includes a number of laws and theological tenets that articulate this duty, and later Jewish law and thought expand upon that base. Classical Jewish sources depict our duties as a series of concentric circles, with primary duties to ourselves, our family, our local community, the larger Jewish community, and then the world at large. While that continues to be the principle that defines Jewish duties to others, as Jews were accepted more fully into general society in post-Enlightenment times, they became all the more interested in making society as a whole not only fair and equitable, but also supportive and, as much as possible, ideal.

This book presents some of the most important aspects of the social component of the Jewish tradition. After examining the grounds for Judaism's fundamental conviction that we should indeed care for others, using alleviating poverty as an example, the book turns to areas of life in which this concern takes concrete expression. Specifically, it first explores the ways in which fixing the world applies to the social arena, such as how we should speak with and about others, heal the sick, celebrate with brides and grooms, and comfort mourners. Repairing the world (*tikkun olam*) is then discussed regarding family, such as duties of spouses to each other as well as obligations of children to parents and of parents to children.

Several important topics that might also reasonably fit within a book on *tikkun olam* are not treated here. We might fix the world literally by taking care of the environment and by repairing what we have befouled. But that is beyond the scope of this book, which limits itself to fixing the world in our relationships with other human beings. In this arena, two important components of repairing the world are our relationships with people of other faiths and our business dealings. This book's theoretical section lays the groundwork in articulating why we should care about other human beings at all.

Because Judaism's social message is a significant part of Judaism, and because the surveys cited above indicate that this aspect of Judaism is a, if not *the*, fundamental mainstay of the Jewish identity of a large percentage of America's Jews, this book will help Christians understand this aspect of their Jewish neighbors as it informs Jews about why and how Christians manifest some of the same concerns, albeit sometimes in different ways or degrees. It will also help many Jews understand the foundations and directions of their Jewish social commitments and their Jewish identity altogether.

PART ONE

REPAIRING THE WORLD (*TIKKUN OLAM*) IN THEORY

1

THE MEANING AND SIGNIFICANCE OF TIKKUN OLAM

Jews today speak of repairing the world—*tikkun olam*—as a central Jewish precept, and concern for literally "fixing the world" by making it a better place through activities we often call social action is certainly at the heart of a Jewish perspective on life. This meaning of *tikkun olam*, however, is very new in Jewish history. Historically, it has meant all of the following, each of which I discuss at further length elsewhere[1]:

1. Changes that the Rabbis of antiquity instituted in Jewish law to avoid or resolve unfair treatment caused by the law as originally formulated.
2. Changes that God institutes in order to perfect the world to be the Kingdom of the Almighty.
3. Fulfilling Jewish law in order to fix both God and this broken world.
4. Freeing human beings from the desire to do evil.
5. Making the world work efficiently by following common manners, which Jews should do if they are more stringent than what Jewish law requires but not if they are more lenient.

6. Fixing the concrete world of objects, animals, and persons through everyone's efforts to prevent harm to, or to restore, the environment and social and familial ties.

This last meaning, derived from Jewish scholar Leonard Fein in the 1950s, is the one that most Jews today have in mind when they speak of *tikkun olam,* and it is the one we shall be using throughout this book.

OLDER RELATED TERMS AND CONCEPTS

Although this last meaning of *tikkun olam* is relatively new, the concepts and duties underlying it are anything but. Classical Judaism used other terms for what we mean today by it. On a personal level, the equivalent term was *hesed,* and on a social level the terms that refer to aspects of what we mean by *tikkun olam* were *tzedek* and *mishpat.*

Hesed originally meant loyalty—to God and to your neighbor. It therefore came to mean what you do in faithfulness to God and your neighbor, namely, acts of love and kindness and care.

Tzedek means justice, as in the verse, "Justice, justice shall you pursue" (Deut. 16:20). The Torah's vision of justice includes both procedural and substantive elements. That is, it demands that in court we ensure fairness by following specific procedures in judging people (procedural justice), and in society generally we must guarantee that there is a substantial safety net so that the poor, orphans, and widows are provided with what they need to live, get an education, and find a mate (substantive justice).[2]

Mishpat comes from the root meaning *shofet,* "judge," and thus *mishpat* originally meant the decision of a judge, or a precedent. It has that meaning, for example, in the very first verse of Exodus 21. Biblical scholars have pointed out that the norms contained in that section of the Bible probably originated as judicial rulings.[3] From this origin the word *mishpat* expands to mean law generally, especially in its plural form, *mishpatim*, and so the new American translation of the Bible published by the Jewish Publication Society translates *mishpatim* as "rules." For example, "See, I [Moses] have imparted to you laws [*hukkim*] and rules [*mishpatim*], as the Lord my God has commanded me" (Deut. 4:5; see also Ps. 147:19–20 and Neh. 9:13).[4] Finally, already in the Bible the word *mishpat* expands yet further to mean justice. For example, "The Rock!—His deeds are perfect, Yea, all His ways are just [*mishpat*]" (Deut. 32:4), and this famous verse from Micah 6:8: "He has told you, O man, what is good, and what the Lord requires of you: Only to do justice [literally, "to do *mishpat*"], to love goodness [*hesed*], and to walk modestly with your God."[5]

In the Bible the values of justice and kindness are often spoken of together to indicate that they balance and reinforce each other. For example, in a verse Jews recite three times each day, the psalmist asserts, "Adonai is righteous [*tzadik*] in all His ways and kind [*hasid*] in all His actions" (Ps. 145:17).[6] More expansively, using many of the Hebrew words we have encountered as parts of the way *tikkun olam* was expressed in the past, the psalmist declares:

> O Lord, Your faithfulness [*hasdikha*] reaches to heaven;
> Your steadfastness [*emunatkha*] to the sky;
> Your beneficence [*tzidkatkha*] is like the high mountains;
> Your justice [*mishpatkha*] like the great deep;
> man and beast You deliver, O Lord.
> How precious is Your faithful care [*hasdikha*], O God!
> Mankind shelters in the shadow of Your wings.
> —Psalm 36:6–8

This intermixing of terms continues in rabbinic literature—the subsequent commentaries and discussions of the Rabbis of antiquity—as in this passage:

> Rabbi Elazar quoted this verse, "He has told you, O man, what is good, and what the Lord requires of you: Only to do justice [literally, "to do *mishpat*"], to love goodness [*hesed*], and to walk modestly with your God" (Micah 6:8). What does this verse imply? "To do justice" means to act in accordance with the principles of justice. "To love goodness" means to let your actions be guided by principles of loving-kindness. "To walk modestly with your God" means to assist needy families at their funerals and weddings [by giving humbly, in private]....
>
> —B. *Sukkah* 49b

Clearly, then, from the Jewish perspective doing justice is not restricted to abiding by or judging according to the rules; it certainly does demand that,[7] but it also requires that we balance justice with kindness.

The rabbinic tradition goes further than that. It values acts of kindness for the objective good they accomplish, regardless of the motive that prompted the person to do them. Thus it prefers acts of kindness to charity, though it values those as well, for kindness can fix the world in more ways than charity can:

> Our Rabbis taught: Deeds of loving-kindness are superior to charity in three respects: Charity can be accomplished only with money, while deeds of loving-kindness can be accomplished through personal involvement as well as with money. Charity can be given only to the

poor, while deeds of loving-kindness can be done for both rich and poor. Charity applies only to the living, while deeds of loving-kindness apply to both the living and the dead.

—B. *Sukkah* 49b

At the same time, the Rabbis were not blind to the importance of motive. Regardless of the reasons people do acts of kindness, the Rabbis judge their moral worth according to the degree to which they are done with selfless, benign motives:

Rabbi Elazar said: The reward for acts of justice [charity, *tzedakah*] depends upon the degree of loving-kindness [*hesed*] in them, as it is written, "Sow righteousness [justice, charity, *tzedakah*] for yourselves. Reap according to [your] goodness [*hesed*]" (Hosea 10:12).

—B. *Sukkah* 49b

Our acts of kindness must, if possible, affect our inner being as well as the world at large. Here, though, we must remember the fundamental rabbinic educational psychology—that is, although it is best to do good things for the right motives, we should do the right thing even for the wrong reasons for "from doing the right thing not for its sake one will come to do it for its sake" (B. *Pesahim* 50a). Thus we should to do the right thing now rather than wait for the proper motive for three reasons. First, the right motive may never come. Second, even if we do the right thing for an improper motive (e.g., to get a good reputation or a favor from someone else), the good act hopefully accomplishes an objective good in society. Third, as the Rabbis say, we learn good motives by doing good acts.

THE IMPORTANCE OF *TIKKUN OLAM*

The values we are discussing are among the most important in the Torah. The Rabbis assert that kindness (*hesed*) runs through the Torah from beginning to end:

> Rabbi Simlai taught: The Torah begins with deeds of loving-kindness and ends with deeds of loving-kindness. It begins with deeds of loving-kindness, as it is written, "And the Lord God made garments of skins for Adam and for his wife and clothed them" (Genesis 3:21). It ends with deeds of loving-kindness, as it is written, "And He buried him [Moses] in the valley in the land of Moab" (Deuteronomy 34:6).
>
> —B. *Sotah* 14a

It is also the way we atone for our sins:

> Once, as Rabbi Yohanan was walking out of Jerusalem, Rabbi Joshua followed him, and upon seeing the Temple in ruins, he said: "Woe unto us that this place is in ruins, the place where atonement was made for the Israel's iniquities!" Rabbi Yohanan responded: "My son, do not grieve, for we have another means of atonement that is as effective. What is it? It is deeds of loving-kindness, concerning which Scripture says, 'I [God] desire goodness [*hesed*], not sacrifice'" (Hosea 6:6).
>
> —*Avot d'Rabbi Natan* 4:5

Further, to refuse to care for others is to deny God: "Rabbi Judah said: When a man denies the duty of loving-kindness, it is as though he had denied the Root [that is, God]" (*Ecclesiastes Rabbah* 7:1, par. 4). Conversely, engaging in acts of kindness (*hesed*) is nothing less than modeling yourself after God:

"To walk in all His ways" (Deuteronomy 11:22). These are the ways of the Holy One: "compassionate and gracious, slow to anger, abounding in kindness [*hesed*] and faithfulness, extending kindness to the thousandth generation, forgiving iniquity, transgression, and sin," (Exodus 34:6). This means that just as God is compassionate and gracious, you too must be compassionate and gracious.... Just as God is kind, you too must be kind.... "The Lord is righteous in all His ways and kind in all His actions" (Psalm 145:17): Just as the Holy One is righteous, so you too must be righteous; just as the Holy One is kind (loving, *hasid*), so too you must be kind (loving).

—*Sifre Deuteronomy, Ekev*

Finally, it is one of the three values on which the very existence of the world depends, as we learn in this famous passage from the Mishnah's tractate *Ethics of the Fathers* (*Pirkei Avot* or just *Avot*), famous both because it comes at the very beginning of the tractate and also because in modern times it is often sung:

Simeon the Just ... used to say: The world depends on three things: on Torah, on worship, and on acts of loving-kindness [*gemillut hasadim*].

—M. *Avot* 1:2

The other ancient terms that describe aspects of what we now mean by *tikkun olam* are *tzedek* (justice) and *mishpat*, especially in the latter term's broadest sense of justice. In contrast to kindness (*hesed*), which denotes the personal, individual aspects of *tikkun olam*, these terms for justice, *tzedek* and *mishpat*, denote its social elements. As such, *tzedek* and *mishpat* are also core values of the Jewish tradition. Thus at the end of the first chapter of *Ethics of the Fathers,* we read an alternative list of values on which the world depends:

> Rabbi Simeon ben Gamliel says: The world depends on three things, on justice [*ha-din*], truth, and peace, as the Bible says, "Judge in your gates truth and justice [*u'mishpat*] and peace" (Zechariah 8:16).
>
> —M. *Avot* 1:18

Like kindness, the justice aspects of repairing the world are also part of God's very essence: "Righteousness and justice [*tzedek u'mishpat*] are the base of Your throne, steadfast love and faithfulness [*hesed ve'emet*] stand before You" (Ps. 89:15; see also 97:2). Consequently, to seek God is to seek justice: "Listen to Me, you who pursue justice, You who seek the Lord ... For teaching [*torah*] will go forth from Me, My way [*mishpati*, my justice] for the light of peoples ... Listen to Me, you who care for the right [*tzedek*], O people who lay My instruction to heart!" (Isa. 51:1, 4, 7). From the Torah's point of view, then, the tasks of discerning the just and the good and then acting on that knowledge are not just central to Jewish identity; they are what God demands of us: "Do what is right and good in the sight of the Lord" (Deut. 6:18).

Many philosophical questions immediately arise from this verse and the other passages we have been considering: What do we mean by the terms "kind," "just," "right," and "good" in the first place, and how are they different from each other? How shall we determine the courses of action that are right or good in morally ambiguous situations? And how is God related to our moral discernment and action? I deal with these important philosophical issues elsewhere.[8] Now we shall turn to another critical question: Why should I care for others in the first place, and how?

2

WHY SHOULD I CARE?
THE EXAMPLE OF
CARING FOR THE POOR

The very idea of *tikkun olam* assumes that we should try to fix
the world in both its natural and social aspects. But why should
we? The reasons we should endeavor to preserve and repair the
natural world are important, but in this book, where we focus
on the *human* world, our question boils down to this: Why
should I care about the plight of other people?

Caring for others takes many forms, including caring for
your elderly parents, paying attention to the needs of your
spouse and friends, spending time and effort in raising your
children, talking to and about others in ways that do not harm
them or others, visiting the sick, educating others, providing
cultural opportunities for others, diminishing (if not eliminat-
ing) crime and abuse, and alleviating poverty. Because people
often think of the last of these when they think of fixing the
world, this chapter uses caring for the poor as the example of
its broader topic of why we should care for others.

WHY I SHOULD *NOT* CARE

Both Jews and Christians know almost instinctively that their
religion requires them to care about and for others, so it may
seem superfluous to rehash a series of reasons for doing
so. Caring for others is not obvious, though, as this section
will demonstrate. That makes the claims of Judaism and

Christianity on their adherents serious duties taken in the face of, and despite, these important reasons for letting people take care of themselves:

1. *Justice: I earned this money, they did not.* The poor often do not work for a living and therefore do not deserve our help. This is substantive justice in its libertarian meaning.
2. *Dignity: Taking help is demeaning.* Begging, or even getting help from a social service agency, is inherently humiliating. Therefore as individuals and as a society we should not encourage behavior that cheapens our collective sense of the dignity of human beings.
3. *Benevolence: I may be reinforcing physically harmful forms of behavior if I help the poor.* Sometimes giving money to the poor actually contributes to their harmful habits and thus injures them. Stories of poor people turning down offers of food or coupons that can be exchanged only for food reinforce the impression that many poor people use money they gain from begging for alcohol or drugs.
4. *Self-sufficiency: By giving the poor aid, I am encouraging them to stay poor.* To offer aid to the poor may ultimately be detrimental to them not only physically but also psychologically and economically, for they may come to depend on it and never take the initiative to extricate themselves from poverty, hence the cycle of poverty that affects so many generations of the poor. If people need money, we as a society should help them with education and jobs, not alms, public housing, or health care (the politically conservative version of this argument). Personally helping someone or an institution by donating money or services takes the

pressure off the government to do its proper job, which is to furnish education and job training to those who can work and become self-sufficient and to provide a meaningful safety net if they cannot (the politically liberal version of this argument).

5. *Deception: The people who seem poor may not be.* When people on the streets ask me for a handout, I never know whether they really need it. The possibility of falling prey to deception is great, and nobody likes to be duped. If I am going to give some of my money away, I at least want to know that it is going to needy people.

6. *Danger: I may be subjecting myself to injury or theft if I open my wallet to give to the poor.* Beggars on the streets might even pose a danger to you, for if they do not get what they want, they may attack you or steal from you, especially if they are on drugs.

7. *Discomfort: Beggars make me feel guilty and invade my space.* Even if beggars do not pose a physical threat to pedestrians or to drivers stopped at a light, they are surely bothersome. The quality of life of society as a whole deteriorates if people cannot walk the streets without being accosted by beggars.

8. *Guilt: Beggars make me feel that I am somehow immoral for being able to support myself and have some luxuries.* Beyond the sheer aesthetics of wanting to live life without constantly being confronted by poor people and the problems of poverty is a moral dimension: beggars and other manifestations of poverty instill a sense of guilt in us. Even if I earned each penny of my own resources legitimately, how is it that I have enough (and maybe even more than enough) and these people do not? Yes, some may be lazy or deceptive, but I know

that some cannot find a job despite really trying to do so, some have family members who just suffered a catastrophic illness, and some are just down on their luck. Why am I fine but they are not? And why do I feel guilty when I did not cause their situation and cannot possibly make it so that there are no poor people in the world? Frankly, I resent feeling guilty when I did nothing wrong.

9. *Bad for business: Beggars lead to a deterioration of the business environment.* People will not come to your store if they have to go past beggars to get there.

10. *Hard to decide: There are simply too many individuals and institutions that deserve help for me to decide whom to help and how much to give.* My duty to help others, coupled with sheer compassion for the plight of the truly unfortunate, makes me want to give money to each and every one I pass. Pandering thus makes it hard to make good decisions about how to spend that part of my own private resources that I can devote to helping the poor. Like the vast majority of people, I am not rich, and I surely cannot support everyone in the world who needs help. But how can I walk past this particular person who seems so needy? Even in the privacy of my own home, without the complications of facing beggars on the street, how can I decide which of the many worthy charities to help and how much should I give? What about my duties to myself, my family, my friends, and my close community? In the face of poverty, do I have a right to spend some of my money on luxuries for myself or my family? If so, why and how much?

11. *Futility.* Finally, any efforts to alleviate poverty are like throwing a stone in an ocean in order to try to fill it.

As Deuteronomy 15:11 and Matthew 26:11 affirm, there will always be poor people. Why bother to help when it will not solve the ultimate problem anyway?

WHY I *SHOULD* CARE?

From the perspective of the Jewish tradition, then, why should anyone care about the welfare of others? We shall now focus on taking care of the poor, but many of the same rationales apply to other forms of *tikkun olam* as well.

God's Sovereignty

Many contemporary Jews who are skittish about their belief in God but strongly committed to helping others may be disturbed by the centrality of the belief in God in motivating Judaism's commitment to others. Jewish sources provide a series of rationales for caring for others, but some of them, as we shall see, invoke God much less than others. As a result, atheistic or agnostic Jews can find ample grounds for the duty to help others in the Jewish tradition, and even those who affirm a belief in God will at times be motivated more by Judaism's nontheistic reasons than by its theistic ones. At the same time, it would be misleading to pretend that the Jewish conception of and belief in God plays only a minor role in Judaism's demand that we care for others. On the contrary, God is very much at the center of that Jewish duty.

The ultimate theological foundation for Judaism's command to help others is the belief that God created the world and therefore owns it. The Torah (Gen. 14:19, 22) describes God as "*koneh shamayim va'aretz*," which in biblical Hebrew means both creator of heaven and earth and also owner of heaven and earth. ("Heaven and earth" is a merism, a biblical device that names the ends of a spectrum and means

15

everything in between as well.) The Bible also spells this out in verses such as these:

> Mark, the heavens to their uttermost reaches belong to the Lord your God, the earth and all that is on it!
>
> —Deuteronomy 10:14

> The land and all that is on it belongs to God, the earth and those who dwell on it.[1]
>
> —Psalm 24:1

How does creation convey ownership? In modern times, the Industrial Revolution divided the creation of many things into small parts, with a given person repeatedly doing the same task as one small part of the process of making something. This enabled companies to train people to do only one thing rather than everything necessary to make the object, and the resulting assembly line made things faster, cheaper, and with greater quality control. These advantages, though, came at the cost of separating people from the things they were creating. Thus we are no longer used to thinking of the maker of something as automatically its owner.

At the same time, we moderns still recognize that when individuals create a complete thing, they own it. So, for example, artists own their paintings until and unless they decide to sell them, and authors own their books until they sign over rights to a publisher. In fact, we have developed rather sophisticated patent and copyright laws to protect even our intellectual property—that is, our ideas, apart from any particular object embodying them. So even though we are more used to cooperative efforts in which none or all of the makers of an object own it, we do have many examples in our modern lives in which creating something—and even the idea of something—conveys ownership of it.

In the case of the universe, the Jewish doctrine of monotheism makes God's claim to own the earth and everything on it similar to that of the modern-day artist or author. That is, because Jews believe that God is one, no other party was involved in the creation of the world, and so God alone is both the sole creator and owner of the earth and all that is on it. That alone would be sufficient to establish God's ownership of everything in the world; after all, creators of a work of art or an idea do not have to do anything else to own what they have created. Jewish liturgy, though, takes this idea further: the morning prayers describe God as benignly renewing creation each day,[2] and so God's ownership of the world is justified not only by what God did in the distant past but also by God's re-creation of the world each and every day.

As owner of all assets, God has the right to distribute them as God wills and to make demands about their use. Human beings may, at God's behest, own property, but only vis-à-vis other human beings. All property that humans own, though, ultimately belongs to God, and we have it only as a temporary lease. As the ultimate owner, God requires us, as the Torah's commandments indicate, to give charity from "our" resources. Those who refuse to provide for the poor and for others in need thus effectively deny God's sovereignty, for such people dispute God's ultimate legal claim to all the earth and the right of God to demand that some of God's property be redistributed to those in need. Consequently, the Rabbis deemed refusal to assist the poor as nothing less than idolatry.[3]

The National Conference of Catholic Bishops, in *Economic Justice for All: Pastoral Letter on Catholic Social Teaching and the U.S. Economy*, strike the very same note:

> *From the patristic period to the present, the Church has affirmed*
> *that misuse of the world's resources or appropriation of them by*
> *a minority of the world's population betrays the gift of creation*
> *since "whatever belongs to God belongs to all"* [italics in the
> original].[4]

God's sovereignty also requires us to take care of the
world that God has entrusted to us. For example, because God
owns our bodies, we have a fiduciary duty to God to take care
of them through proper diet, exercise, hygiene, and sleep, even
if we would rather eat too much and sleep too little.
Conversely, we have a duty to God to avoid endangering ourselves unnecessarily, a duty that modern rabbis have used to
prohibit smoking and hallucinatory drug use.[5] Both the positive and negative parts of our responsibility to take care of
God's creation—that is, the duties to fix what is broken and to
avoid damaging activities in the first place—also apply to the
environment, the topic of another book in this series.[6]

It is important to note that for both Judaism and
Christianity, God's ownership of the world does not necessar-
ily mean that we should divest ourselves of all our assets or that
poverty is the ideal. Judaism has certainly denied this, for it has
a keen understanding of the indignity involved in poverty, and
it imposes limits on how much of your assets you may give
away lest you fall into poverty yourself.[7] Poverty is not a crime
in the Jewish tradition, as it was in England and other countries that had debtors' prisons, but it is not the ideal either. You
should try to earn enough to sustain yourself and your family
and also give some of your resources to those in need.

Christianity comes closer to seeing poverty as an ideal;
indeed, Catholic priests belonging to orders to this day are
required to take a vow of poverty. New Testament passages
such as these support such a view:

No one can serve two masters; for a slave will either hate the one and love the other, or be devoted to the one and despise the other. You cannot serve God and wealth.

—Matthew 6:24

There is great gain in godliness combined with contentment; for we brought nothing into the world, so that we can take nothing out of it; but if we have food and clothing, we will be content with these. But those who want to be rich fall into temptation and are trapped by many senseless and harmful desires that plunge people into ruin and destruction. For the love of money is a root of all kinds of evil, and in their eagerness to be rich some have wandered away from the faith and pierced themselves with many pains.

—1 Timothy 6:5–10

Note, however, that in the latter excerpt, it is not money itself but the love of money that is the root of all evil, for that love can all too easily lead you to make money an idol, the center of all your thoughts and actions. Dallas Willard, a contemporary Christian writer, says this:

The idealization of poverty is *one of the most dangerous illusions of Christians in the contemporary world.* Stewardship—which requires possessions and includes giving—is the true spiritual discipline in relation to wealth. There can be no doubt that we often fail to give of our goods when we should. But it must be noted that such failures concern the *use* of goods, not their possession. Poverty and wealth, on the other hand, have to do with the *possession* of things. Condemnation and guilt over mere possession has no part in scriptural faith and is, in the end, only a barrier to the right use of the riches of the earth.[8]

Similarly, The National Conference of Catholic Bishops asserted:

> Catholic social teaching does not require absolute equality in the distribution of income and wealth. Some degree of inequality not only is acceptable, but also may be considered desirable for economic and social reasons, such as the need for incentives and the provision of greater rewards for greater risks. However, unequal distribution should be evaluated in terms of several moral principles we have enunciated: the priority of meeting basic needs of the poor and the importance of increasing the level of participation by all members of society in the economic life of the nation. These norms establish a strong presumption against extreme inequality of income and wealth as long as there are poor, hungry, and homeless people in our midst.[9]

God may own everything, but that does not deprive humans of the right to possess parts of God's world to the exclusion of other people, as long as the basic needs of the poor are met and as long as those well-off attend to and ameliorate the plight of the needy.

God's Commandment

As owner of everything, God also has the prerogative to make demands about how God's property is distributed. Thus the most straightforward reason in the tradition that we must care for others is that God commands us to do so. With regard to the poor, the Torah says this:

> If there is a needy person among you, one of your kinsmen in any of your settlements in the land that the Lord your God is giving you, do not harden your heart and

shut your hand against your needy kinsman. Rather, you must open your hand and lend him sufficient for whatever he needs.... For there will never cease to be needy ones in your land, which is why I command you: open your hand to the poor and needy kinsman in your land.

—Deuteronomy 15:7, 8, 11

Note that this responds to the argument that it is futile to help poor people because the world will always contain poor people, as the book of Deuteronomy and Matthew openly admit. As contemporary evangelical writers Ronald Sider and Heidi Unruh have said:

Some have taken this statement [of Jesus in Matthew 26:11 that there will always be poor people among us] to mean that social ministry is ultimately futile and that Christians should concentrate on saving souls. But it is important to understand Jesus' words in the context of the passage in Deuteronomy to which he was referring: "There will always be poor people in the land. Therefore I command you to be openhanded toward your brothers and toward the poor and needy in your land" (Deuteronomy 15:11, NIV). Jesus' words do not justify sidelining poverty and focusing on the world to come. Rather, the overwhelming reality of poverty in this world is an urgent call for people of faith to open their hands freely to those in need.[10]

The language of "commandment" is not as central to Christianity as it is to Judaism, but it is certainly not absent either. Richard Mouw, president of Fuller Theological Seminary in Pasadena, California, has written an entire book exploring the meaning of divine commands for Christians.[11] Thus it is not surprising that some Christians speak in these terms with regard to caring for others in general and for the poor in particular. Consider this statement by Ronald Sider and Heidi Unruh:

> Yet it is not riches alone that provokes God's wrath, but two dangers associated with wealth. First, Scripture harshly warns those who acquire wealth by exploiting the poor. "You who make iniquitous decrees ... that widows may be your spoil, and that you may make the orphans your prey! What will you do on the day of punishment?" (Isaiah 10:1–3; see also Isaiah 3:14–15; Amos 2:7 and Micah 2:1–5). Second, God's anger is also aroused by people who have plenty, yet neglect the needy. In Ezekiel 16:49, God proclaims regarding the destruction of the city of Sodom: "This was the guilt of your sister Sodom: she and her daughters had pride, excess of food, and prosperous ease, but did not aid the poor and needy" (see also Luke 16:19–31). In God's eyes, ignoring the needs of the poorest is as grievous as idolatry and sexual abominations.[12]

Although the Torah likewise asserts that God will punish those who fail to care for others, including the poor, it was keenly aware that enforcement, even by God, would not suffice to motivate people to obey God's commandments. After all, a mere forty days after the People Israel stood at the foot of Mount Sinai, with thunder, lightning, and earthquakes—truly an impressive display of God's power if there ever was one—they were worshiping the golden calf. The threat of God's punishment for disobedience and the promise of God's reward for obedience are thus not adequate grounds to produce conformity to the law. (The threat of being arrested is not enough to produce obedience of American law either; the vast majority of us must obey it for many other reasons for the American legal system to function.) Therefore, it is not surprising that the Torah and other classical Jewish texts describe additional reasons to live by God's commandments, rationales that I discuss elsewhere.[13] Knowledge that God will enforce God's commandments, including those that demand that we care for the poor, is nevertheless an important, if not a totally adequate, motivation for doing so.

The Divine Dignity of God's Human Creature

Jewish tradition places strong emphasis on the worth of the individual. Human worth derives first from being created in God's image, a concept that the Torah repeats three times in the opening chapters of Genesis to ensure we take note of it:

> And God created the human being in His image, in the image of God He created him: male and female He created them.
>
> —Genesis 1:27

> This is the record of Adam's line. When God created man, He made him in the likeness of God; male and female He created them. And when they were created, He blessed them and called them Human.
>
> —Genesis 5:1-2

> Whoever sheds the blood of man, by man shall his blood be shed; for in His image did God make man.
>
> —Genesis 9:6

As this last verse indicates, the divine image in each of us is not only a philosophical conception; it also justifies and explains specific laws. The most obvious, the one in Genesis 9, is that murder is to be banned, for human beings have divine worth. The divine image in each and every human being does not require that we like each and every person or approve of their actions, but it does require that we respect their ultimate worth.

The Rabbis took this further. That we were created in God's image is a manifestation of God's love for us; our *awareness* of the divine image within us is a mark of yet more divine love:

> Beloved is man, for he was created in the image of God; but it was by a special love that it was made known to him that he was created in the image of God, as the Torah says, "For in the image of God He made man" (Genesis 9:6).
>
> —M. *Avot* 3:18

Exactly which feature of the human being reflects this divine image is a matter of debate within the Jewish tradition. The Torah itself seems to tie it to humanity's ability to make moral judgments—that is, to distinguish good from bad and right from wrong, to behave accordingly, and to judge our own actions and those of others on the basis of this moral knowledge.[14] Another human faculty connected by the Torah and by the later tradition to divinity is the ability to speak.[15] Maimonides, perhaps the most important medieval Jewish scholar of Jewish law and philosophy, claims that the divine image resides in our capacity to think, especially discursively.[16] Locating the divine image within us may also be the Torah's way of acknowledging that we can love, just as God does,[17] or that we are at least partially spiritual and thus share God's spiritual nature.[18]

The Rabbis, like the Torah before them, invoke the doctrines that God created human beings in the divine image and uniquely not only to *describe* aspects of our nature, but also to *pre-*

scribe behavior. Specifically, the Rabbis maintain that because human beings are created in God's image, we affront God when we insult another person.[19] Conversely, "one who welcomes his friend is as if he welcomes the face of the Divine Presence."[20] Moreover, when we see someone with a disability, we are to utter this blessing: "Praised are you, Lord our God, *meshaneh habriyyot,* who makes different creatures," or "who created us different." Precisely when we might recoil from a deformed or incapacitated person, or thank God for not making us like that, the tradition instead bids us to embrace the divine image in such people—indeed, to bless God for creating some of us so.[21] Finally, the nonutilitarian basis of the Rabbis' assertion of human worth is graphically illustrated in their ruling that no one person can be sacrificed to save even an entire city unless that person is named by the enemy or guilty of a capital crime.[22]

This demand that we respect each other means we must help others while preserving their dignity as much as possible. Thus the Torah says:

> When you make a loan of any sort to your neighbor, you must not enter his house to seize his pledge. You must remain outside, while the man to whom you made the loan brings the pledge out to you.
>
> —Deuteronomy 24:10-11

Preserving the dignity of the poor, despite the inherent indignity of poverty, is also the underlying value in Maimonides's famous ladder of the levels of charity:

> [7]There are eight gradations in the giving of charity, each higher than the other. [1] The highest of these, which has no superior, is to take the hand of a fellow Jew and offer him a gift, or a loan, or enter into a business

partnership with him, or find him a job, so that he may become economically strong and no longer need to ask others for help. Concerning this Scripture says, "You shall strengthen him ... so that he may live with you ..." that is, you shall assist him so that he does not fall into poverty and need charity.

[8][2] Less praiseworthy than this is giving charity to the poor so that the donor does not know to whom he gave and the recipient does not know who gave it. In this way the act of giving charity is done for its own sake. This is like the Chamber of the Discreet in the Jerusalem Temple. The righteous would secretly deposit funds, and the poor, just as secretly, would enter and be sustained by what they took (M. *Shekalim* 5:6). Another way of giving charity in this fashion is to give to the community charity fund....

[9][3] Less praiseworthy than this is the charity in which the donor knows the recipient, but the recipient does not know the donor. This is like the practice of our sages who would go about discreetly leaving money in the doorways of the needy....

[10][4] Less praiseworthy than this is the situation when the needy knows the donor, but the donor does not know the recipient. This is like the practice of the greatest of our sages, who would tie coins in their shawls that would trail behind them, so that the needy could come and take without any embarrassment (B. *Ketubbot* 67b).

[11][5] Less praiseworthy than this is personally giving a gift to someone before being asked.

[12][6] Less praiseworthy than this is giving after being asked.

[13][7] Less praiseworthy than this is giving less than is appropriate, but doing so graciously.

[14][8] Less praiseworthy than this is giving, but resenting having to do so.

—*M. T. Laws of Gifts to the Poor* 10:7–14

Ultimately, the duty to protect the dignity of the poor is evident in the Talmud's demand that "Even a poor person who lives entirely on charity must also give charity to another poor person"[23]; the indignity of receiving must be balanced by the dignity of giving.

The duty to care for others because of the divine stamp inherent in each one of us is a theme that evangelical Christians, brought together in Lausanne, Switzerland, in 1974 largely through the efforts of the evangelist Dr. Billy Graham, expressed in the Lausanne Covenant, a part of which states this:

Christian Social Responsibility

We affirm that God is both the Creator and the Judge of all men. We therefore should share his concern for justice and reconciliation throughout human society and for the liberation of men and women from every kind of oppression. Because men and women are made in the image of God, every person, regardless of race, religion, colour, culture, class, sex or age, has an intrinsic dignity because of which he or she should be respected and served, not exploited. Here too we express penitence both for our neglect and for having sometimes regarded evangelism and social concern as mutually exclusive. Although reconciliation with other people is not reconciliation with God, nor is social action evangelism, nor is political liberation salvation, nevertheless we affirm that evangelism and sociopolitical involvement are both part of our Christian duty. For both are necessary expressions of our doctrines of God and man, our love for our neighbour and our obedience to Jesus Christ.... Faith without works is dead.[24]

Community: Love of Your Neighbor

In another book I describe in detail the differences between the American, Christian, and Jewish conceptions of community.[25] For our purposes, it is sufficient to note that with the possible exception of some right-wing Orthodox groups, all modern Jews, like modern Christians, see the world through an Enlightenment perspective in which the individual is the fundamental reality. All individuals are independent agents who may choose to associate themselves with others for specific purposes. Further, this view implies that even if other people happen to belong to a group to which I too belong, what they do in other areas of their lives is none of my business, and their needs are none of my concern unless all members of the group have specifically undertaken duties to care for each other in some way or unless the other person's actions have a direct effect on me, for even within groups Americans retain their fundamental identity as individuals.

This perspective stands in stark contrast to the traditional Jewish view, shared with most pre-Enlightenment theories,[26] in which the individual is defined by his or her membership in the group. This membership is not voluntary and cannot be terminated at will; it is a metaphysical fact over which people have no control. God speaks to the entire People Israel at Sinai; it is the people as a whole with whom God makes the covenant and who will be punished or rewarded according to their adherence to that covenant; it is the community's leaders, who know the theology and legal stipulations of the covenant, who bear the responsibility and have the right to interpret and apply God's word in each generation; and it is the People Israel as a whole who will ultimately be redeemed

WHY SHOULD I CARE?

in messianic times. Thus, contrary to the concept of the group in Christianity or American secular thought, in Jewish thought the community has not only practical but also theological status.

Moreover, the Jewish community is organic. That is, in the perspective of traditional Judaism, membership in and commitment to the Jewish community is not voluntary for those born Jewish any more than your foot has a right to dissociate itself from the rest of your body. Thus Jews who convert to another religion lose their *privileges* as Jews—they may not be married or buried as a Jew or count as part of a prayer quorum (minyan)—but even as apostates (*meshumadim*) they retain all the *responsibilities* of Jews. The same is true for converts to Judaism: they clearly choose to convert, but once they have completed the conversion process, they become an organic part of the People Israel and cannot leave the Jewish fold any more than can someone born Jewish.

Judaism's theological and organic sense of community has some important implications for our purposes. The indissoluble linkage between the individual and the group means that each person is responsible for every other simply by being part of the Jewish people, without any specific assumption of that duty by the individual Jew and even against his or her will:

> Love your neighbor as yourself: I am the Lord.
> —Leviticus 19:18

> All Jews are responsible for each other.[27]
> —B. *Shevu'ot* 39a

It is this sense of a strong community that, according to a recent poll, is the primary meaning that most Jews find in their Jewish identity. The second most important factor is the Jewish community's social action activities to help those in need.[28] As Jacob Neusner, a well-respected Jewish scholar, has pointed out, in our own day, when Jews differ sharply in beliefs, practices, and customs, and when Jews live and work among non-Jews to a much greater extent than in the past, the shared work of collecting and distributing charity and working in other ways as well to help those in need is a significant mechanism through which individual Jews *become* a Jewish community.[29]

A person's duty to help the local community provide for those in need depends on how deep his or her roots are within a given community:

> One who settles in a community for thirty days becomes obligated to contribute to the charity fund together with the other members of the community. One who settles there for three months becomes obligated to contribute to the soup kitchen. One who settles there for six months becomes obligated to contribute clothing with which the poor of the community can cover themselves. One who settles there for nine months becomes obligated to contribute to the burial fund for burying the community's poor and providing for all of their needs of burial.
> —Maimonides, *M. T. Laws of Gifts to the Poor* 9:12

Even though Jews are part of a universal community, with duties to all other Jews and, as we shall see, to non-Jews as well, their primary duties are to their local communities. Similarly, in Jewish law a person's right to claim assistance also works in concentric circles, with greatest claim on that person's family, then his or her local community, and then the larger Jewish community.

Compassion for and Love of Neighbor and Stranger

Beyond recognition of familial and communal duties, the Torah demands that we love our neighbor as we love ourselves (Lev. 19:18). Although this may seem like an impossible demand—and, frankly, in some ways it is—it nevertheless is central to both Judaism and Christianity.

Rabbi Akiva, one of the most important rabbis of the late first century and early second century CE, calls the Torah's commandment to love our neighbor a (or perhaps the) fundamental principle of the Torah.[30] The Rabbis of the Midrash and Talmud, in interpreting this verse, determine that it does not require us to love everyone, which they knew was impossible, but to have concern for others and, more importantly, to act out of that sense of commitment and loyalty to others even if we do not feel love toward them. For example, they use this verse to explain a man's duty to marry a woman who is fitting for him; to forbid a man from having sexual intercourse with his wife during the day lest he see something loathsome in her; to permit a child to draw blood from his or her parent in an effort to heal him or her despite the Torah's prohibition of injuring your parents (Exod. 21:15); and to require that a person who is to be executed be killed in the least offensive way possible.[31]

Maimonides uses this verse as the basis for yet other laws: that you must tell the praises of others, avoid self-aggrandizement through defaming others, and concern yourself for other people's money as you would care for your own.[32] Furthermore, Maimonides maintains that loving your neighbor as yourself is one of the grounds for the demand that we rescue captives;[33] and he asserts that although the commands to visit the sick, bury the dead, comfort mourners, and help a bride and groom celebrate their wedding are of rabbinic rather than biblical status, they are rooted in this biblical command to love your neighbor as yourself.[34]

This love of and compassion for your neighbor that we are to have is illustrated in some specific demands of the Torah vis-à-vis the poor. For example, a lender who has taken a poor person's cloak as a pledge must return it to him by nightfall, "for in what else will he sleep?" (Exod. 22:26). If you oppress a widow or orphan and they cry out to God, God "will kill you by the sword and your wives will be widows and your children orphans" (Exod. 22:21–23). Similarly, "You shall not abuse a needy and destitute laborer, whether a fellow country-man or a stranger in one of the communities of your land. You must pay him his wages on the same day, before the sun sets, for he is poor and urgently depends on it; else he will cry to the Lord against you, and you will incur guilt" (Deut. 24:14–15).

But certainly the most repeated of the Torah's demands is not to love your neighbor, but to love the stranger in our midst. While God's special love for and covenant with the Jewish people would seem to lead to the conclusion that Jews have duties to help only other Jews, that has not been the his-tory of the covenant idea. Quite the contrary, according to the Talmud's count,[35] thirty-six times the Torah requires Jews to treat foreigners within their midst fairly and even to love the stranger. This is rooted not only in a general humanitarian feel-ing of sharing in the human species but also in the concrete experience of being strangers in Egypt:

> You shall not subvert the rights of the stranger or the fatherless; you shall not take a widow's garment in pawn. Remember that you were a slave in Egypt and that the Lord your God redeemed you from there; therefore do I enjoin you to observe this commandment.... When you gather the grapes of your vineyard, do not pick it over again; that shall go to the stranger, the fatherless, and the

widow. Always remember that you were a slave in the land of Egypt; therefore do I enjoin you to observe this commandment.

—Deuteronomy 24:17–18, 21–22

Christian sources, both ancient and modern, share this conviction that the command to love your neighbor is an important source of our duty to care for the poor. Jesus illustrates this principle by recounting the story of the Good Samaritan (Luke 10:25–37), who helps a total stranger who had been robbed, stripped, and beaten.

Civil rights activist and Baptist preacher Dr. Martin Luther King Jr. explains Jesus's message in this parable:

(The Samaritan's) goodness was not found in a passive commitment to a particular creed, but in his active participation in a life-saving deed; not in a moral pilgrimage that reached its destination point, but in the love ethic by which he journeyed life's highway. "Who is my neighbor?" "I do not know his name," says Jesus in essence. "He is anyone toward whom you are neighborly. He is anyone who lies in need at life's roadside. He is neither Jew nor Gentile; he is neither Russian nor American; he is neither Negro nor white. He is 'a certain man'—any needy man—on one of the numerous Jericho roads of life." So Jesus defines a neighbor, not in a theological definition, but in a life situation.[36]

The Rabbis of the Talmud maintained that you should fulfill a commandment even if it is not for its own sake, for out of doing the right action for the wrong reason, you may come to do it for the right reason.[37] (In the meantime, moreover, others benefit from the good act.) C. S. Lewis, an important twentieth-century Christian thinker, suggests a similar approach to loving your neighbor as a rationale to help others in need—namely, that acting as if you loved another, even if you do not, has the potential to produce love:

> Do not waste your time bothering whether you "love" your neighbor; act as if you did. As soon as we do this we find one of the great secrets. When you are behaving as if you loved someone, you will presently come to love him. If you injure someone you dislike, you will find yourself disliking him more. If you do him a good turn, you will find yourself disliking him less.[38]

Puritan pastor Jonathan Edwards is often pigeonholed as a "preacher of wrath" for such sermons as "Sinners in the Hands of an Angry God." In his sermon and writings on the Christian call to charity, however, Edwards develops an expansive ethic of sacrificial giving to *all* from the doctrine of God's sovereign grace that extends to all humanity, even those who might harm us in the process:

> We are particularly required to be kind to the unthankful and to the evil; and therein to follow the example of our heavenly Father, who causes his sun to rise on the evil and on the good, and sendeth rain on the just and on the unjust. We are obliged, not only to be kind to them that are so to us, but to them that hate, and that despitefully use us.[39]

Judaism, and presumably Christianity as well, would caution that in the context of a beggar approaching you, you must take steps to ensure that your generosity does not expose you to danger,[40] and they would certainly not encourage someone to aid someone in accomplishing nefarious intentions. Here, though, Edwards is using God's love of us to urge us to go quite far in helping even people whom we detest. In this, he is following the lead of the Torah, which demands that you help not only your friend whose animal has been lost or has fallen under its burden (Deut. 22:1–4), but even your enemy (Exod. 23:4–5), for until and unless the other person intends to do you harm, you must respond to God's love of all human beings, including those you do not like, in recognizing and fulfilling the duty to help them.

Our Covenant with God: Mutual Promises and Love

Although birth to a Jewish woman or conversion to Judaism defines who is "a member of the tribe," the substance of what it means to be a Jew is defined in the covenant between God and the Jewish people. Beginning with Abraham and finding its quintessential expression at Mount Sinai, that covenant is, in part, a contract between God and the Jewish people in which both parties promise to fulfill their parts of the bargain. It is, though, more than that: it is a covenant similar to a covenant of marriage, in which the two parties not only agree to do specific things for each other, but also enter into a long-term *relationship* in which they each care for the other. The terms of the covenant, then, are obligatory in part as a function of the morality of *promise keeping*—every Jew in every generation was at Sinai and promised there to fulfill the covenant—and, in larger part, a function of the ongoing *relationship* that was consecrated there. As a Jew, then, I need to care for all other Jews because they are part of my people covenanted to each other and to God in all ages and places. The following passages describe a covenant of mutual promises:

Then he [Moses] took the record of the covenant and
read it aloud to the people. And they said, "All that the
Lord has spoken we will do and obey."

—Exodus 24:7

The Lord our God made a covenant with us at Horeb. It
was not with our fathers that the Lord made this
covenant, but with us, the living, every one of us who is
here today.

—Deuteronomy 5:2–3

Because Israel's acceptance of the Covenant at Mount
Sinai occurred amid thunder, lightning, and earthquakes, one
might conclude that the Israelites were coerced, but the
Bible records two later instances in which the Covenant (or
part of it) was reaffirmed voluntarily by the People Israel:
Joshua 24 and, most impressively, in Nehemiah 8–10. As the
following passage indicates, the last of those occasions
involved every Israelite—men, women, and children—and
was preceded by seven days of hearing the Torah and having
it translated and explained so that they all knew what they
were accepting:

In view of all this, we make this pledge and put it in writing; and on the sealed copy [are subscribed] our officials,
our Levites, and our priests.... And the rest of the people,
the priests, the Levites, the gatekeepers, the singers, the
temple servants, and all who separated themselves from
the peoples of the lands to [follow] the Teaching of God,
their wives, sons and daughters, all who know enough to
understand, join with their noble brothers and take an
oath with sanctions to follow the Teaching of God, given
through Moses the servant of God, and to observe care-

fully all the commandments of the Lord, our Lord, His rules and laws.

—Nehemiah 10:1, 29–30

In each and every generation, each person must see him/herself as if he or she left Egypt.

—The Passover Haggadah

The following passage describes a covenant of love:

Love, therefore, the Lord your God, and always keep His charge, His laws, His rules, and His commandments.

—Deuteronomy 11:1

Caring for others as a duty growing out of love of God is a common theme in Christianity as well. While Jews see this love of God as expressed in the covenant, Christians often express this as a demonstration of their love for Jesus, as, for example, this passage from Matthew 25:31–46, in which Jesus speaks to the righteous:

I was hungry and you gave me something to eat, I was thirsty and you gave me something to drink, I was a stranger and you invited me in, I needed clothes and you clothed me, I was sick and you looked after me, I was in prison and you came to visit me." Then the righteous will answer him, "Lord, when did we see you hungry and feed you, or thirsty and give you something to drink? When did we see you a stranger and invite you in, or needing clothes and clothe you? When did we see you sick or in prison and go to visit you?" The King will reply, "I tell you the truth, whatever you did for one of the least of these brothers of mine, you did for me."[41]

Among evangelical Christians, this theme was expressly articulated in the second meeting of the Lausanne Movement, held in Manila in 1989 and including 3,600 leaders from 190 nations. Their Manila Manifesto includes the following paragraphs:

> The authentic gospel must become visible in the transformed lives of men and women. As we proclaim the love of God, we must be involved in loving service; as we preach the Kingdom of God, we must be committed to its demands of justice and peace.
>
> Evangelism is primary because our chief concern is with the gospel, that all people may have the opportunity to accept Jesus Christ as Lord and Saviour. Yet Jesus not only proclaimed the Kingdom of God, he also demonstrated its arrival by works of mercy and power. We are called today to a similar integration of words and deeds. In a spirit of humility we are to preach and teach, minister to the sick, feed the hungry, care for prisoners, help the disadvantaged and handicapped, and deliver the oppressed. While we acknowledge the diversity of spiritual gifts, callings and contexts, we also affirm that good news and good works are inseparable.
>
> The proclamation of God's kingdom necessarily demands the prophetic denunciation of all that is incompatible with it. Among the evils we deplore are destructive violence, including institutionalized violence, political corruption, all forms of exploitation of people and of the earth, the undermining of the family, abortion on demand, the drug traffic, and the abuse of human rights. In our concern for the poor, we are distressed by the burden of debt in the two-thirds world. We are also outraged

by the inhuman conditions in which millions live, who bear God's image as we do.

Our continuing commitment to social action is not a confusion of the kingdom of God with a Christianized society. It is, rather, a recognition that the biblical gospel has inescapable social implications. True mission should always be incarnational. It necessitates entering humbly into other people's worlds, identifying with their social reality, their sorrow and suffering, and their struggles for justice against oppressive powers. This cannot be done without personal sacrifices.[42]

Similarly, Rick Warren, author of *The Purpose Driven Life* and founder and senior pastor of Saddleback Church, a megachurch in Southern California, in speaking to the issue of global poverty, urged Evangelicals to take practical actions to alleviate the plight of others. In his advocacy letter for the One campaign to eliminate poverty, he wrote:

I deeply believe that if we as evangelicals remain silent and do not speak up in defense of the poor, we lose our credibility and our right to witness about God's love for the world: "If anyone has material possessions and sees his brother in need but has no pity on him, how can the love of God be in him?" (1 John 3:17)

Perhaps no other person in recent history, though, has taken the words, "For I was hungry and you gave me something to eat," more seriously than Mother Teresa and her co-workers in Calcutta, India. According to the constitution of the International Association of Co-Workers of Mother Teresa, life, care, and community are to be extended to "all castes and creeds," especially the "poorest of the poor" whom no one else is willing to attend to.[43]

In saying this, Mother Teresa is echoing the catechism of the Catholic Church, which, in turn, echoes Deuteronomy 11:1, quoted previously:

> Above all—charity.
>
> The whole concern of doctrine and its teaching must be directed to the love that never ends. Whether something is proposed for belief, for hope or for action, the love of our Lord must always be made accessible, so that anyone can see that all the works of perfect Christian virtue spring from love and have no other objective than to arrive at love.[44]

Aspirations to Holiness

Finally, a very different kind of reason to help those in need appears in Jewish sources: the aspiration to holiness. This is not the morality of owing God, of promise keeping, or of community involvement; it is rather the morality of doing something because the person I want to be and the kind of community I want to be part of requires that I do this. In theological terms, this translates into aspiring to be like God:

> The Lord spoke to Moses, saying: Speak to the whole Israelite community and say to them: You shall be holy, for I, the Lord your God, am holy.... When you reap the harvest of your land, you shall not reap all the way to the edges of your field, or gather the gleanings of your harvest. You shall not pick your vineyard bare, or gather the fallen fruit of your vineyard; you shall leave them for the poor and the stranger: I the Lord am your God.
>
> —Leviticus 19:1–2, 9–10

I have made you a light of nations to be [the vehicle of]
My salvation to the ends of the earth.

—Isaiah 49:6

Rabbi Hama, son of Rabbi Hanina, said: What is the
meaning of the verse, "You shall walk behind the Lord
your God" (Deuteronomy 13:5)? ... [It means that] a
person should imitate the righteous ways of the Holy
One, blessed be He. Just as the Lord clothed the naked
... so too you must supply clothes for the naked [poor].
Just as the Holy One, blessed be He, visited the sick ...
so too you should visit the sick. Just as the Holy
One, blessed be He, buried the dead ... so too you
must bury the dead. Just as the Holy One, blessed be
He, comforted mourners ... so too you should comfort
mourners.

—B. *Sotah* 14a

Christian texts speak to the same aspiration for religion—undefiled by selfish motives: "Religion that is pure
and undefiled before God, the Father, is this: to care for
orphans and widows in their distress, and to keep oneself unstained by the world" (James 1:27). Similarly, Paul
explained that unlike Peter's form of belief in Christ, which
demanded adherence to Jewish law, the religion of the Spirit
that he was espousing did not require adherence to the
Torah's laws except for one: care for the poor (Galatians
2:7–10).

Caring for the poor is thus central to authentic Christian
faith, discipleship, and vocation. In Jewish terms, it is how a
person aspires to be holy—that is, to be as much like God as
possible.

The Wisdom of Multiple Motivations

In sum, the Jewish and Christian traditions provide multiple reasons to help those in need. In all human acts, we are motivated by many things, some more prominent in our consciousness and more compelling at the moment than others, perhaps, but all playing a role in getting us to do what we do. Furthermore, what goads us into action today may be different tomorrow. Thus even though one particular ground for helping others may dominate a person's thinking and acting today, other rationales for doing so may nevertheless play a role now and may become primary at another time. Both Judaism and Christianity were wise in suggesting multiple reasons to help others in need.

Limits on Giving

Some people have no difficulty understanding why they should give to the poor; in fact, they are so convinced by one or more of the rationales described in this chapter that they give up all or most of their assets to help others. The Talmud knows of such people:

> When the charity collectors saw Elazar Ish Biratha, they would hide from him, for otherwise he would give them everything he had. One day he went to the market to provide a dowry for his daughter. The charity collectors saw Elazar and hid from him. He, however, ran after them and said to them: "I adjure you, tell me what you are collecting for?" They said to him, "We are collecting for an orphan boy and an orphan girl [so that they may marry]." He said to them: "By the Temple Service [the form of making an oath]! The orphans take precedence over my

daughter." He took all that he had and gave it to them. He kept, though, one *zuz* [a small denomination of money], and with it he bought wheat, which he brought home and placed in his storehouse. His daughter asked him, "Father, what did you get?" He said to her, "All that I bought I placed in the storehouse." When she went to open the door to the storehouse, she saw that the storehouse was filled with wheat so that it was bursting out of the door lock, so much so that the door would not open [because its openings on the top and bottom were stuffed with wheat]. Elazar's daughter went to the house of study and said to him, "Come and see what your Beloved [God] did for you!" He said to her, "By the Temple Service! This wheat is consecrated [and hereby given to the Temple], and you must only draw from it along with the other poor of Israel."

—B. *Ta'anit* 24a

There are some voices in rabbinic literature that express appreciation for such extravagant levels of giving, even though such generosity inevitably produces an ascetic way of living:

One who says, "Mine is yours and yours is yours" is a pious person [*hasid*].

—M. *Avot* 5:12

The general thrust of the rabbinic tradition, though, is that divesting yourself of all or most of your assets to help the poor is not the proper path for either yourself or your family, or even for the community at large. Thus, except for the German pietists (*hasidai ashkenaz*) of the thirteenth and four-teenth centuries, the Jewish tradition did not value asceticism, contrary to the model of Catholic monks, priests, and nuns.

You instead have a duty to care for your own life and health first, then for the needs of your family, and then for the poor and other social needs.

> Decreasing one's wealth is not an act of piety if such wealth has been gained in a lawful way and its further acquisition does not prevent one from occupying himself with study of Torah and good deeds, especially for one who has a family and dependents and whose desire is to spend his money for the sake of God.... For you are, as it were, enjoying the Lord's hospitality, being invited to God's table, and should thank God for God's bounty, both inwardly and outwardly.
> —Judah Halevi (before 1075–1141)
> *The Kuzari* 11:50

Furthermore, the Rabbis were worried that those who give too much to the poor will themselves become poor and dependent on the society for their sustenance. Consequently, the Rabbis of the Talmud specify that giving 5 percent or less of your income each year to charity is "mean" and that 10 percent is "middling," and they impose a limit of 20 percent (B. *Ketubbot* 50a; Maimonides, *M.T. Laws of Gifts to the Poor* 7:5).

These limits affect yearly contributions. What about estate planning, though? We could argue that the wealthiest among us can and should give more than a fifth of their assets to charity when they plan their estate; for after death they obviously no longer need to sustain themselves, and although people clearly need to provide for a surviving spouse if there is one, leaving too much to your children can diminish their own drive to be productive. Thus for the welfare of your own children as well of society, the wealthy among us should probably give more than a fifth of their estate to the poor and other social causes such as education and health care.

Christians have wrestled with proper limits for giving too. One of the most thoughtful thinkers on this is influential evangelical minister Timothy Keller, who has written this:

> God's mercy comes to us without conditions, but does not proceed without our cooperation. So too our aid must begin freely, regardless of the recipient's merits. But our mercy must increasingly demand change or it is not really love.... At what point, then, do we begin to set conditions? What is the guideline? It is this: We must let mercy limit mercy. Sometimes we let revenge limit mercy. "Look at all I've done for that person," we say, "and what thanks do I get?" Perhaps you have looked foolish to others for your involvement with a needy person, and his lack of response has embarrassed you. In other cases, we may let selfishness limit mercy. "That family is bleeding me dry. I quit!" But in the final analysis, only mercy can limit mercy. We may cut off our aid only *if it is unmerciful to continue it.* It is unmerciful to bail out a person who needs to feel the full consequences of his own irresponsible behavior.[45]

On the other end of the financial spectrum, contrary to those who maintain that "money is the source of all evil," the Jewish tradition maintains that wealth and piety can coexist. In fact, the rich in particular should be thankful to God for their bounty, and they should give to the poor and to other social needs generously in accordance with their wealth.

Most of the wealthy, though—and, for that matter, the well-off, the near-wealthy, and even the rest of us with fewer assets—do not give what we should. In the mid-1980s, when estates in the United States over $600,000 were taxed at 50 percent, my attorney told me that he made it crystal clear to his wealthiest clients that even with employing all of the legal tax shelters available, estate taxes would take close to half of their estates and that the only way to avoid giving that money to the government was to give it to charities. Furthermore, he showed them that they could arrange to do that in their lifetime in a way that did not prevent them from doing what they wanted for the remainder of their lives; they could enjoy and even be honored for the good they were doing for the causes that mattered to them. Even with all that information, he told me, most wealthy people failed to be generous; they just could not think about parting with their money, even after they died. So the most important part of the Jewish tradition to learn for the vast majority of us is not so much the limits on what we should give, but the imperative to give in the first place.

RESPONSIBILITIES OF THE POOR

The well-off have duties to the downtrodden for the reasons described above, but Jewish law imposes duties on the poor as well. Aside from the duty of giving to other poor people, the poor must strive to find work to support themselves. Nobody may avoid work on the presumption that God and compassionate human beings will provide for his or her needs.

> A person should not say, "I will eat and drink and see prosperity without troubling myself since Heaven will have compassion upon me." To teach this Scripture says, "You have blessed the work of his hands" (Job 1:10), demonstrating that a man should toil with both his hands and then the Holy One, blessed be He, will grant His blessing.
> —*Tanhuma Vayetze*, Section 13

Fill in this card and return it to us to be eligible for our quarterly drawing for a $100 gift certificate for Jewish Lights books.

We hope that you will enjoy this book and find it useful in enriching your life.

Book title: _____

Your comments: _____

How you learned of this book: _____

If purchased: Bookseller _____ City _____ State _____

Please send me a free JEWISH LIGHTS Publishing catalog. I am interested in: (check all that apply)

1. ☐ Spirituality
2. ☐ Mysticism/Kabbalah
3. ☐ Philosophy/Theology
4. ☐ History/Politics

5. ☐ Women's Interest
6. ☐ Environmental Interest
7. ☐ Healing/Recovery
8. ☐ Children's Books

9. ☐ Caregiving/Grieving
10. ☐ Ideas for Book Groups
11. ☐ Religious Education Resources
12. ☐ Interfaith Resources

Name (PRINT) _____

Street _____

City _____ State _____ Zip _____

E-MAIL (FOR SPECIAL OFFERS ONLY)

Please send a JEWISH LIGHTS Publishing catalog to my friend:

Name (PRINT) _____

Street _____

City _____ State _____ Zip _____

JEWISH LIGHTS PUBLISHING

Tel: (802) 457-4000 • Fax: (802) 457-4004

Available at better booksellers. Visit us online at www.jewishlights.com

WIN A $100 GIFT CERTIFICATE!

Fill in this card and
mail it to us—
or fill it in **online** at

**jewishlights.com/
feedback.html**

—to be eligible for a
$100 gift certificate for
Jewish Lights books.

Place
Stamp
Here

This has direct implications in our own day for some, primarily in the ultra-Orthodox community, who devote themselves solely to study of classical Jewish texts. It is fine to do that for a year or two, as many do immediately after high school or during or after college and as some do on a sabbatical later in life. Some pursue Jewish study further and become rabbis, earning their living through the many activities that rabbis are called upon to do in teaching, counseling, worship, life cycle events, and social service; and others may like the life of the mind so much that they become professors, earning a living by teaching and doing research in a university or seminary setting. But a person may not study throughout his or her life, contribute nothing to the life of others on the basis of that study, and depend on others for support:

> [On the one hand,] one should not say: I will first accumulate wealth and then devote time to the study of the Torah, or I will delay study until I acquire what I need and retire from my work, for if you think in that way, you will never merit the crown of Torah study. Rather, make your study of Torah a set part of your calendar and your work temporary, and "Do not say, 'When I have time, I will study,' lest you never have time" (*M. Avot 4:10*)....
> [On the other hand,] anyone who decides to study Torah, not work, and sustain himself through charity has desecrated God's Name [reputation] and disgraced the Torah ... Sacred study that is not accompanied by gainful employment is itself null and void and leads to sin, for in the end such a person will rob others.
> —Maimonides, *M. T. Laws of Studying Torah* 3:7, 10

Those who try to find work but cannot must nevertheless engage in some useful activity, because that will at least contribute to the society that is supporting them and also because "a man only dies through idleness" (*Avot, D'Rabbi Natan,* 11).

Some people, of course, cannot work, and they are exempted from this requirement. What happens, though, if a poor person is simply lazy and does not seek work? The Jewish tradition did not contemplate such a possibility, probably for a combination of reasons. First, the work ethic was strongly ingrained in Jews, and so refusing to work when you could would be seen as shameful. Second, Jews by and large lived in small communities, so people could not be anonymous and thus deceive others as to the reality of their needs as readily as they could in a large community. Furthermore, the degradation of begging is all the greater if the ones from whom you beg know you. Finally, until the twentieth century, Jewish communities were seldom wealthy, and so while a person could subsist on the support provided by the community, he could not live comfortably on that aid. This made depending on the community unattractive for economic reasons as well as moral, psychological, and social ones.

PRINCIPLES AND METHODS FOR DISTRIBUTING AID TO THOSE IN NEED

In some ways, the distribution of relief to those who need it was radically different in times past from what we know today. Governments did not provide such relief; it was totally a matter of generous individuals and religious and social agencies. Nowadays, part of our tax dollars are used to provide a safety net for the poor and needy, and you might legitimately ask whether you can count that percentage of your taxes toward what you are required by Jewish law to give to those in need. (That percentage would decrease, of course, if the government reduced its support for the poor and others in need, as the American government has done in recent years.) Furthermore, we now live in much larger communities than we did earlier, and so the need for contributing and the sense that we should support our community may well be weaker. At the same time, modern media bring news of the destitute around the world into our living rooms, so we are more aware of the extent of poverty not only in our local community but also literally around the world. Therefore, when we consider Jewish sources on how to collect and distribute funds, we must take into consideration the differences between contemporary conditions and those of times past.

Even during the years when the government provided generously for social programs, there has been a consistent need for individuals to contribute to charitable institutions—religious, educational, and cultural ones as well as those dedicated to helping the poor or needy. The Jewish community can take pride in its long history of ensuring that people—both Jews and non-Jews—do not starve or lack clothing. Maimonides went so far as to say this:

> We have never seen nor heard of an Israelite community that does not have a charity fund.
>
> —*M. T. Laws of Gifts to the Poor* 9:3

What a given Jewish community could provide depended on its resources, but the historical record offers an estimable model and motivation for our own contemporary efforts. Moreover, Jewish sources give us some guidance in how Jewish social service agencies should distribute their aid.

First, as we saw in Maimonides's ladder of the degrees of charity quoted previously (see p. 25–26), lending money to people is preferable to giving them support directly—similar to the old adage of teaching a person to fish rather than giving him one. Investing in a common business with poor people is even better than giving them money for their enterprises, because working with poor people trains them in the skills they need to succeed. It also affords an even greater measure of dignity to them: after all, the donor thinks enough of the person not only to invest money in his or her future, but also to invest time and effort and, furthermore, to interact with him or her on an ongoing basis. Although Maimonides spells out this hierarchy in greater detail than had been previously done, its origins are in the Talmud:

> Rabbi Abba said in the name of Rabbi Simeon ben Lakish: He who lends money [to a poor person] is greater than he who gives charity; and he who throws money into a common purpose [to form a partnership with the poor person] is greater than either.
>
> —B. *Shabbat* 63b

In modern times, Christian writer Ron Sider has delineated seven principles for working with those in need that are clearly based on the same principle that Maimonides used—namely, providing for the needs of the poor while preserving their dignity:

1. Practice hospitality and live in solidarity
2. Share resources
3. Empower self-sufficiency
4. Invest in development
5. Promote justice
6. Break the cycle of poverty
7. Share the good news with the poor[46]

The National Conference of Catholic Bishops' *Pastoral Letter on Catholic Social Teaching* also echoes Maimonides, for the first five of its principle speak directly to helping people help themselves before turning attention to giving out doles:

> a. *The first line of attack against poverty must be to build and sustain a healthy economy that provides employment opportunities at just wages for all adults who are able to work....*
>
> b. *Vigorous action should be undertaken to remove barriers to full and equal employment for women and minorities....*
>
> c. *Self-help efforts among the poor should be fostered by programs and policies in both the private and public sectors....*
>
> d. *The tax system should be continually evaluated in terms of its impact on the poor....*
>
> e. *All of society should make a much stronger commitment to education for the poor....*
>
> f. *Policies and programs at all levels should support the strength and stability of families, especially those adversely affected by the economy.*
>
> g. *A thorough reform of the nation's welfare and income-support programs should be undertaken.... Public assistance programs should be designed to assist recipients, wherever possible, to become self-sufficient through gainful employment.... Welfare programs should provide recipients with adequate levels of support....* [italics in the original][47]

Along these lines, in 1970 the United States Conference of Catholic Bishops created the Catholic Campaign for Human Development with a mission to help "people lift themselves out of poverty" by "breaking the cycle of poverty" through funding low-income, controlled empowerment projects and through legislative efforts to spur states and local communities to pass living wage ordinances.[48]

According to the Rabbis, it is also better to come to people's aid when their problems are just beginning rather than after they have become destitute:

> "If your kinsman, being in straits, comes under your authority, you shall uphold him" (Leviticus 25:35). Do not allow him to fall into utter poverty. The injunction may be explained by analogy with a load on a donkey: as long as he is standing up, one may grab him [to keep him from falling] and keep him standing upright. Once he has fallen, however, five men cannot make him stand up again.
>
> —*Sifra Leviticus*, on Leviticus 25:35
> (ed. Weiss, p. 109b)

If the first lesson of Jewish sources is that prevention is better than cure, the second is that the extent to which a person should be eligible for the community's aid should depend, at least in part, on the depth of that person's roots in the community.

> The soup kitchen [provides enough food] for a full day, but the communal fund gives [sufficient food to last] from one week to the next. The soup kitchen [provides food] for anybody, but the communal fund [gives support only] to the poor of that locale. [A poor person] living there for thirty days attains the status of being a resident of the locale for [purposes of receiving assistance] from the communal fund. But [to receive] shelter [he must have lived there] for six months, and to be liable to the town tax [he must have been a resident] for twelve months.
>
> —*Tosefta Pe'ah* 4:9

Presumably, the extent of a person's need would be another factor that the community must take into account, but there was a strong sense that the community must first help its own. What results are concentric circles of care and concern:

> The Torah commands that the needy of his household come first, then the poor of his city, and they, in turn, have priority over the poor of another city.... Rabbi Saadia (882–942) wrote that a person is required to put his own sustenance first, and is not obliged to give charity to others until after providing for his own. The Torah says, "And your brother shall live with you" (Leviticus 25:36), a verse that clearly establishes that your life comes first and only then the other person [following the Babylonian Talmud, *Bava Metzia* 62a]. Also remember what the widow of Tzarefat said to the prophet Elijah [1 Kings 17:12]: "And I have done this for me and my son," first for herself and afterward for her son, a comment Elijah approved of because he said [v. 13], "Do it for yourself" [first] "and your son" only afterward. After one has seen to his own sustenance, he may then give priority to the sustenance of his needy parents over that of his adult children, and then he should see to the sustenance of his adult children.[49]
>
> —Jacob ben Asher (d. 1340),
> *Arba'ah Turim, Yoreh De'ah,* chap. 251

Third, the community has a duty to ensure that funds collected for charity are distributed honestly and fairly.

> Our Rabbis taught: The charity fund is collected by two persons [jointly] and distributed by three. It is collected by two because any office conferring authority over the community must be filled by at least two persons. It must be

distributed by three, on the analogy of monetary cases [that
are, according to Jewish law, decided by a court consisting of
three judges. Here three are necessary because the people
involved have to judge the merits of various claimants].

—B. *Bava Batra* 8b

Furthermore, those who distribute the funds have to be
trusted to be both morally beyond reproach and efficient:

Only a person who is as trustworthy as Rabbi Haninah
ben Teradyon is qualified to administer the communal
charity fund. But a ... person who is forgetful should not
be nominated as administrator, no matter how upright and
moral he may be, for he will forget how much he paid out,
and he cannot be trusted to receive donations [either], for
it [the donation] may slip his mind.... You cannot satisfy
everybody. Sometimes a treasurer of a charity fund gives
money to dignified people who are in straits. He should
tell only two or three of the leading members of the community because if the matter became public knowledge, it
would be a source of deep embarrassment to the recipient.... The treasurer should not pay attention to vile char-
acters who say that they do not trust him. But if the
majority of the community expresses displeasure and
wants to depose him, he should say to the board of directors, "Because the majority of the members are opposed to
me, go ahead and elect someone who is to your liking."

—Rabbi Yehudah He-Hasid, *Sefer Chasidim*
192–193 (Avraham Finkel, trans. [Northvale, NJ:
Jason Aronson, 1997], 116)

Fourth, Jewish law recognizes that it is not just physical
needs that must be supplied, for poverty makes people

ashamed. As Maimonides's ladder of methods to help the poor (see pp. 25–26) illustrates, you must attend to the psychological needs of the poor to the extent that you can. Thus, on the basis of Deuteronomy 15:8, "You shall open your hand [to the poor person] and provide him sufficient for his need, whatever it may be," the Rabbis ruled that those managing the community's charity fund must take into account the standard of living poor people enjoyed before falling into poverty. The fund must then afford whatever they need to regain their dignity—even if that means providing a horse and herald.[50] This does not mean that the community is obligated to restore the poor to their former wealth.[51] Instead, the officers who distribute funds must differentiate between the *legitimate* call to sustain a poor person's honor and an *illegitimate* demand on the part of the poor to live lavishly at the community's expense.

Another factor obviously plays a role in how much aid the poor receive, namely, the funds available. Throughout history, most Jewish communities were themselves poor. Consequently, few poor people, if any, were provided with "a horse to ride upon and a herald to run before him," or the equivalent. Indeed, the limited resources of Jewish communities made it especially imperative that they balance the individual needs of each poor person with due regard for their obligation to aid *all* the needy.[52] No wonder the Talmud says that the distribution of charitable funds is more onerous than the collection![53]

The Baptist minister Tony Campolo has similarly argued for attending, when possible, to the spiritual needs of the poor as well as their physical needs in order to help them maintain their dignity—in his case, through music:

> People—especially poor people whose lives tend to be very drab—need beauty for their souls. Some Roman

Catholic missionaries in Haiti made a Herculean effort to get together enough money to build a concert hall and establish a symphony orchestra in the city of Port-au-Prince. There were some who criticized their work and argued that it was crazy to provide concerts for starving people. I, myself, had serious doubts as to the wisdom of the project until opening night. Those who saw the faces of the ragged people who jammed that concert hall to hear the symphony were left with no doubt that the money had been used wisely. There was something mystically beautiful being taken in by these poverty-beaten people. There was something given to them that evening that made life a little more bearable. There was something that happened under the spell of the music that made people who had been hardened by need into softer, kinder folk. Everyone at the concert could feel God at work, providing something precious for the poor.[54]

Finally, the Talmud and codes have an amazing provision: Jews must care for non-Jews as well as Jews. In light of the concentric circles described previously, the degree of aid that Jews provided to non-Jews would surely be less than that given to Jews; but the fact that Jewish law requires Jews to help non-Jews at all is truly remarkable, for historically non-Jews were much more likely to maim and kill Jews than to help them:

> In a city with both Jews and idolaters [non-Jews], the collectors raise funds for charity from Jews and non-Jews for the sake of peace; we support the poor among non-Jews along with the Jewish poor for the sake of peace; [we visit the sick among non-Jews with the sick among Jews;][55] we mourn and bury the non-Jewish dead [assuming that they

do not do that themselves] for the sake of peace; and we comfort those mourning non-Jews for the sake of peace.

—*Tosefta Gittin* 3:18; see B. *Gittin* 61a

In our own day, where the world has become a global village, we certainly can no longer think about caring for others, including the poor, by thinking exclusively of our own local community. Jewish organizations, perhaps especially the American Jewish World Service, have thus created programs for aiding people around the world. Christianity has historically done this and continues to do so as part of its missionary work. Many thinkers in the nineteenth and twentieth centuries—including, among Jews, some very antireligious people, like Karl Marx, who nevertheless articulated a very Jewish conception of the urgency of aiding those in need—have led us to apply to the global community Jewish and Christian principles that until then usually focused only on local needs.

Christians have articulated the same concern. For example, Walter Rauschenbusch, the father of the social gospel, has done so in many of his writings.[56] The World Council of Churches likewise spoke of this in its December 1998 statement on the topic.[57]

Thus we return to the opening chapters of Genesis and the theme with which this chapter began: God is sovereign over the entire world and our obligations flow from that. When Cain asks God, "Am I my brother's keeper?" (Genesis 4:9), God does not answer him directly because the answer should be obvious. That question, and the Bible's expected answer to it, ring through the centuries as a clarion call for us to care for others, a call that now applies worldwide.

PART TWO

Tikkun Olam
in Practice

Individuals and Society

3

THE POWER OF WORDS

On Yom Kippur (the Day of Atonement), the holiest day of the Jewish year, at each of the five services of the day Jews recite a long litany of sins for which we ask God's forgiveness. A large portion of that list involves sins we commit through speaking. Clearly, then, the Jewish tradition takes the ethics of speaking very seriously. In fact, the Rabbis of the Talmud note that if you embarrass someone else in public, the victim's face often turns white, and they compare that to the pale face of the dead so as to say that embarrassing a person is akin to killing him or her:

> Someone taught before Rabbi Nahman bar Isaac: If a man put his neighbor to shame, it is as if he shed blood. Rabbi Nahman said to him: Well have you spoken, for we see how the red disappears [in the victim's face] and the pallor comes.
>
> —B. *Bava Metzia* 58b

In fact, they go further: such a remark also "kills" both the speaker and the listener. The Rabbis therefore call slander "the third tongue" (*lishan telitae*) because "it slays three people: the speaker, the listener, and the one spoken about" (B. *Arakhin* 15b). Not only do speech violations cause death, they also deprive a person of a place in the world to come:

> There are four great sins that correspond to four great virtues, in that a person is punished for them in this world, and their capital, or stock, remains in the form of punishment dealt out to him or her in the world to come. These four are idolatry, incest, murder, and slander, the last of which is as bad as all the other three put together.
>
> —J. *Pe'ah* 1:1 (15d)

As the Book of Proverbs (18:21) succinctly puts it, "Death and life are in the hands of the tongue."

Words obviously are not altogether a bad thing; like all our other faculties, the moral quality of our speech depends on how we use it. The following rabbinic story makes this point eloquently:

> Rabbi Shimon ben Gamliel said to his servant Tabbai: "Go to the market and buy me good food." He went out and brought back a tongue. He told him, "Go out and bring me bad food from the market." He went out and brought him a tongue. He then asked him: "Why is it that when I said 'good food' you brought me a tongue, and when I said 'bad food' you also brought me a tongue?" He replied: "It is the source of good and evil. When it is good, it cannot be surpassed; when it is evil, then there is nothing worse."
>
> —*Leviticus Rabbah* 33:1

The exact same understanding of the power of the tongue to do both good and bad appears in the New Testament:

> For all of us make many mistakes. Anyone who makes no mistakes in speaking is perfect, able to keep the whole body in check with a bridle. If we put bits into the mouths of horses to make them obey us, we guide their whole bodies. Or look at ships: though they are so large that it

takes strong winds to drive them, yet they are guided by a very small rudder wherever the will of the pilot directs. So also the tongue is a small member, yet it boasts of great exploits. How great a forest is set ablaze by a small fire! And the tongue is a fire. The tongue is placed among our members as a world of iniquity; it stains the whole body, sets on fire the cycle of nature, and is itself set on fire by hell. For every species of beast and bird, of reptile and sea creature, can be tamed and has been tamed by the human species, but no one can tame the tongue—a restless evil, full of deadly poison. With it we bless the Lord and Father, and with it we curse those who are made in the likeness of God. From the same mouth come blessing and cursing.

—James 3:2–10

THE MISUSE OF WORDS

We human beings have been quite creative in developing ways to misuse words, and, as the Yom Kippur liturgy reminds us, we therefore have to be especially careful in how we speak about and to others. Why do we have to take such precautions? Because we must have respect for others and care for them for all the reasons described in Chapter 2. Moreover, as people created in the image of God, we must have respect for ourselves as well; when we abuse our power to speak, we besmirch ourselves as well as the people to or about whom we are speaking.

In making those values concrete, the Rabbis warn us against the following forms of speech: foul language, lies, gossip, negative talk, and oppressive speech.

Foul Language—Nivvul Peh

People use swear words to dishonor others and/or to emphasize some point that they are trying to make. Degrading others is prohibited by Jewish tradition for the reasons discussed in Chapter 2: we do not have to like everyone, and we certainly do not have to approve of what everyone does, but we must respond to others—even when condemning their behavior—with respect for the image of God within them. The topic of the next section of this chapter focuses on how to criticize what others do while upholding their honor.

If the point of using foul language is to stress how intensely you feel about a given point, that use of language involves several problems. First, if you do that often—some teenagers and adults use foul language in virtually every sentence—then verbal inflation takes place and the swear words lose their power. Nobody recognizes that your swear words indicate that you feel especially strongly about a given topic if you use them too much; it is like crying wolf.

Furthermore, people with a good education can express intense feelings without using swear words, and they are well advised to do so. Nobody respects you more because of your use of swear words; at best, good friends will excuse that behavior. Thus just as much as respect for others demands that you avoid swear words, so too does self-respect.

Another factor reinforces the point that you should desist from using foul language to protect your own self-respect. An article assigned in my college freshman English course argued that the swear words various societies use bespeak the aspects of life that they find troubling. In the United States, with its Puritan heritage, foul language is primarily sexual. In Germany, with its focus on cleanliness, swear words are based on bathroom functions. Italians swear using various epithets for the Church.

For Americans, this means that when people swear, they are revealing their discomfort with their own sexual functioning. Jewish sources, though, depict our bodies, including their sexual parts, as made by God no less than our minds, our emotions, our wills, and all other parts of our inner being (our souls). Consequently, using sexual terms to curse or denigrate others is not only to insult the people at whom the remarks are directed, but also to slur God.

Finally, obscenities befoul the social atmosphere, making it rough and uncouth rather than respectful and polite. It is, as this source suggests, a form of pollution:

> Rabbi Elazar ben Jacob said: A person who uses rough language is like a pipe spewing foul odors in a beautiful room.
> —*Derekh Eretz Rabbah* 3:3

Although it is not completely clear that Matthew is speaking about foul language specifically, he expresses a similar sentiment:

> For out of the abundance of the heart the mouth speaks. The good person brings good things out of a good treasure, and the evil person brings evil things out of an evil treasure. I tell you, on the day of judgment you will have to give an account for every careless word you utter; for by your words you will be justified, and by your words you will be condemned.
> —Matthew 12:34b–37

Lies—Sheker

Knowingly and intentionally telling someone something you know to be false undermines people's trust in one another. Indeed, at the extreme—if everyone lied so often that we could never assume that the next person was telling the truth—social cooperation, commerce, and even friendships and family relations would become impossible.

We would all be living in a fantasy world, and a terrifying one at that. It is not surprising, then, that the Torah specifically prohibits lying and the Book of Proverbs calls it "an abomination":

> You must not carry false rumors [*shaima shav*, literally, "worthless words to be heard"] ... Keep far from falsehood [*sheker*].
>
> —Exodus 23:1, 7; see also Leviticus 9:11

> Lying speech is an abomination to the Lord,
> But those who act faithfully please Him.
>
> —Proverbs 12:22

In remarkably parallel statements, both the Rabbis and Jesus assert that your "yes" should mean yes and your "no" should mean no:

> "You shall have an honest balance, honest weights, an honest *ephah*, and an honest *hin*:" (Leviticus 19:36). Why did the Torah specify an honest *hin*? After all, a *hin* is included in an *ephah*. It is to tell you that your "yes" [*hain*, a play on words on *hin*] should be honest and your "no" should be honest.
>
> —B. *Bava Metzia* 49b

> Say "yes" when you mean yes and "no" when you mean no. Anything beyond that is from the evil one.
>
> —Matthew 5:37

The New Testament maintains that lying is a clear sign that a person lacks Christian faith, that his or her religion is "worthless":

If any think they are religious, and do not bridle their tongues but deceive their hearts, their religion is worthless.

—James 1:26

Catholic moral theologian Father Gerard Sloyan has noted that neither the Hebrew nor the Christian Bible specifies a reason for its ban on lying:

No philosophical rationale is provided for statements like this in the Bible, no epistemology that explains why tongue and mind must always conform. The assumption is that the liar is a diminished human being, that no satisfactory way exists to do business with a cheat or a deceiver.[1]

Similarly, the talmudic Rabbis understood the social consequences of lying:

This is the penalty for the liar: even when he tells the truth, no one believes him.

—B. *Sanhedrin* 89b

They also condemned it as a form of theft, indeed the worst form of theft:

Stealing a person's thought [*genevat da'at*, i.e., deception] is the worst form of theft.

—*Tosefta Bava Kamma* 7:8

Why did the Rabbis say that lying is the worst form of theft? Why is it worse than stealing money or property from a person? There are many possible answers. One is that even though people who have been robbed often feel personally violated, in the end it is their property that the thief has encroached upon, not their person. Often the thief does not even know the person from whom he or she has stolen. Deception, though, is immediately and directly personal: the liar did not think enough of you to tell you the truth, and so you rightly feel dishonored and molested. We will see below how the Rabbis make the same kind of distinction between property and person with regard to slander.

Of course, sometimes you tell a falsehood without knowing or intending to do so. In such cases, the level of moral culpability is much less; you have simply made a mistake. Nevertheless, the Rabbis warn us against our very human desire to be seen as someone who knows everything, for that may lead us to give people false information:

> Teach your tongue to say "I do not know," lest you invent something and be trapped.
>
> —B. *Berakhot* 4a

"I do not know" is a really important phrase to include in our common speech patterns, for then the hearer knows exactly how much you trust what you say if you then venture a guess. Under those circumstances nobody is deceived. The hearer may just accept the guess or suggest one of his or her own if the matter does not mean very much to either person. But if the hearer really needs to know the answer for some practical or personal purpose, the speaker has put him or her on notice that even though the speaker *thinks* that the answer is X, the hearer will have to go elsewhere to find out conclusively. By saying "I do not know," the speaker transfers responsibility for discovering the answer back to the hearer. In the case of doctors, for example, if a physician can tell a patient exactly what is wrong and what needs to be done, then he or she should surely do so. Often, however, the diagnosis or prognosis is much less clear, in which case a patient feels much more respected if the doctor acknowledges that fact, or even suggests that the patient consult another doctor, instead of pretending to know what he or she really does not know.

Does such an admission, though, undermine our own self-respect and the honor that others will give us? Not really, for in our heart of hearts we all know that none of us is all-knowing, as God is believed to be. Therefore you should not be embarrassed to admit not knowing something. Even if the question is in what is supposed to be the hearer's area of expertise, the questioner will appreciate an honest admission of a lack of knowledge—especially if the person asked then goes to the trouble to find the answer. Honesty about what you know and do not know is always the best policy so that you can avoid telling even unintended falsehoods and thus be trusted.

In the end, then, as both the psalmist and the New Testament proclaim, we must avoid deceit, even when unintended:

> Who is the man who is eager for life,
> who desires years of good fortune?
> Guard your tongue from evil,
> your lips from deceitful speech.
> Shun evil and do good,
> seek peace and pursue it.
> —Psalm 34:13–15

For those who desire life and desire to see good days, let them keep their tongues from evil and their lips from speaking deceit; let them turn away from evil and do good; let them seek peace and pursue it.
—1 Peter 3:10–11

Gossip—Rekhilut

The Hebrew word for gossip comes from the root *rokhel*, which means a peddler. Gossips spread news about people, just as peddlers hawk their wares. Even though gossip, by definition, consists of truths about other people—or, at least, what the speaker thinks is true—and even though the speaker tells of matters that do not in and of themselves degrade the person being described, nevertheless the Torah forbids spreading gossip:

> Do not spread tales [*lo talekh rakhil*] among your people.
> —Leviticus 19:16

Similarly, Paul in the New Testament fears that people will engage in gossip among a number of other common offenses:

> For I fear that when I come, I may find you not as I wish, and that you may find me not as you wish; I fear that there may perhaps be quarreling, jealousy, anger, selfishness, slander, gossip, conceit, and disorder.
> —2 Corinthians 12:20

Unfortunately, neither the Torah nor the New Testament defines gossip. What, then, is it, and how does it differ from ordinary conversations in which friends sometimes describe what other people are doing?

The Mishnah identifies at least one aspect of gossip that is interdicted, and it quotes that verse from the Torah (Lev. 19:16) and another from Proverbs that uses the same Hebrew phrase (*holekh rakhil*) to make its point:

> How do we know that when one of the judges leaves the court, he may not say [to the litigant who lost the

case], "I voted to acquit you, but my fellow judges made you liable. What could I do, given that my colleagues outnumbered me?" On such speech the Torah says, "Do not spread tales among your people," and the Bible says, "One who spreads tales reveals secrets [but a trustworthy soul keeps a confidence"] (Proverbs 11:13).

—*M. Sanhedrin* 3:7

Maimonides expands on this when he offers a more general definition of gossip and describes its consequences:

[1]One who spreads rumors about someone else violates the negative commandment, "Do not spread tales among your people" (Leviticus 19:16). And even though we do not whip a person who violates this negative commandment [despite that fact that flogging is the usual punishment for violating a negative commandment], nevertheless it is a great sin and causes the killing of many souls of Israel. Therefore, this part of the verse is juxtaposed to the next part, "Do not stand idly by the blood of your brother." Go and learn from what happened to Do'eg the Adumean [whose disclosure of information to Saul led to the killing of 85 innocent men and their wives and children: 1 Samuel, chap. 22, 23].

[2]What is "a tale-bearer"? It is someone who claims things and goes from one person to another, saying: "This is what so-and-so said," and "This is what I heard about so-and-so." Even if it is true, such speech destroys the world.

—*M. T. Laws of Ethics (De'ot)* 7:1–2

Although Maimonides clarifies some things, he leaves us with two important questions. First, does this verse prohibit ordinary conversation? Second, why do the forms of speech Maimonides is describing "destroy the world"?

Obviously, if this prohibition of tale-bearing is interpreted to mean that we cannot speak to each other about the normal things that are going on in our lives, including news about other people, it will set an impossible demand. Moreover, it would do clear harm, for part of the way we satisfy our deep need for companionship is by talking with one another, and some of those conversations naturally center on the people in our lives.

What, then, is true speech about others that is not negative and yet "destroys the world"? Maimonides's own example indicates one type of such speech. Do'eg revealed to Saul that David had been in the city of Nob, a city of priests (*kohanim*) and their families, and that one of the priests there had prayed for David and had given him provisions and the sword of Goliath. This led to the deaths of the whole community, for the priests did not know that King Saul saw David—and therefore also anyone who supported him—as an enemy. Sometimes, then, true speech about people can ultimately harm them if the hearer wants to do that.

Rabbi Joseph Telushkin[2] suggests another kind of true speech that can have bad consequences—namely, great praise. Sometimes, as he points out, great praise for a person can be accompanied by mentioning the one thing that the speaker does not like about the person, and then the only thing that anyone remembers is the negative factor.

The folktale in the first two chapters and the last chapter of the Book of Job combines both of these problems. God heaps praises on Job before Satan, who clearly wants to harm Job. God's praise sets the stage for Satan to challenge Job's piety by getting God to test it by inflicting all sorts of tragedies on him. While the story ends with Job triumphing, his life certainly would have been better without his incurring the misfortunes in the first place. Because we can never know who likes or dislikes whom, except, perhaps, among our closest friends, the best policy is to share as little as possible about other people, especially in the company of people we do not know well.

The lesson in both of these kinds of speech, then, is that we must beware what hearers will make of information about another person, even when it is true and even when the speaker intends no ill. This is especially true when in the company of people that the speaker does not know well, and where the less said about other people, the better. The more you know the listener, the more you can share about family and friends, and so normal conversation with such people is fine. Frictions often exist, though, even among family and friends, and so even in that context you must tailor your remarks to the listener in order to avoid bad consequences for the person described.

Negative Talk When True—Lashon Ha-ra—and False— Motzi Shem Ra

If the Jewish tradition warns us against revealing neutral or even praiseworthy things about others, lest they be misunderstood or misused, it even more harshly condemns negative remarks about another person. Slander—saying false, negative things about a person—is condemned in the New Testament as well:

> Rid yourselves, therefore, of all malice, and all guile, insincerity, envy, and all slander.
>
> —1 Peter 2:1

While saying false, negative things about a person is obviously problematic, in most situations Jewish law also prohibits negative comments that are true. It even prohibits comments that are not themselves defamatory but that imply negative things about someone (*avak lashon ha-ra*, "the dust of saying bad things" or "the dust of slurs").

> ²There is a sin much greater than this [that is, greater than telling tales about someone else], and it is included in this negative prohibition, namely, slurs (literally, "talk about the bad," *lashon ha-ra*). That is someone who talks negatively about someone else, even if he speaks the truth. But one who [additionally] tells lies is called "one who spreads a bad name" (*motzi shem ra*) about someone else. ⁴There are also words that are "the dust of slurs" (*avak lashon ha-ra*). How so? If A says to B, "Who would have ever thought that C would be as he is now?" Or A says, "Don't ask about C; I don't want to tell you what happened," and similar talk. Also, anyone who compliments a person in front of his enemies speaks the dust of slander, for that [positive talk] will cause his enemies to speak negatively of him.
> ⁶All these are people who slur others. It is forbidden to live in their neighborhood, and even more to sit with them and listen to them. "The decree against our ancestors in the wilderness [to wander in the wilderness for forty years] was sealed only because of the slur [of the Land of Israel by the ten spies described in Numbers 14]" (B. *Arakhin* 15b).
>
> —Maimonides, *M. T.*
> *Laws of Ethics (De'ot)* 7:2, 4, 6

Spreading false, negative comments about a person clearly attacks his or her integrity and reputation, and that is, as Maimonides says, akin to murder. But even slurs—true but negative comments about someone (*lashon ha-ra*)—can be nothing less than lethal. Oliver Sipple is a woeful case of this. Sipple, an ex-Marine who saved the life of President Gerald Ford by deflecting the gun directed at him by Sara Jane Moore, became an instant national hero. Despite his request to reporters, "Don't publish anything about me," many noted in their articles that Sipple was active in the gay community. This led to rejection by his parents, who had not known about that aspect of his life—even to the point of his father telling him that he was not welcome at the funeral of his mother—which, in turn, led Sipple to drink heavily and to die alone at age forty-seven. The reporter who first publicized Sipple's homosexuality made this postmortem comment: "If I had to do it over again, I wouldn't."[3]

This case illustrates that what constitutes negative information depends largely on how the hearers will respond to it. After all, being gay is not in and of itself a bad thing; for many young people now, it is simply a fact of life, like the fact that some people have blue eyes rather than the more common brown eyes. Sipple knew, though, that his parents would think ill of him if they knew he was gay, and that was all that mattered.

The prohibition of uttering negative speech applies all the more if everyone knows that what the person is saying is negative, for then there is a clear intention to defame a person. We may not defame a person for we are required to respect each and every person as being created in the image of God.

> Ben Azai said, "This is the record of Adam's line. [When God created man, He made him in the likeness of God; male and female He created them]" (Genesis 5:1–2). This is a great principle in the Torah. Rabbi Akiva said: "Love your neighbor as yourself" (Leviticus 19:18). This is a great principle of the Torah, for one should not say that because I have been shamed, let my fellow person be shamed with

me, because I have been disgraced, let my fellow person be disgraced with me. Rabbi Tanhuma said: If you did so, know whom you are shaming, for "God made him [the human being] in the likeness of God" (Genesis 5:1).

—*Genesis Rabbah* 24:7

Note well that the respect demanded by the Jewish tradition for each and every human being does not mean we must accept everything that anyone does. After all, the Torah is filled with laws that categorize certain forms of human behavior as prohibited and others as required, and if Jews fail to abide by those laws, the Torah demands to "Reprove your kinsman and bear no guilt because of him" (Lev. 19:17). But that reproof must be in private so as not to disgrace the person in public and must be done constructively and with respect for the ultimate human dignity that each of us has. The Torah recognizes such dignity even in someone who is to be flogged for violating a negative commandment:

He may be given forty lashes, but not more, lest being flogged further, to excess, your brother be degraded before your eyes.

—Deuteronomy 25:3

Certainly, then, in everyday speech we must respect the dignity of each person by avoiding defamatory speech, even if the negative information is true and all the more if it is false.

Father Gerard Sloyan eloquently articulates the same requirement of Catholic moral theology:

Detraction—or at its gentlest, belittling—is a sin that most of us are prone to. We hear a name in conversation. We have to cite a character flaw or a foible—some tidbit that the assembled company may not have heard. Silence is called for in such circumstances. We bear no burden so heavy in our little piece of information that it has to be laid down for relief at every opportunity. If the person's weakness must come to light, it ultimately will. We have no obligation to hasten the process. And we have a serious obligation in justice *not* to.[4]

When, though, may you say something negative about someone else? Indeed, when *should* you do so?

You may and actually should share negative information about someone with someone else when the hearer will be making practical decisions based on that information. In such cases the Rabbis interpreted "do not put a stumbling block before a blind person" (Lev. 19:14) as a ban on misleading those who are blind to the facts of a situation (B. *Bava Metzia* 58b, 75b) and on knowingly giving bad advice (*Sifre Kiddoshim* on Lev. 19:14).

If, for example, A has asked you to write a letter of recommendation for him or her to be sent to B, a potential employer, you have a duty to B to be honest about A's qualifications for the job as you see them. Presumably A would not ask you unless A thinks that you will be generally positive, and you should definitely point out A's positive qualifications for the job, but you must also share with B whichever of A's weaknesses you anticipate will affect A's performance at that job. (You should also be sure to indicate where you have no grounds for assessment about how A would function in specific aspects of the job so that B will not think that by omitting mention of those areas you want to indicate that you evaluate A negatively in those respects—a form of "dust of negative speech"). If you really do not think that A is qualified, you may want to tell A that and refuse to write the letter. The same would apply to letters of recommendation for schools.

Father Sloyan maintains that Catholicism would endorse a similar position:

> Only when testimony to a person's character is required of us—in serious matters like a recommendation for or against employment—are we allowed and even obliged to disclose our experience of that person. The usual course of character assassination, sometimes mild but more often vicious, goes along other lines than the obligatory disclosure. We pass along what someone else has said of another for its mere amusement value. Anything for a laugh. But the person we report on is diminished by our action and so are we. We do not rise very high by climbing on others, least of all when we [ourselves] have brought them low in the first place.[5]

Both the Jewish and Christian traditions demand more honesty in writing letters of evaluation than what currently happens under American law, where many employers are reticent to share negative information—and sometimes even positive information—about a former employee lest they be sued. Similarly, teachers will write honestly about a former student—or agree to write at all—only if the student waives his or her rights under the Buckley Amendment, the section of a 1974 federal law that grants students the right to see any letters of recommendation about them. Jewish law requires people who have been asked about a person applying for a job or for acceptance to a school to be honest and forthcoming about both the positive and negative things they know because such information has practical implications for the potential employer or school. To refuse to do that, or to lie in favor of the person, ultimately harms the third party, and that we may not do.

Another kind of situation in which a person should say something negative both to and about someone else is if that person is doing something wrong. That is precisely the case where the Torah demands that we reprove someone. In the extreme, where the person is misleading people into worshiping other gods, the Torah (Deut. 13:7–12) demands that even the closest of relatives shun the person and contribute to putting the person to death. Jewish courts no longer have the authority to execute people, but if someone is leading Jews astray theologically (e.g., to maintain that one can believe that Jesus as the messiah and still adhere to Judaism) or morally (e.g., to take drugs or to harm someone), then we clearly must argue against what they advocate, maybe even to the point of suggesting (or, in the case of family or close friends, urging or even demanding) that others stay away from such people.

Oppressive Speech—Ona-at Devarim

Aside from lies and slander, which you might have anticipated that the Jewish tradition would ban, and aside from telling tales, negative truths, and even the "dust" of such language, which readers might not have thought about previously, Jewish law bans another form of speech that it calls "oppressive." The foundation for this prohibition is two verses in the Torah that assert that we must not wrong one another:

> When you sell property to your neighbor, or buy any from your neighbor, you shall not wrong one another.
> —Leviticus 25:14

> Do not wrong one another, but fear your God; for I, the Lord, am your God.
> —Leviticus 25:17

The Rabbis, following their interpretive principle that nothing in the Torah is superfluous or redundant, determine that the first verse applies to wronging one another in material goods, as the context suggests, and the second, which actually ends the same section about buying and selling, nevertheless refers to wronging people through words.[6]

The Mishnah and Talmud then define what this ban on verbal oppression includes:

> Just as there is wronging others in buying and selling, so too there is wronging others through words. [So, for example,] one must not ask another, "What is the price of this article?" if he has no intention of buying it. If a person repented [of his sin], one must not say to him, "Remember your former deeds." If a person is a child of converts, one must not say to him, "Remember the deeds of your ancestors," because it is written [in the Torah], "You shall neither wrong a stranger nor oppress him" (Exodus 22:20).
> —M. *Bava Metzia* 4:10 (58b)

Several things about this list are noteworthy. First, it is not oppressive to ask a merchant the price of an object if you are thinking of buying something like it, even if not for awhile. It is also not oppressive speech to ask the price if you know that a friend of yours is in the market for such an object and you will convey to him or her how much it costs at a given store. After all, the merchant's business is to sell the object, and sellers know that buyers have the right to compare prices from one shop to another. The only time asking the price becomes oppressive is if you or anyone you know has no intention of buying such an object now or in the near future. For example, if you just bought something and see the same thing in another store and ask the price to see if you got a bargain, that is oppressive. You are then stealing the merchant's time and deceiving him or her into thinking that there is a chance for a sale here. As the Talmud adds, in the end only those asking prices know whether they are doing so legitimately, and so the verse forbidding verbal oppression ends with "and you shall fear your God," who presumably knows what you are thinking at the time you ask a price.

The Mishnah's second example is rather remarkable. The Jewish tradition demands quite a lot of someone who has harmed another person in requiring the wrongdoer to complete the process of return (*teshuvah*) described in Jewish sources. That process includes acknowledgment of the wrongdoing, remorse expressed in words to the harmed party, compensation to the victim to the extent that it is possible, and ultimately better behavior when the same kind of situation arises again.[7] In some ways, this is even harder than serving time in prison, for some convicts never acknowledge that they have done anything wrong, let alone try to make amends to the people they hurt.

Once a person has completed the process of *teshuvah*, however, this Mishnah demands that people in society not even mention the person's former troubles with the law, for that would be to engage in oppressive speech. Why? Because one thereby labels the person by his or her former offense, undermines and distrusts the process of return, and denies the person the possibility of righting his or her former wrong and taking on a new, better identity—writing a new personal script, as it were. This Mishnah thus starkly contrasts with the practice in many American states, where former convicts have to list their convictions on any job application, are ineligible to apply for any government job, and, in some states, lose the right to vote.

Similar to what we saw earlier with regard to negative but true speech, however, there is an exception to this rule.

If the person applies for a job that entails dealing with situations similar to the one in which he or she committed the offense and thus the job would tempt him or her to do the same thing again, people who know of the person's past may describe the offense to potential employers in that line of work, and those employers may refuse to take the chance of exposing the person to the same temptations again. In fact, people privy to this information have a duty to take these steps to protect the employer and even the applicant, for the Rabbis interpret "Do not place a stumbling block before the blind" (Lev. 19:14) to include not only those who are physically blind, but those who are morally blind as well.[8] For example, people may tell potential employers in a school, camp, or youth group that they should not hire a given person because he or she has abused children in the past.[9]

Finally, the Mishnah's third example—not to remind converts to Judaism of their former religious affiliation and that of their family—may seem strange to modern Jews and non-Jews. After all, the Jewish community has come to know and welcome many Jews by choice, and it is not particularly embarrassing for such people to acknowledge the religious heritage of their past and that of their family. Still, this passage warns us against doing what some Jews still do—talking to and about Jews by choice as if they were not really Jews. They are fully Jews, and any aspersions cast on their Jewish identity (often by Jews who are less religious than the Jew by choice) are forbidden as oppressive speech, aside from being just plain nasty. Furthermore, any words asserting that Jews by choice behave or think in a particular way that does not follow typical Jewish ethnic patterns and is therefore "goyish" (gentile) is also interdicted by this Mishnah as oppressive speech.

The Talmud adds two more examples of oppressive speech:

If a person is visited by suffering, afflicted with disease, or has buried his children, one must not speak to him as Job's companions spoke to him, "Is not your piety your confidence, your integrity your hope? Think now, what innocent man ever perished? Where have the upright been destroyed? As I have seen, those who plow evil and sow mischief reap them" (Job 4:6–8). If ass-drivers sought grain from a person, he must not say to them, "Go to so-and-so, who sells grain" when knowing that he has never sold any. Rabbi Judah said: One must not feign interest in a purchase when he has no money, since this is known to the heart only, and of everything known only to the heart it is written [in the Torah], "And you shall fear your God" (Leviticus 25:17).

—B. *Bava Metzia* 58b

The first of the Talmud's examples of oppressive speech is telling sick people that their past sins are the reason they are suffering. Even if a person with lung cancer smoked three packs of cigarettes a day or a person with a stroke is obese so that there is indeed a probable link between his past behavior and his illness, you may not mention that when visiting the ill person. Again, if the person will recover, the doctor may—and probably should—describe the connection between his past lifestyle and current illness, together with suggesting ways to stop smoking or avoid overeating to prevent recurrence of the disease; but even a doctor should refrain from blaming people for diseases they have if they have no hope for recovery. People outside the field of medicine who have no practical reason to mention this linkage are definitely prohibited from commenting on it, and the Mishnah compares those who do to Job's "friends" who similarly blamed Job for his troubles and who were ultimately chastised by God for doing so (Job 42:7–9). (Note that in asserting that such language is oppressive speech, the Rabbis of the Mishnah are preferring the way that the Book of Job addresses human suffering to the theology of Deuteronomy 28:58–61, which does link sickness to sin.)

The Talmud's second example of oppressive speech—telling someone seeking grain to go to someone whom the speaker knows has none—is another instance of warning us against "placing a stumbling block before the blind" (Lev. 19:14)—this time, before the cognitively blind, those who lack information and can be misled by those who give them false directions. To do that is oppressive speech, for it steals not only the questioner's time but also his or her trust in other people and even his or her self-respect as someone whom others will not intentionally lead astray. Clearly, this does not apply to games where the whole point is to deceive one another (card games like poker and I Doubt It come to mind), for everyone enters into the game with the intention of having fun by seeing how acute you are in identifying false information. It certainly does constitute oppressive speech, though, when children taunt each other in this way. Even in less personally charged situations, when, for example, you are asked for directions, you should say, "I don't know" if you in fact do not know rather than send someone "on a wild goose chase."

Harming another's money or property is clearly prohibited, as Leviticus 25 spells out in detail. Even so, after explaining what is included in the category of oppressive speech, the Talmud poignantly indicates why verbal oppression is even worse than that:

> Rabbi Johanan said on the authority of Rabbi Simeon bar Yohai: Verbal wrong is worse than monetary wrong because with regard to the former it is written, "And you

shall fear your God" (Lev. 25:17), but not of the second [in Lev. 25:14, which the Rabbis interpret to prohibit monetary wrongs]. Rabbi Eleazar said: The former [verbal oppression] affects his [the victim's] person, the other [only] his money. Rabbi Samuel bar Nahmani said: For the latter [monetary wrongs] restoration is possible, but not for the former [verbal wrongs].

—B. *Bava Metzia* 58b

The New Testament does not go into detail about oppressive speech, but it too bans the kind of talk that expresses anger, evil intentions, and argument:

Thieves must give up stealing; rather let them labor and work honestly with their own hands, so as to have something to share with the needy. Let no evil talk come out of your mouths, but only what is useful for building up, as there is need, so that your words may give grace to those who hear. And do not grieve the Holy Spirit of God, with which you were marked with a seal for the day of redemption. Put away from you all bitterness and wrath and anger and wrangling and slander, together with all malice, and be kind to one another, tenderhearted, forgiving one another, as God in Christ has forgiven you.

—Ephesians 4:28–32

RATIONALES FOR FUDGING THE TRUTH OR OUTRIGHT LYING

The Jewish tradition values truth very highly, not only for the practical reason that social relations depend on our being able to trust what others say, but also because God demands it and is even the paradigm of truth-telling:

The seal of God is truth.

> —B. *Shabbat* 55a, *Yoma* 69b, *Sanhedrin* 64a

God hates the person who says one thing with his mouth and another with his mind.

> —B. *Pesahim* 113b (cf. *Sotah* 42a, *Bava Metzia* 49a)

As a result, the general Jewish maxim is that you should tell the truth:

> Rabbi Jose ben Judah said: "Let your 'yes' be yes and your 'no' be no."
>
> —B. *Bava Metzia* 49a

Rabbinic literature, though, describes some exceptions to telling the whole truth.

Tact

When there is no practical purpose requiring the truth and those hearing it will only have their feelings hurt, the Rabbis tell us to prefer tact over truth, especially when the truth is a matter of judgment in the first place. In the following excerpt, the Rabbis' first example is what we say about a bride on her wedding day: Do we tell the brutal truth and describe her as she is—beautiful or ugly—or do we describe her as beautiful no matter what she looks like? What is gained by calling her ugly? More importantly, consider what is lost by doing that—her self-esteem, her joy, and the exuberance of those attending the wedding. Similarly, although somewhat less graphically, it is one thing to advise a person before he or she buys something, but after the sale people should refrain from criticizing the item (assuming that it cannot be returned):

What words must be used when dancing before the bride? The School of Hillel said: "Say, 'O bride, beautiful and gracious.'" The School of Shammai said: "If she is lame or blind, is one to say, 'O bride, beautiful and gracious?' Does it not say in the Torah, 'Keep far from lying?'" (Exodus 23:7). The Hillelites said, "Then, if someone makes a bad purchase in the market, is one to commend it or run it down? Surely one should commend it." Hence the wise say, "Always make your disposition sympathetic to that of your neighbor."

—B. *Ketubbot* 17a

Peace

A second exception to the requirement to tell the truth is when someone is engaged in an effort to bring peace. The Rabbis deduce this exception from the very words of God, who reported to Abraham that Sarah was worried that she was too old to have children rather than, as she had said, that he was; from the lie Joseph's brothers told him after Jacob's death to try to attain Joseph's forgiveness and peace among the brothers; and from God's advice to Samuel to lie to Saul that he was coming to bring a sacrifice even though his real purpose was to tell him that God had decided to wrest the throne from him and give it to David:

Bar Kappara said: Great is peace, for even Scriptures [allow a lie] when there is a possibility to bring peace between Abraham and Sarah. "And Sarah laughed to herself, saying, 'Now that I am withered, am I to have enjoyment—with my husband so old?'" But to Abraham God does not quote her thus but rather says, "Why did Sarah laugh, saying, 'Shall I in truth bear a child, old as I am?'" (Genesis 18:11–14). Scripture does not quote God as saying what Sarah said, "that my husband is old," but rather "old as I am."

—*Genesis Rabbah* 48:18

One may properly tell a lie for the sake of peace, as did Joseph's brothers when they said: "Before his death your father left this instruction: 'So shall you say to Joseph: "Forgive, I urge you, the offense and guilt of your brothers who treated you so harshly"'" (Genesis 50:16–17). Rabbi Nathan said: "[Not only may one tell a lie in the name of peace, but] one should tell a lie [for that purpose], for the Bible says: 'And Samuel said: "How can I go? If Saul hears it [that You are taking the throne from him], he will kill me." The Lord said: 'Take a heifer with you, and say, "I have come to sacrifice to the Lord."'" (1 Samuel 16:2).

—B. *Yevamot* 65a

All lies are forbidden unless they are spoken for the sake of making peace.

—*Baraita Perek Ha-Shalom*

One of the earliest and most thorough Catholic theologians to discuss the various levels of lying was St. Augustine of Hippo. He wrote a "Book on Lying" and "Against Lying" before writing in 395 CE *De Mendacio,* "Of Lying," in which he synthesizes his theory. He identifies eight kinds of lies, listed from the most severe offense to the least:

1. Lies in religious teaching.
2. Lies that harm others and help no one.
3. Lies that harm others and help someone.
4. Lies told for the pleasure of lying.

5. Lies told to "please others in smooth discourse."
6. Lies that harm no one and that help someone.
7. Lies that harm no one and that save someone's life.
8. Lies that harm no one and that save someone's "purity."[10]

Augustine does not permit any of these, but he clearly sees the types at the bottom of the list as less immoral than the ones at the top. White lies—number 6 on his list—are the type that describes God's report to Abraham, changing Sarah's disdain for Abraham's ability for fathering a child to a remark about her own inability to have one, and the Rabbis explicitly permit such lies for the sake of peace. Lies that save a person's life—as, for example, intentionally misleading an irate and violent husband as to the whereabouts of his wife—would, for the Rabbis, be not only permissible but also required, for in Judaism saving a life takes precedence over the prohibition against lying. Judaism generally bans lying, but it does permit lies for peace and actually demands them for saving lives and so differs from Augustine, who sees such lies as less culpable than others but nevertheless prohibited.

There are some important limits to Judaism's openness to lying for the sake of peace. Lies have a way of being discovered, and so lying even in the interests of making peace may not only fail to work, but may also make the parties angry at the peacemaker. Moreover, lies cannot cover up realities; if the parties really hate each other, no false reports that the other party said something nice will magically make things right. On the contrary, both parties, upon finding out about the false report, may now be reconfirmed in their animosity toward each other and also distrust the reporter who was trying to make peace. Peace, it if is to be had, must rest on stronger foundations than lies. Take the example of how God revised Sarah's words when transmitting them to Abraham with the proverbial grain of salt. You surely may and should omit nasty comments if you are trying to make peace; you may speak of each party's benign, broader intentions; and you may even interpret remarks made by one party about the other more positively than the speaker probably meant them; but actually changing what someone said is asking for trouble, even if it is in the name of making peace.

Hope

Finally, rabbinic literature records some rabbis who condone and even demand that those visiting very sick people lie to them about the seriousness of their disease so as to help them retain hope for recovery. Those who take this position base themselves on the biblical stories of Elisha's lie to the emissary of Benhadad, King of Aram, and the change of fate of King Hezekiah:

> The king said to Hazael: "... Inquire of the Lord through Elisha, saying, 'Shall I recover from this illness?'" So Hazael went to meet him ... and said [in the king's name] ... "Shall I recover from this illness?" Elisha said: "Go say to him, 'You shall surely recover,' even though the Lord has shown me that he shall surely die." ... Then he departed from Elisha and came to his master ... and answered, "He told me that you would surely recover."
>
> —2 Kings 8:8–10, 14

> In those days Hezekiah was sick unto death. Isaiah, the prophet, the son of Amoz, came to him and said to him: "Thus the Lord said: 'Set your house in order, for you shall die and shall not live.'" Then Hezekiah turned his face to the wall and prayed to the Lord.... Then the word of the

Lord came to Isaiah, saying: "Go and say to Hezekiah:' ... I have heard your prayer, I have seen your tears, and I will add to your days fifteen years.'"

—Isaiah 38:1–7 (also 2 Kings 20:1–7)

"For through the multitude of dreams and vanities there are also many words; but fear the Lord" (Ecclesiastes 5:6). This was the case when Hezekiah, king of Judah, took sick, and God told Isaiah to tell him, "Put your house in order, for you will die and not live." Hezekiah said to Isaiah: "Normally, when a person visits the sick, he says, 'May God show compassion to you.' And when a physician visits a patient, he tells him, 'Eat this and not that, drink this and not that.' And even if it is obvious that he is about to die, one does not tell the sick to put his house in order, in order that he not experience mental distress. And yet you tell me to put my house in order, for I am about to die! I will not accept this nor listen to your words. Instead I will rely on my forbear, who said, 'Through the multitude of dreams and vanities, there are also many words.'"... [Later] Isaiah said to God, "God, first you told me one thing, and now you tell me another. How can I go now and tell him this [that God will add fifteen years to Hezekiah's life]?" God said: "Hezekiah is a humble man and will accept your words; besides, the original decree has not gone forth."

—*Midrash Rabbah, Ecclesiastes* 5:6

If the close relative of a sick person dies, we do not inform the sick person lest he be emotionally overwhelmed (*titaref da'ato*).

—B. *Mo'ed Katan* 26b

These sources elevate the value of retaining hope for recovery over truth. They do so for two different reasons. First, the visitor never really knows whether the patient will get better or worse, even if God declares that he or she will die of the illness, for God may decide otherwise in response to the patient's prayers. In our own day, where people cannot depend on a revelation from God for the prognosis but only on the training and experience of physicians, we surely cannot know for certain whether the patient will live or die.

Furthermore, even if you are convinced that there is little, if any, hope for the patient's recovery, you may not deprive the patient of hope; to do so would be cruel. Despite the sexism in its formulation, the *Shulhan Arukh*, an important sixteenth-century code of Jewish law, clearly has this concern:

> When a man is about to die, we tell him to say Viddui [the confessional prayer]. We tell him, "Many have uttered the confession and not died, and many have not said the confession and died. The reward for saying the confession is that you will live, for whoever says the confession will acquire a place in the afterlife." If he cannot say the confession, he should verbalize it in his heart. Such things should not be said to him in presence of the ignorant or women or children lest they cry and thereby break his heart.
>
> —S. A., *Yoreh De'ah* 338:1

Moreover, depriving the patient of hope for recovery may actually hasten the patient's death, for he or she may then stop following the regimen prescribed by the doctor to stay alive as long as possible. According to some studies, people from a variety of different cultures and even animals who are convinced that there is no hope for survival give up trying and die earlier than they would have had they tried to live.[11]

This is the line of reasoning that led Rabbi Immanuel Jakobovits, author of the first book on Jewish medical ethics and chief rabbi of the British Commonwealth, to write to me when I was chair of the Jewish Hospice Commission in Los Angeles. Rabbi Maurice Lamm, an Orthodox rabbi, had been its first chair, and I took over when he moved to the East Coast. Hospice care involves a patient's recognition that he or she has an irreversible, terminal illness. At that point a Jew may choose to enlist any or all experimental therapies, even if their toxicity may hasten the person's death if they do not bring a cure. But a Jew may also, Rabbi Lamm and I concluded, choose hospice care, where he or she is still under a physician's care but the goal of that care is to enable the patient to do as much as possible in fulfilling his or her goals and minimize pain ("palliative care") rather than to cure the illness that has been diagnosed as incurable.

Rabbi Jakobovits wanted to know how Rabbi Lamm and I justified hospice care in light of the Jewish sources that require that we maintain a patient's hope for recovery. I responded that while the Jewish tradition certainly wants us to reinforce a patient's hope, it cannot be plausibly read to require us to instill unrealistic hope, for the tradition has a keen awareness—from the Garden of Eden story on—that we are mortal; that, in fact, is one critical factor that distinguishes us from God. Even if the prognosis is terrible, a person can legitimately hope for many things—for as little pain as possible; for seeing family and friends or completing a trip or project before dying; for reconciliation with estranged family members or friends—but we human beings cannot hope to live forever. It was after that exchange of letters that Rabbi Jakobovits permitted hospice care under Jewish auspices in England.[12]

My perspective on hospice care is based, in part, on my experience that the vast majority of people who are seriously ill do much better if they are told the truth than if it is withheld from them, even for the benign purpose of keeping their spirits up. Patients know from their own bodies that things are not good. If everyone around them pretends that everything is fine when in fact it is not, patients will cease to trust anyone. They may go along with the rouse out of their concern that those around them not suffer, but that is the patient caring for the healthy rather than what should be happening—namely, the healthy caring for the sick. A context of secrets and lies also prevents patients from sharing what they really feel and thus makes it impossible for family and friends to come to their aid. It is downright sad to spend your last days, weeks, or months not being able to trust or talk truthfully with the most important people in your life.

If, on the other hand, doctors and families communicate honestly about the prognosis—including what the doctor really does not know—families, friends, doctors, nurses, rabbis, social workers, and anyone else involved in the patient's care can work effectively to make his or her life as long and as meaningful as possible. Doctors in the past knew less about any patient's chances of recovery than they do now, so dissembling then may have had a justification in that lack of knowledge. Today, though, patients expect doctors to know much more and to communicate that knowledge to them so that they can make important decisions in their lives. Doctors should be supportive and compassionate and describe the medical alternatives and the degree to which things are not clear. When that is done, I maintain, contrary to these earlier sources, helping the patient honestly is the best policy.

USING WORDS FOR GOOD PURPOSES

The Rabbis were all too aware of the power of the tongue to do bad things despite the many safeguards that God provided in creating it:

> Rabbi Joseph ben Zimra said: [God said to the tongue:] "All the limbs of the human body are vertical, but I made you horizontal; all of them I put outside the body, but you I put inside; and I have even surrounded you with two walls, one of bone and one of flesh."
>
> —B. *Arakhin* 15b

Not surprisingly, then, the tradition includes, as we have seen, many prohibitions and cautions about our use of words, to the point that some would prefer that we not talk at all!

> Shimon, his [Rabban Gamliel's] son, says: All my life I have grown up among the wise, and I have not found anything better for the body than silence.
>
> —M. *Avot* 1:17

> Rabbi Akiva says: ... A hedge around wisdom is silence.
>
> —M. *Avot* 3:13

Jews, though, have had no trouble speaking up. Just consider the immense body of literature Jews have produced, the intense debates on almost every page of the Talmud, and even the standard joke that where there are two Jews there are at least three opinions. (Someone recently asked me whether you really need two Jews for three opinions!) While this verbosity and feistiness may seem to Jews like a universal human trait—Jews tend to think that the whole world acts the way they do—

the fact is that many cultures encourage much more passive and silent behavior. Jews are anything but reticent to talk, and in this vein they have been shaped by their tradition.

While normal conversation about what is going on in your life, pragmatic matters, and talk related to work or play are clearly sanctioned forms of speech, Judaism especially appreciates three kinds of speech: words of Torah, words of gratitude, and words of support and comfort.

Words of Torah

Many rabbinic texts encourage us to speak words of Torah—so many, in fact, that you might think that every tradition encourages its adherents to study its texts. That, however, is not true: many traditions presume that only the elite will know the texts, and some (like the Mormons) even bar anyone but the elite from knowing the secrets of the religion. The Torah makes it clear that this is not going to be the Jewish way when God tells Moses twenty-seven times to "speak to the Children of Israel" rather than to the elders alone and when it requires that the Torah be read every seven years to everyone assembled, "men, women, and children and the stranger within your midst."[13] The rabbinic tradition takes this much further, putting at least a bit of the rabbinic tradition in the early-morning service, inserting many biblical passages in the liturgy, and claiming that Jewish learning should not be restricted to the house of study but rather should pervade our daily activities:

> Rabbi Shimon says: Three who ate at the same table and did not speak words of Torah are as if they ate sacrifices to the dead ... but three who ate at the same table and spoke words of Torah are as if they ate from the table of the Holy Blessed One ...
>
> —M. *Avot* 3:3

Words of Gratitude

It is only right and proper to acknowledge when someone has done you a favor. After all, we do not enter this world entitled to everything we need, let alone everything we want. Consequently, when someone provides for our needs or desires, we minimally owe that party an expression of our gratitude.

First we owe gratitude to God. Jewish prayer is replete with thanksgiving to God. Two examples will suffice:

It is good to give thanks to the Lord, to tell of Your faithfulness in the morning and your trustworthiness at night.
—Psalm 92:1

We thank You, for You are Adonai, our God and God of our ancestors throughout all time, Rock of our lives, the Shield of our salvation in every generation. We thank You and praise You morning, noon, and night for Your miracles that daily attend us and for Your wondrous kindnesses.... Praised are You, Adonai, whose reputation is for goodness and to whom it is fitting to give thanks.
—*Amidah* (said three times daily and four times on Sabbaths and Festivals)

Given that something like 80 percent of the traditional Jewish prayer book (the *Siddur*) consists of prayers that either praise or thank God, we might aptly ask whether that is just too much, whether we are making ourselves far too humble and acting like sycophants. Why should God need our praises and thanksgiving in the first place?

This goes to the heart of the meaning of Jewish prayer. The English word "prayer" misleads us into thinking that the essence of prayer is asking God for things, as in the expression,

"Do this, I pray." The Hebrew word for prayer, though, does not mean that. The root *hitpalel* instead means to submit yourself to judgment, to leave your status of a privileged person to whom everything is owed and instead to recognize that you depend on much that you have done nothing to deserve—good health, family, friends, food, liquids, air. This is extremely hard for human beings to do; we tend to be egocentric, thinking only from our own perspective and about our own needs and desires. It is precisely because of that prevalent human trait that Jewish liturgy spends so much time on getting us out of ourselves so that we can gain a proper, humble assessment of who we are, what we have, and what we deserve.

It is not only God whom we should thank; we should also express our gratitude to people who do good things for us. This seems obvious to us, and it probably did to the Rabbis as well. Saying "thank you" for a favor done or expressing our gratitude in other ways seems like elementary manners, a function of necessary humility about ourselves and appropriate respect for others, and Jews probably always saw it as that. Interestingly, though—and, I would say, unfortunately—Jewish sources requiring that we express gratitude to other people who benefit us are remarkably sparse. This is probably an area where we modern Jews need to add to the tradition by articulating what is only implicit in it.

The tradition certainly does encourage gratitude toward other human beings; it just does not demand that we express it. For example, in the following talmudic passage, the rabbinic sage Ben Zoma combines thankfulness for the many people who enable him to live his life with ease with thankfulness to God for creating such people:

> Ben Zoma once saw a large crowd on the steps of the Temple Mount. He exclaimed: "Blessed is the One who

has created all these people to serve God." Ben Zoma also customarily said: "What labors did Adam have to carry out before he obtained bread to eat? He plowed. He sowed. He reaped. He bound the sheaves, threshed the grain, winnowed the chaff, selected the ears, ground them, sifted the flour, kneaded the dough, and baked it. Only then was he able to eat. I, on the other hand, get up and find that all these things have already been done for me. Similarly, how many labors did Adam have to carry out before he obtained a garment to wear? He had to shear the sheep, wash the wool, comb it, spin it, and weave it. Then did he have a garment to wear. All I have to do is get up and find that these things too have been done for me. All kinds of artisans have come to my home so that when I awake in the morning, I find these things ready for me."

—B. *Berakhot* 58a

Similarly, the Jerusalem Talmud understands the command to "honor your father and mother" (Exod. 20:12) as "paying a debt" to them for bringing you into the world and raising you (J. *Pe'ah* 1:1 [3b]). Another talmudic passage asserts that those who name the person who first said something significant or wise "brings salvation to the world" (B. *Megillah* 15a; *Hullin* 104b; *Niddah* 19b). The codes, however, never make this a legal requirement, while in modern times we would say that failure to do that is plagiarism.

The one thing we can say in defense of the tradition's silence on this score is that it clearly demands that we thank God multiple times each day; aside from psalms and prose expressions of such gratitude to God, the Talmud requires that we utter a hundred blessings of God each day.[14] Since God serves as our model, expressing our gratitude to God may serve as training for us to express our gratitude to human benefactors as well. In any case, words used to do that are certainly a good use of language.

Words of Support and Comfort

Another genre of words that the Jewish tradition especially lauds are those used to support and comfort others.

> Rabbi Isaac said: Whoever gives a small coin to a poor man has six blessings bestowed on him [citing Isaiah 58:7–9], but the one who speaks a kind word to him obtains eleven blessings [citing Isaiah 58:10–12].
>
> —B. *Bava Batra* 9b

> Better is one who shows a smiling countenance than the one who offers milk to drink.
>
> —B. *Ketubbot* 111b

In using words and body language to support others, we are modeling ourselves after God:

> Rabbi Hamma, son of Rabbi Hanina, said: What is the meaning of the verse, "You shall walk behind the Lord your God" (Deuteronomy 13:5)? ... [It means that] a person should imitate the righteous ways of the Holy One, blessed be God. Just as the Lord clothed the naked, ... so too you must supply clothes for the naked [poor]. Just as the Holy One, blessed be God, visited the sick, ... so too you should visit the sick. Just as the Holy One, blessed be God, buried the dead, ... so too you must bury the dead. Just as the Holy One, blessed be God, comforted mourners, ... so too you should comfort mourners.
>
> —B. *Sotah* 14a

SPEECH CAN DESTROY OR CREATE WORLDS

The way we speak to one another, is a critical part of how we can destroy worlds if we use language badly or how we can build and support them if we use it well. Indeed, in the Bible's opening chapter, God creates the world through speech—a graphic way to symbolize the power and promise of speech. Although we often think of "fixing the world" in more concrete actions taken to aid others, the way we speak to people is at the forefront of the Jewish tradition's concerns in how to build a better world. Like every other capacity that we have, the ability to speak is morally neutral; it gains moral character according to the way we use it. The tradition's warnings about how easily we can use speech badly should make us aware of the power and pitfalls of speech, and the tradition's encouragement to use speech to fix the world should encourage us to talk in those ways. In the end, we bear full responsibility for how we use our faculty of speech.

4

THE MINISTRY OF PRESENCE

We often think of repairing the world (*tikkun olam*) in terms of practical things that one person or one group of people does for another. *Tikkun olam* certainly includes such things, as this book demonstrates. It also, however, includes supporting people emotionally in their time of need. The most obvious cases of this occur when people feel diminished—when, for example, they are sick or are mourning a loved one. People also need the presence of other people, though, when they want to celebrate a joyous event in their lives, like a birth or a wedding. This chapter focuses on such kinds of *tikkun olam*, where the fixing involves fulfilling emotional needs at least as much as practical ones.

HEALING PEOPLE'S BODIES

For the last two thousand years, Judaism has had a virtual love affair with medicine. Many rabbis were also physicians, including some of the most famous ones (such as Maimonides). God is our ultimate healer:

> God said: "If you will heed the Lord your God diligently, doing what is upright in His sight, giving ear to His commandments and keeping all His laws, then I will not bring

upon you any of the diseases that I brought upon the
Egyptians, for I the Lord am your healer."

—Exodus 15:26

Bless the Lord, O my soul
and do not forget His bounties.
He forgives all your sins,
heals all your diseases.

—Psalm 103:2–3

God's role in healing, however, does not preclude human
efforts to heal as well. On the contrary, the last words of the
following passage, according to the Talmud, give us permission
to attempt to heal:

When men quarrel and one strikes the other with stone or
fist, and he does not die but has to take to his bed, if he then
gets up and walks outdoors on his staff, the assailant shall go
unpunished, except that he must pay for his idleness (time
lost) and he must surely cure him [ve-rapo yerapeh].

—Exodus 21:18–19

"And he shall surely be healed": from this verse we derive
the permission [of human beings] to heal.

—B. Bava Kamma 85a

On the basis of the command to "love your neighbor as
yourself" (Lev. 19:18), the Rabbis conclude that this permission
even extends to treatments that require inflicting a wound, for
they presume that we would all prefer to suffer from a temporary wound to get well.[1] This, incidentally, also establishes the
basis for judging therapies in terms of the balance of their risks
and benefits, for in each case—and especially if the patient is
unconscious or mentally incompetent—we must think of what

we would want done for ourselves and do the same out of love for our neighbor. On the basis the specific words used in the Hebrew text of Deuteronomy 22:2, the Talmud declares that the Torah imposes an *obligation* to restore another person's body as well as his or her property and hence to come to the aid of someone in a life-threatening situation.[2] That duty also stems from Leviticus 19:16, which the Talmud uses not only to ground our duty to do what we can do personally to save lives but also to spend our money to hire others who are more qualified to heal others:

> If you see your fellow's ox or sheep gone astray, do not ignore it; you must take it back to your fellow. If your fellow does not live near you or you do not know who he is, you shall bring it home and it shall remain with you until your fellow claims it; then you shall give it back to him [*ve-hashevato lo*].
>
> —Deuteronomy 22:1–2

> On what biblical basis can it be derived that it is obligatory to restore the body of a fellow human being [when ill or in danger, just as it is obligatory to restore his or her lost property]? Because the Torah says: "And you shall restore it to him" (Deuteronomy 22:2). ["To him" is superfluous, for to whom else would you return it? The Rabbis, assuming that nothing in the Torah is superfluous, therefore use that extra word [*lo*] to assert that the Torah imposes a duty on us not only to restore lost property to its owner, but also a person's body to him or her (*'avedat gufo*, the loss of one's body) when it is lost through illness or danger. See Rashi on the *Sanhedrin* passage, s.v., *talmud lomar ve'hashevato lo.*]
>
> —B. *Sanhedrin* 73a (also *Bava Kamma* 81b)

Do not stand idly by the blood of your neighbor.

—Leviticus 19:16

Our Rabbis taught: How do we know that one who sees that someone [literally, "his friend," *haveiro*] is drowning in the river or that a wild animal is dragging him or that highway robbers are attacking him is obligated to save him? Because the Torah says, "Do not stand idly by the blood of your neighbor."

—B. *Sanhedrin* 73a

In contrast, only a few American states have established a legal duty to rescue; in fact, until the recent adoption of "Good Samaritan" laws in most states, if you tried to help someone in a jam and injured the person in the process, you could be sued. It still is the case in most states that if you simply do nothing when you see someone in distress, you have violated no laws.[3]

Furthermore, in Jewish tradition the duty to strive to heal, which includes the obligation to rescue, takes precedence over all but three of the other commandments:

It was taught: How do we know that saving a life supersedes the laws of the Sabbath? Rabbi Judah said in the name of Samuel: For it is written, "And you shall observe My statutes and judgments that a person should do *and live by them*" (Leviticus 18:6), [meaning] that he should not die by them.

—B. *Yoma* 85b

With regard to all transgressions in the Torah except for idolatry, sexual licentiousness, and murder, if enemies say to a person, "Transgress and then you will not be killed," the person must transgress and not be killed. What is the reason? "And you shall live by them [My command-ments]" (Leviticus 18:6) [implies] and not that he should die by them.

—B. *Sanhedrin* 74a

Ultimately, Joseph Karo, author of the important six-teenth-century code, the *Shulhan Arukh*, says:

The Torah gave permission to the physician to heal; moreover, this is a religious precept and is included in the category of saving life, and if the physician withholds his services, it is considered as shedding blood.

—S. A. *Yoreh De'ah* 336:1

But is it not the case that engaging in medicine is a vio-lation of God's prerogatives? The following midrash is a beau-tiful rabbinic response to that theological problem, indicating that, on the contrary, practicing medicine is exactly what God would have us do:

It once happened that Rabbi Ishmael and Rabbi Akiva were strolling in the streets of Jerusalem accompanied by another person. They were met by a sick person. He said to them, "My masters, tell me by what means I may be cured." They told him, "Do thus and so until you are cured." The sick man asked them, "And who afflicted me?" They replied, "The Holy One, blessed be He." The sick man responded, "You have entered into a matter that does not pertain to you. God has afflicted, and you seek to cure! Are you not transgressing His will?"

Rabbi Akiva and Rabbi Ishmael asked him, "What is your occupation?" The sick man answered, "I am a tiller of the soil, and here is the sickle in my hand." They asked him, "Who created the vineyard?" "The Holy One, blessed be He," he answered. Rabbi Akiva and Rabbi Ishmael said to him, "You enter into a matter that does not pertain to you! God created the vineyard, and you cut fruits from it."

He said to them, "Do you not see the sickle in my hand? If I did not plow, sow, fertilize, and weed, nothing would sprout."

Rabbi Akiva and Rabbi Ishmael said to him, "Foolish man! ... Just as if one does not weed, fertilize, and plow, the trees will not produce fruit, and if fruit is produced but is not watered or fertilized, it will not live but die, so with regard to the body. Drugs and medicaments are the fertilizer, and the physician is the tiller of the soil.

—*Midrash Temurrah* as cited in *Otzar Midrashim,*
J. D. Eisenstein, ed. (New York, 1915) II, 580–581

Similarly, although circumcision is not justified in the Jewish tradition in medical terms, it is instructive that the Rabbis maintained that Jewish boys were not born circumcised specifically because God created the world such that it would need human fixing:

Everything that was created during the six days of Creation needs work. For example, the mustard seed needs sweetening; lupines need sweetening; wheat needs to be ground; even the human being needs to be fixed [through circumcision].

—*Genesis Rabbah* 11:6 (end; also
Pesikta Rabbati 22:4)

TIKKUN OLAM IN PRACTICE: INDIVIDUALS AND SOCIETY

Indeed, this source endorses not only healing the sick but the project of *tikkun olam* as a whole.

Although the duty to heal applies first and foremost to physicians and then to the whole community, another duty applies to all Jews: to live in a community where there is a doctor so that they can get expert help in carrying out their obligation to preserve God's property, their own bodies:

> It is forbidden to live in a city in which there is no physician.
> —J. *Kiddushin* 66d (see also B. *Sanhedrin* 17b)

What happened, then, to the role of God in causing illness and healing? The Jewish tradition sees no contradiction in asserting both that God has ultimate control of these matters and that a Jew must use physicians in seeking to prevent and cure sickness, for it depicts human beings generally, and physicians in particular, as God's agents and partners in the ongoing act of creation and healing.[4] In fact, in B. *Sanhedrin* 38a, the Rabbis (Pharisees) specifically assert that the Sadducees were wrong in claiming that angels or any being other than humans participate with God in creation. Judaism thus recognizes the ultimate power and authority of God and yet honors human beings enough to give them the role and responsibility to seek to cure. We therefore must pray for healing and also use the services of doctors toward that end. What a remarkable balancing of honor for God and human beings!

The topic of this book is repairing the world (*tikkun olam*) generally, and healing the sick is only one aspect of that broader theme. This volume therefore cannot treat how the Jewish tradition applies this mandate to heal to issues at the beginning of life (birth control, abortion, infertility treatments, genetic testing and engineering), at the end of life (withholding and withdrawing life support systems, organ transplantation), or the complicated issue in modern times of the distribution of health care. Space contraints also preclude a discussion of other ways people's souls are healed, including mental health interventions and treating the disabled effectively and honorably. Those interested in a Jewish approach to such topics are encouraged to consult my book *Matters of Life and Death: A Jewish Approach to Modern Medical Ethics* and some of the other references in this endnote[5]; those interested in a Christian treatment of such matters may consult the references in this endnote.[6] One aspect of the mandate to heal, though, deserves more attention in this volume, namely, the duty to visit the sick.

HEALING PEOPLE'S SOULS

Most of us do not like to visit the sick, especially when they are in hospitals, for reasons that include these:

1. On a sheerly physical level, we do not want to catch a disease from the person we visit or any of the other people in the hospital, whether this fear is warranted or not.
2. Even if the ill present no physical danger to us, they remind us of our own vulnerability to illness and even our own mortality, neither of which is something we like to contemplate. The very smells, sights, and sounds of hospitals make those of us not used to such phenomena feel as if we are in a threatening, strange place.
3. Engaging with the sick is often depressing, for we cannot do with them what we like to do together.

4. Then there is the inconvenience of it all. You are not going to see your family member or friend in the usual places. You have to reserve time for your visit, go to an unusual place, pay for parking, and then find the room where the patient is. Worse, once you get there, the patient is likely to be either sleeping or out of the room for tests—and that will surely not encourage you to visit again.

5. If the patient is in the room and awake, you then face another problem—what do you say? Visitors and patients both tire of talking about the food and the weather in about ten seconds. You do not want to dwell on the depressing topic of the patient's illness, but if you do not mention it, it becomes the elephant in the room that nobody wants to recognize and that everyone dances around. So what do you talk about, and how?

We moderns are by no means the first to feel this way. Our ancestors did not have to go to hospitals to see ill friends or family members, for until very recently in human history, people endured their illnesses at home. But, the lack of medical knowledge about which diseases are contagious must have made our ancestors fear visiting the sick even more than we do. It is precisely because people often have an aversion to visiting the sick that the Jewish tradition made it a *mitzvah*, not just in the sense of a nice thing to do, but in the original sense of that word as a commanded and obligatory act. Jews are therefore duty-bound to visit the sick, whether we want to or not.

There are other reasons the tradition supplies, however, to visit the sick. First, the Rabbis assert that in doing so, as in providing for the poor and the bereaved, *we imitate God:*

Rabbi Hamma, son of Rabbi Hanina, said: What is the meaning of the verse, "Follow the Lord your God" (Deuteronomy 13:5)? Is it possible for a mortal to follow God's Presence? After all, the Torah says, "For the Lord your God is a consuming fire" (Deuteronomy 4:24). Rather, the verse means to teach us that we should follow the *attributes* of the Holy One, praised be He. As God clothes the naked ... you should clothe the naked; the Holy One, blessed be He visited the sick, as it says, "The Lord appeared to him by the terebinths of Mamre" (Genesis 18:1) [after the account of Abraham's circumcision], so too you should visit the sick. The Holy One comforted those who mourned.... you should comfort those who mourn. The Holy One buried the dead.... you should also bury the dead.

—B. *Sotah* 14a

Second, the tradition understood that *illness is isolating.* People, though, are social beings. Although we need some time to be alone, and although some of us are more gregarious than others, all of us crave company, at least from time to time. That is why the harshest punishment in prison settings, short of execution and torture, is solitary confinement. Thus it is not surprising that the isolation of illness adds to its ill effects, if not to the illness itself:

Visiting the sick is an obligation incumbent on everyone. Even the great [those of high social status] visit the small [those of low social status]. And we should visit many times each day, and all who add visits are to be praised as long as they do not burden [the sick person]. And anyone who visits the sick is as if he took away a part of his illness and made things easier for him; anyone who fails to visit the sick is as if he sheds blood.

—Maimonides, *M. T., Laws of Mourning* 14:4

(see also *S. A., Yoreh De'ah* 335)

What, then, should you do while visiting the sick? Here too the Jewish tradition has much to tell us. First, sit down (doctors take note!). Why? Because we communicate at least as much through our body language as we do through our words. Visitors who stand while the patient is lying down communicate that they are strong and the patient is weak. That, though, is the very last thing you want to convey, for *illness is debilitating.* You surely should not add to the patient's sense of loss of ability that the illness has already inflicted by emphasizing through your standing that you can do more than the patient can. In fact, reflecting his time when patients lay on mattresses on the ground rather than on raised beds, Maimonides requires that the visitor lie down so that his or her head is *below* the level of the patient, a goal that Joseph Karo, writing four centuries later when there were beds, acknowledges can be achieved in his time by sitting on a chair:

> One who enters a room to visit a sick person [who is lying on a mattress on the ground with his or her head on a pillow] should not sit on the mattress or on a chair or a bench or in an elevated place or above the sick person's head but rather should wrap himself in humility [for, according to the Talmud (*Shabbat* 12b), "the Presence of God rests above the head of a sick person"] and sit lower than the sick person's head [presumably lying on the ground] and ask God's mercy for him before leaving.
>
> —*M. T. Laws of Mourning* 14:6

This, though, applies only when the ill person is lying on the ground such that a visitor who sits will be higher than he or she; but if the patient is lying on a bed, it is permissible to sit on a chair.

—*S. A. Yoreh De'ah* 335:3

What, then, do you talk about? Here a third aspect of illness comes into play: *illness is infantilizing.* In robbing people of what they were able to do before, sickness makes you feel like a child or even, when incontinent, an infant. Moreover, fourth, *illness is boring;* you cannot do what normally occupies your day and week, and so you seek anything that will pass the time in an interesting way. To counteract both the sense of diminishment that illness conveys and its boredom, *visitors should talk about the same adult topics that they would discuss with the ill person if he or she were not sick,* whether that is the family, business, politics, sports, movies, novels, the synagogue, or anything else they normally discuss. As I myself learned when I was asked to give three lessons on Jewish theology at a Jewish home for the aged, you can even do things that will stretch the minds of the ill to consider things they had never studied before, for unless a person suffers from a mental illness, the mind continues to like to be stimulated. I am not suggesting that visitors discuss Jewish theology with patients, but my own experience in doing so illustrates just how adult the subjects of conversation with physically ill people can and should be.

Visitors can also help the patient create an ethical will, especially for patients with chronic illnesses who can benefit from a long-term agenda for conversations. A product of Jews of the Middle Ages, ethical wills were originally letters that a parent wrote to his or her children, and it can still take that form. Nowadays, though, many instead use an audiotape or a videotape. An ethical will includes the family story; this involves helping the patient recall early memories of childhood, including descriptions and stories of all the relatives, as well as the patient's account of his or her later life. Ethical wills commonly also include mention of the person's convictions and moral values (hence the name "ethical will"), his or her suggestions and hopes for the future of the family, and expressions of love. Even if the person's adult children may be tired of hearing the stories, the patient's grandchildren will eagerly want such a record. Patients who know that someone is coming to help them with this project have a real reason to get up in the morning and look forward to the day, for they are clearly doing something meaningful. Conversely, because creating such a document or tape can take days or weeks, it helps visitors pass the time and even look forward to the visits.[7]

Finally, Jewish law asserts that you have not fulfilled the duty to visit the sick unless you pray with the patient. The prayer need not be long, and it need not use the traditional liturgy, although sometimes people like to use old and familiar prayers or psalms. It can also be whatever comes to mind at the moment or a prayer that the visitor or patient creates after some thought. It can be in Hebrew or in English. The point of insisting on a prayer, though, is to link the patient with God and to enable him or her to express hope—for recovery, if that is possible, or at least for as little pain as possible. The patient may also use the prayer to express hopes for other personal things, like reconciliation with a family member before death. Even those visitors and patients who have problems with belief in God or who have not been very religious in their lives should find a way to contemplate and express realistic hopes, to act on them to the extent possible, and to find blessings in each other's company.

Visiting the sick is not, of course, foreign to Christians either. On the contrary, in the second and third centuries, when the Roman Empire was stricken by several epidemics that claimed the lives of thousands of people, the Christian bishop Dionysius recounted the efforts of many Christians who risked death in order to nurse the sick and bury the dead. Rodney Stark, professor of sociology and comparative religion at the University of Washington, has explored the historicity of Dionysius's writings:

> It seems highly unlikely that a bishop would write a pastoral letter full of false claims about things that his parishioners would know from direct observation. So if he claims that many members of the diocese have perished while nursing the sick, it is reasonable to believe that this happened. Moreover, there is compelling evidence from pagan sources that this was characteristic Christian behavior. Thus, a century later, the emperor Julian launched a campaign to institute pagan charities in an effort to match the Christians. Julian complained in a letter to the high priest of Galatia in 362 that the pagans needed to equal the virtues of Christians, for recent Christian growth was caused by their "moral character, even if pretended," and by their "benevolence toward strangers and care for the graves of the dead." In a letter to another priest, Julian wrote, "I think that when the poor happened to be neglected and overlooked by the priests, the impious Galileans observed this and devoted themselves to benevolence." And he also wrote, "The impious Galileans support not only their poor, but ours as well, while everyone can see that our people lack aid from us."[8]

Visiting the sick has been a Christian form of fixing the world from Christianity's earliest times, and it remains so today.

Comforting Mourners

If people understand and act on the need to visit the ill, they more readily recognize that friends and family members who have lost a loved one need to have others surrounding them at that time to help them cope with their loss. This is especially true if the loss is sudden, unexpected, and tragic; but it is also true if the deceased suffered through an illness for a long time, such that death was ultimately a blessing for everyone, including (perhaps especially) the deceased. After all, every death is a loss, and relatives and friends need help in making their peace with it. Even more importantly, they need others to help them mourn.

Some forms of aid that mourners need is material and easy to recognize. Thus Jewish tradition mandates that people bring food with them so that the mourning family does not have to worry about such matters during the seven days of mourning (*shiva*). Coordinating who is bringing what and making sure that people are there to set the food out on the table and clean up afterward are essential parts of this duty, and those who perform these tasks are doing a real, concrete service for the mourners. Similarly, helping the family with carpool duty for their children and other mundane but essential tasks in life are doing a real service. Finally, showing up for a minyan (prayer quorum) during each morning and evening of the *shiva* period and walking the mourners around the block after the last morning service of the week to symbolize their reentry into life are clear, physical things we can and should do.

The harder parts of being there for mourners is to help them mourn. What does it mean to mourn, and how can anyone help? Mourning is the process by which relatives and friends separate themselves first physically and then psychologically from the deceased. We separate ourselves physically from the person who has died through the funeral and burial. To make that separation clear to everyone, it is customary for all those attending the interment to shovel three shovelfuls of earth onto the casket once it has been lowered into the ground. The thud the dirt makes as it hits the casket communicates to everyone in a very graphic way that the deceased will no longer be part of our physical world.

That, though, only begins the process of separating ourselves from the deceased psychologically. To do that everyone who knew him or her, especially close relatives and friends, must express (literally, "press out of themselves") their memories of the deceased. People do that by talking out their memories, crying as they think of some of them, and laughing as they think of others.

How do you help mourners do that? When I was a child, I was told that you should talk about anything but the deceased in order to get the mourners' minds off their loss. "Talk about baseball," I was told. *That is exactly the wrong advice.* If you do that, the subtext you are communicating very clearly to the mourners is that you do not want to hear about the deceased, that you either cannot bear the emotional stress or do not want to endure it. Mourners will understand that and will not share their memories with you. They probably will not talk much about baseball either, for that is just not where their heads and hearts are.

What you need to do is to help the mourners mourn, that is, to call up memories of the deceased and express them. How do you do that? There is a very simple way: Just ask questions. I cannot recount the number of times that I visit a family on the third or fourth day of *shiva* and all I do is ask a leading question. If it is a spouse that died, I ask when the widow or widower first met him or her. If it is a parent that died, I ask about the earliest memories that the children have of him or her. In doing that I am communicating that I am willing to listen, and usually it is forty-five minutes before I find myself asking a second question, for finally someone has really let the memories flow.

Notice that I ask about early memories. Mourners tend to fixate on the last days or hours of the deceased's life, both because that is when the physical separation took place and also because mourners sometimes worry that others—or perhaps they themselves—will think badly of what they did in the last few days and hours for "letting" the person die. (Such feelings also lead some people to pursue medically inappropriate and futile measures to keep the person's body functioning when there is no chance of recovery, often at great emotional and financial expense as well as physical injury to the patient.) Mourning can only bring psychological separation, however, if the whole life of the person is remembered. Moreover, it is an honor to the deceased to remember how he or she lived, for even in heroic deaths, the meaning and value of the person's life comes from the whole expanse of his or her life rather than just the last few days or hours.

Attending to the physical and psychological needs of mourners is clearly a boon to them, but the Jewish tradition saw it also as a favor to the deceased. Burying the dead is even more obviously an act of love and care, for the deceased can never pay you back:

> And when the time approached for Israel [Jacob] to die, he summoned his son Joseph and said to him: "Do me this favor: place your hand under my thigh as a pledge of your steadfast loyalty (*hesed v'emet*; or, more literally, "Do for me

an act of loving-kindness and truth"). Please do not bury me
in Egypt" (Genesis 47:29). Is there an act of loving-kindness
that is a lie such that he has to say "an act of loving-kindness
and truth"?.... He said to him: "If you do this for me after
my death, it will be an act of kindness and truth."

—*Genesis Rabbah* 96:5

An act of kindness and truth (hesed v'emet). An act of loving-
kindness that one does for the dead is an act of
loving-kindness of truth (*hesed shel emet*, an authentic act
of loving-kindness) because one does not expect to be
repaid [because the dead person cannot do that].

—Rashi on Genesis 47:29

For more on Jewish rites, laws, and customs about death
and mourning in all four modern movements in Judaism
(Conservative, Orthodox, Reconstructionist, Reform), see the
books listed in this endnote.[9]

Nicholas Wolterstorff, a modern Christian writer, has
suggested similar practices:

What do you say to someone who is suffering? Some
people are gifted with words of wisdom. For such, one is
profoundly grateful ... But not all are gifted that way ...
Your words don't have to be wise. The heart that speaks
is heard more than the words spoken. And if you can't
think of anything to say, just say, "I can't think of anything
to say. But I want you to know that we are with you in
your grief." Or even, just embrace. Not even the best
words can take away pain. What words can do is testify
that there is more than pain in our journey on earth to a
new day. Of those things that are more, the greatest is love.
Express your love ... But please: Don't say it's not really so

bad. Because it is. Death is awful, demonic. If you think your task as comforter is to tell me that really, all things considered, it's not so bad, you do not sit with me in my grief but place yourself off in the distance away from me. Over there, you are of no help. What I need to hear from you is that you recognize how painful it is. I need to hear from you that you are with me in my desperation. To comfort me, you have to come close. Come sit beside me on my mourning bench.[10]

Celebrating Births and Marriages

Burying the dead and comforting mourners by helping them remember the deceased may seem obvious acts of love and kindness (*hesed*) and repairing the world (*tikkun olam*), for they respond to people in clear need. The Jewish tradition recognized, however, that people celebrating joyous events in their lives also need companionship.

Why is that so? In part it is because as social beings, we want our family and friends to celebrate with us. Their absence diminishes our own joy, and their presence makes it all the more exuberant. It is also because people celebrating a wedding, birth, bar or bat mitzvah, or even a birthday also recognize that something important is going on in their lives, that in some ways they will be different after the event than they were before it, and they want their family and friends there to help them through this life passage. They also want help unpacking such events' meaning, which they feel in their gut but cannot always consciously articulate. As a result of all these factors, people celebrating these events are often quite nervous, partially because they do not want to look bad in front of their family and friends, but also because they know that these events will transform them in important ways.

Similarly, the meal after the circumcision of a baby boy is called a *se'udat mitzvah*, a meal accompanying a commanded act or, possibly, even a commanded meal. Rabbi Moses Isserles, who contributed additions—"glosses"—to Joseph Karo's code of Jewish law (*Shulhan Arukh*) indicating where the practice of northern European (Ashkenazic) Jews differed from Mediterranean (Sephardic) Jews, says that God comes close to excommunicating someone who refuses to take part in such a meal.[11] It has always been customary for the family of a newborn girl to sponsor a *Kiddush* (a reception after services on Saturday morning) on the day she is named in the synagogue and/or, in our time, to include a celebratory meal as part of a completely separate ceremony (a *simhat bat*).

Family and friends need to help a couple celebrate their wedding, for much of the meaning of weddings is that the couple publicly proclaims before their family and community that they now intend to be viewed as husband and wife. Moreover, joyous events become all the more exuberant in the company of the people near and dear to you. At the other end of the emotional spectrum, the community needs to help people mourn a death that has occurred in their family, which includes attending the funeral and visiting the family through the week of mourning (*shiva*) that follows to help make up a prayer quorum mornings and evenings and to help the family recall memories of the deceased. These duties even take precedence over studying Torah, which demonstrates how seriously Judaism takes our obligations of presence:

> If two scholars sit and study Torah and before them passes a bridal procession or the bier of a dead man, then if there are enough in the procession, they ought not to neglect their study; but if not, let them get up and cheer and hail the bride or accompany the dead.... As Rabbi Judah bar

121

Il'ai sat teaching his students, a bride passed by ... "My sons," he said to them, "get up and attend upon the bride. For we find that the Holy Blessed One attended upon a bride ... and if He attended upon a bride, how much more so should we!" The Holy Blessed One fixed Eve's hair and outfitted her as a bride and brought her to Adam, as the Torah says, "And He brought her to the man" (Genesis 2:22). At the first wedding the Holy Blessed One [also] acted as a best man for Adam; henceforth one must get a best man for himself.

—*Avot d'Rabbi Natan*, chapter 4; B. *Berakhot* 61a

The Apostle Paul also requires that we accompany people in their rejoicing as well as their mourning:

Let love be genuine; hate what is evil, hold fast to what is good; love one another with mutual affection; outdo one another in showing honor. Do not lag in zeal, be ardent in spirit, serve the Lord. Rejoice in hope, be patient in suffering, persevere in prayer.... Rejoice with those who rejoice, weep with those who weep.

—Romans 12:9–12, 15

It is fitting to end this chapter with a statement by Maimonides that summarizes the duties of being there for people in their times of illness, sadness, and joy:

It is a positive commandment of Rabbinic authority to visit the sick, comfort mourners, accompany the dead [to the burial ground], bring the bride under the wedding canopy, to accompany visitors to their destination, and to deal with all the needs of burial, including carrying the casket on one's shoulder, walking before it, saying a eulogy,

tearing one's clothing, and burying the dead. Similarly, [it
is a duty imposed by the Rabbis] to help the bride and
groom rejoice and to provide for all their needs. These acts
are forms of loving-kindness that one does with one's body
[in contrast to those done with one's money], for which
there is no limit [to determine when you have done
enough or too much]. Even though all these commandments are Rabbinic [in origin and authority], they are in
the category of "Love your neighbor as yourself"
(Leviticus 19:18): Everything that you would want others
to do for you, you must do for your fellow Jew [literally,
"for your neighbor in Torah and commandments"]....

—*M. T. Laws of Mourning* 14:1
(see also *S. A. Yoreh De'ah* 335)

PART THREE

Tikkun Olam in Practice

Families

5

DUTIES OF SPOUSES TO EACH OTHER

Our family relationships are in many ways the most important ties to other human beings we have. Therefore it should not be a surprise that Judaism—and Christianity—has much to say about how we relate to our spouses, parents, and children.

In fact, Jewish law has much more to say about those relationships than secular law does, partially because Jewish law is a *religious* legal system. The Bill of Rights in American law specifically denies jurisdiction of the government to many areas of life. Because God is presumed to know and care about everything in our lives, however, Jewish law presumes competence and jurisdiction to govern our personal relationships as well as our social ones.

Furthermore, because people can do bad things to each other in their personal relationships at least as much as in their social ones, Jewish law has a particular agenda of *tikkun olam* in the family as well as in the larger society. In each of the chapters of this section we will look at how the Jewish tradition understands relationships—to our spouse, our parents, and our children—and then explore how it pushes us to acts of *tikkun olam* with regard to those relationships, in each case with comparisons to Christian writers.

Marriage as Covenant, Social Structure, and Sacred Act

The Jewish tradition understands marriage to operate on three independent but interlocking planes: the contractual, the social, and the sacred. That is, marriage is not exclusively a matter of contract between the two people or families, and it is not simply a social structure governed by the rules of society, or a sacred act with solely religious meaning; it is all three at once. Moreover, each element affects the functioning of the others. Arthur Rosett and I discuss the ramifications of each of these three elements in some detail in our book *A Living Tree: The Roots and Growth of Jewish Law.*[1] For our purposes here, I will focus on the basic premise of each element.

The Covenantal Element of Jewish Marriage

Jewish marriage is, first, a covenant between the parties. Like a contract, a covenant is an agreement between two parties in which each gets something and gives something (lawyers call what each party gets "consideration"). Unlike a contract, though, a covenant is not designed to accomplish *a specific task*, after which it terminates; those entering a covenant rather intend to create *a long-term relationship*.

Judaism clearly intends to create long-term relationships in providing for marriage, but the covenantal nature of marriage also ironically enables divorce. As a covenant, the two parties—and, in Jewish law, only they—can create a marriage or dissolve it. Both the man and the woman must agree to be married for the marriage to be valid.[2] Because Deuteronomy 24:1–3 specifies a procedure for divorce, the Jewish tradition does not see divorce as a sin; it is simply a dissolution of the couple's covenant of marriage. (Compare some Christian views that see marriage as creating a new ontological entity, and Matthew 19:6: "What God has joined let no man rend asunder.") Because divorce is almost always sad for the couple and weakens the social fabric, however, the Jewish community historically tried to discourage divorce, especially if children were involved. Nevertheless, if the couple agrees to divorce, they need not provide any grounds to satisfy a court; irreconcilable differences are enough.[3] In addition, both parties have considerable leeway to create prenuptial conditions to their marriage.[4] All these aspects of Jewish marriage flow from its covenantal character.

The Social Element of Jewish Marriage

Marriage is a social phenomenon in several senses of the word "social." It is, first, a social occasion in which family and friends are invited to join in the celebration. Furthermore, because marriage affects the entire community, the seven blessings of the wedding ceremony may only be recited in the presence of a *minyan*, ten adult Jews, which officially marks a Jewish community.[5]

Marriage is social also in the sense that society—in Judaism, Jewish law—establishes conditions that the society imposes on every marriage as to who may marry (for example, age requirements, only those not related by blood) and what they commit themselves to provide for each other. California law is typical: "Husband and wife contract toward each other obligations of mutual respect, fidelity, and support."[6] The civil code then ignores the issues of mutual respect and fidelity, the former probably because it cannot find legal ways to define it and the latter because since the 1970s, state laws in all fifty states have recognized the legality of private, consensual sex between adults, regardless of their marital status. The California Code does, though, spell out some of the elements of its third element of marriage, support, for secular law can and does regulate money and property in marriage as it does in other commercial transactions, although with some differences in deference to the special relationship between the two parties.[7]

Jewish law is much more specific. It establishes a number of "constructive conditions" of marriage—that is, conditions that are built into the very construct of marriage as the Rabbis define it. As a result, whether or not a husband specified these benefits to his wife, they are part of his duties in marriage "as a condition of the court." These include duties to support her and her children; to ransom her from captivity; to pay for her medical expenses and her "adornments"; to allow her continued ties to her family and community; to avoid professions that would make him smell bad as well as diseases that would make him unattractive to her; and to offer to have sexual intercourse with her in reasonable intervals, as measured by the frequency with which his job enabled him to be home.[8]

The wife's duties, according to Jewish law, include the household duties that were expected in the patriarchal society of old. They also include, though, being reasonably modest in her social conduct; enabling her husband to obey Jewish law in eating (through proper tithing of the dough and, it is simply assumed, through making their home kosher) and in sexual intercourse (by informing him as to when she is menstruating so that they avoid sexual intercourse then); and doing work of her own, both to help support the family and to avoid boredom, "for idleness leads to lewdness ... and lightmindedness."[9]

Two things should be noted about this list. First, unlike almost every other tradition both ancient and modern, Judaism presumes that women have sexual needs just as much as men do; most other societies presumed that only men have sexual needs and that their wives accept their sexual advances because women want economic security and children. Furthermore, rabbinic law recognized and banned marital rape,[10] a very recent addition to American law.[11] As a result, if a woman refuses to engage in conjugal relations with her husband, his remedy is not rape, but rather reducing the amount that he would have to pay her in a divorce settlement by a certain amount each week until he can divorce her without paying her anything and marry someone else. Finally, unlike Catholicism, in which, according to Pope John Paul II, "*The two dimensions of conjugal union,* the unitive and the procreative, *cannot be artificially separated* without damaging the deepest truth of the conjugal act itself,"[12] Judaism recognizes two distinct and independent goals for sex within marriage—procreation and the mutual enjoyment and bonding of the couple, marked by two distinct commandments of the Torah (Gen. 1:28; Exod. 21:10)—and so Jewish law requires the couple to seek to satisfy each other sexually even if they are using contraceptives or are unable to have children, as, for example, after menopause.[13] The Calvinist tradition emphasized the unitive function over procreation and affirmed yet a third purpose for sex within marriage, namely, controlling lust,[14] an element that echoes Maimonides's views of sex.[15]

Second, the Mishnah has a keen understanding of the importance of work in the lives of women as well as men. Although family takes precedence over work in Jewish sources, work is also important. The lack of it leads to "lewdness" and "lightmindedness"—whatever those terms mean—and certainly lack of self-esteem, boredom, and possibly even criminal activity. Hence the insistence of the Jewish tradition that we saw in Chapter 2 to help the poor find a job, and hence the Mishnah's provisions that even wealthy women who can carry out their household duties through hired help must do some work themselves. In our own day, that might include volunteer projects as well as work for pay, and in the senior years it may mean volunteer work (such as, helping children or adults learn to read) or helping to care for grandchildren.

The Sacred Element in Jewish Marriage

Two of the Torah's commandments—to "be fruitful and multiply" (Gen. 1:27) and the duty of the man to provide his wife with her "food, clothing, and conjugal rights" (Exod. 21:10)—establish marriage as part of God's plan for us. The Torah also includes God's commandments defining whom we may not marry.[16]

Later Jewish tradition depicts God as personally celebrating human marriages. The Rabbis say, as we have seen, that God acted as Adam's best man and plaited Eve's hair in preparation for their wedding, symbolic of God's involvement in every marriage.[17] Ultimately, the Prophets and, especially, the Jewish mystical tradition depict the People Israel as married to God, indicating just how deeply marriage is rooted in God's universe.[18]

Christians have also affirmed the social and religious meanings of marriage. Typical is this statement of the National Association of Evangelicals:

> *We work to nurture family life and protect children.*
> From Genesis onward, the Bible tells us that the family is central to God's vision for human society. God has revealed himself to us in the language of family, adopting us as his children (Rom. 8:23, Gal. 4:5) and teaching us by the Holy Spirit to call him *Abba Father* (Rom. 8:15, Gal. 4:6). Marriage, which is a lifetime relationship between one man and one woman, is the predominant biblical icon of God's relationship with his people (Isa. 54:5; Jer. 3:20, 31:32; Ezek. 16:32; Eph. 5:23, 31–32). In turn, family life reveals something to us about God, as human families mirror, however faintly, the inner life of the Trinity.

The mutuality and service of family life contrast strongly with the hypermodern emphasis on individual freedom and rights. Marriage, sexuality, and family life are fundamental to society. Whether we are married or single, it is in the family that we learn mutual responsibility, we learn to live in an ordered society with complementary and distinct roles, we learn to submit and to obey, we learn to love and to trust, we learn both justice and mercy, and we learn to deny ourselves for the well-being of others. Thus the family is at the heart of the organic functioning of society.[19]

The following statement of the United States Conference of Catholic Bishops, quoted here in part, recognizes the human and social importance of marriage, but asserts that the divine aspect of marriage is preeminent and cannot be altered by human authorities:

Marriage is both a natural institution and a sacred union because it is rooted in the divine plan for creation. In addition, the Church teaches that the valid marriage of baptized Christians is a sacrament, a saving reality. Jesus Christ made marriage a symbol of his love for his Church (see Eph. 5:25–33). This means that a sacramental marriage lets the world see, in human terms, something of the faithful, creative, abundant, and self-emptying love of Christ. A true marriage in the Lord with his grace will bring the spouses to holiness. Their love, manifested in fidelity, passion, fertility, generosity, sacrifice, forgiveness, and healing, makes known God's love in their family, communities, and society. This Christian meaning confirms and strengthens the human value of a marital union.

Marriage is a basic human and social institution. Though it is regulated by civil laws and church laws, it did not originate from either the church or state, but from God. Therefore, neither church nor state can alter the basic meaning and structure of marriage.

Marriage, whose nature and purposes are established by God, can only be the union of a man and a woman and must remain such in law. In a manner unlike any other relationship, marriage makes a unique and irreplaceable contribution to the common good of society, especially through the procreation and education of children.

The union of husband and wife becomes, over a lifetime, a great good for themselves, their family, communities, and society. Marriage is a gift to be cherished and protected.[20]

Note that the covenantal aspect of Jewish marriage that recognizes the power of the couple to create and dissolve their union is missing in these statements. It was under this Christian influence that the law in all American states except Nevada until the 1970s restricted divorce to cases of adultery or insanity. Thus New York Governor Nelson Rockefeller had to fly to Nevada in 1968 to dissolve his marriage because his wife was neither adulterous nor insane. It was only in the 1970s, with a heightened sense of civil rights, that states gradually replaced such laws with "irreconcilable differences" as being sufficient grounds to grant a divorce, unconsciously following the Jewish model of seeing a covenantal, as well as a social and religious, meaning to marriage.

Forms of *Tikkun Olam* in Spousal Relations

Although Judaism does not consider divorce to be a sin, and although sometimes it is the right thing to do for both members of the couple and even for their children, divorce, even under the best of circumstances, is always sad. After all, the couple minimally must give up and mourn the dreams they had when they married of a long, happy life together. They must also deal with the feelings of frustration and self-doubt that often accompany divorce. Some will be gun-shy for quite some time in looking for a new partner, not daring to trust their instincts.

Moreover, divorce is hard. There are all the legal issues to take care of in both civil and Jewish law, including the disposition of their property. If the couple has children, they face the often difficult and extremely important issues of custody, education, and financial and emotional support for their children so that the divorce harms them as little as possible. Often this means that the couple, despite their distaste for each other, has to interact with each other for a long time to come. The welfare of their children demands that they learn to do that with civility, all the while supporting the children's respect and love for their former spouse, but this is often much easier said than done.

Preparation for Marriage

Because divorce, while not a sin, is nevertheless sad and hard, it is crucial that a couple contemplating marriage engage in some preventive measures to raise the chances that they will stay married. At the initiative of Rabbi Aaron Wise and Dr. Sylvia Weishaus, the University of Judaism (now the American Jewish University) in Los Angeles established a Preparation for Marriage course in 1975, consisting of ten sessions for groups of ten couples who are about to be married or have just been married. Five sessions are led by a marriage counselor, in which the couples discuss such matters as these: how to handle their parents; how to deal with friends of one partner but not the other; how to balance their careers and children; how to please each other sexually when one partner is not in the mood and one is; how to have an argument and still come out married. One session is devoted to economic issues, led by a financial counselor, because especially during the first years of marriage arguments often center around money. Finally, four sessions are devoted to creating a Jewish home. In 1994 the program's directors commissioned a survey of all the couples who had gone through it. Instead of the current American divorce rate—in the neighborhood of 50 percent of all couples who get married—the divorce rate among those who had gone through the program was 8.9 percent.[21] Given those figures, I will not officiate at a wedding in Los Angeles unless the couple has taken that Preparation for Marriage course; I think it is actually rabbinic malpractice to perform the ceremony without such preparation.

Couples sometimes object to such a course because they find the very thought of it demeaning. They believe they can handle themselves and interact with each other in marriage by "doing what comes naturally." If they cannot manage their marriage on their own, they think, they must be either stupid, clueless, or somehow deficient in this most personal of areas.

The fact is that there are many skills involved in marriage that need to be learned. Some couples do indeed intuit these skills, and some learn them through trial and error over time; but all can benefit immensely from some advice from those who have experience in helping couples understand what is important in a marital relationship and how to handle its inevitable ups and downs. As I tell couples, you spend years preparing for your careers; you can spend ten sessions preparing for your marriage. This is preventive *tikkun olam*.

Christians have affirmed this as well. In 2000, key leaders from the Catholic, Baptist, and Evangelical communities came together to consider how the Christian Church should respond to the widespread deterioration of marriages in North America. The outcome of this collaboration was a joint declaration that stated a commitment to work together to strengthen marriage within the Christian community and within society as a whole by, among other things, "educating young people about the meaning and responsibility of marriage" and "preparation for those engaged to be married."[22]

"Booster Shots"

Marriage only begins on the wedding day, and it hopefully lasts long after the honeymoon. As life presents its challenges, couples can and often do deepen their relationship as they face them together and manage them. Children, careers, parents, and friends all demand their attention. In the midst of all of this, it is important that the couple not let the rush of their lives blind them to each other. Too many couples find that after the children have grown up and left the house, their own relationship has to be reborn. It is appropriate that the relationship be redefined as new factors play into the couple's lives, but it is also important that they retain enough connection to each other through thick and thin so that they can build on their mutual commitments to each other to redirect their relationship as needed.

To retain and even deepen that reservoir of love, couples need to take some time off for each other. If they do not have the money to hire a babysitter, they can exchange babysitting nights with another couple. Once every week or two they should go out and do something they enjoy—dinner, a movie, a play, dancing—whatever. The few hours they spend away from their children will not only contribute to their relationship, but ultimately make them better parents and even better at their jobs. Later, when the children are grown, a weekend away every once in awhile, in addition to a vacation together, can ensure that their relationship does not become routine.

Many couples find programs like Jewish Marriage Encounter helpful. While these "booster shots" may seem obvious and even a little silly, they actually are a crucial way to tend to the relationship, fixing and strengthening a couple's personal world in critical ways. Jewish organizations like the American Jewish University and Christian ones like the United Methodist Church have created Jewish Marriage Encounter and Marriage Enrichment, respectively, precisely to foster ongoing communication and commitment within marriages.[23]

Bringing Peace Between Husband and Wife

Sometimes couples find themselves at odds with each other in ways that they themselves cannot resolve. James Dobson has identified the following list of "The Great Marriage Killers":

- Overcommitment and physical exhaustion
- Excessive credit and conflict over how money will be spent
- Selfishness
- Unhealthy relationships with in-laws
- Unrealistic expectations (for marriage)
- Space invaders (lack of boundaries)
- Sexual frustration and its partner, the greener grass of infidelity
- Business collapse
- Business success
- Getting married too young
- Alcohol and substance abuse
- Pornography, gambling, and other addictions[24]

When couples suffer from any or all of these factors to the point that they cannot resolve their disputes on their own, it is important that they find some help, whether a rabbi, a social worker (perhaps through the counseling services of Jewish Family Service), a marriage counselor, or a therapist. Men, in particular, find it hard to admit that they need help, especially in personal areas, and often resist discussing their problems with anyone, even close friends. Men are socialized in our society to be self-reliant and independent. (This also leads to men consulting doctors about their physical ailments much less than they should and often too late to stop a problem before it gets serious.) The fact of the matter, though, is that none of us is God, we all need help in certain areas of life, and it is only smart and wise to reach out for it when we need it. Thus, one version of the Talmud's list of activities that bring immediate benefit and that have a principle that bears fruit for a long time to come includes "bringing peace between a husband and wife."[25]

Domestic Violence

Sometimes problems escalate further, to the point of one spouse battering the other or abusing the other sexually, verbally, and/or psychologically. Physical abuse is relatively easy to see. Sexual abuse, where the man effectively rapes his wife in insisting on having sex with her against her will, is usually clear to both parties but somewhat less easy for others to identify, especially when the man claims that the sex was consensual, at which point it becomes a case of "he said, she said." Verbal and psychological abuse are even harder to identify, but no less real. Verbal abuse consists of cases where one spouse continually demeans the other out of anger and spite for no good reason ("You are so stupid"), to be distinguished from constructive and loving criticism for a specific act. Psychological abuse occurs when one spouse creates an atmosphere of intimidation and fear.

Domestic violence of all these types occurs in families of all religions, as well as among avowedly secular people. It happens at all levels of educational and financial status. Worse, sometimes religion itself is invoked as the justification for such abuse.

In my rabbinic ruling on family violence, approved unanimously by the Conservative movement's Committee on Jewish Law and Standards and reprinted in an earlier book,[26] I define the various kinds of violence—physical, sexual, and verbal—and the most common targets—spouses, parents (especially elderly ones), and children. I then discuss how the Jewish tradition evaluated and responded to each of these sorts of violence and argue for prohibiting in our day even those forms of assault that were permitted by the tradition in the past (for example, wife beating and hitting children). The ruling then successively deals with the responsibilities of victims of abuse, witnesses to it, and batterers.

It is not, however, Judaism's Conservative movement alone that bans family violence. Indeed, religious leaders from all Jewish denominations, most Christian ones, and both Sunni and Shi'ite Muslims have signed on to the following declaration created through the efforts of the Faith Trust Institute:

> We proclaim with one voice as national spiritual and religious leaders that violence against women exists in all communities, including our own, and is morally, spiritually and universally intolerable.
>
> We acknowledge that our sacred texts, traditions and values have too often been misused to perpetuate and condone abuse.

We commit ourselves to working toward the day when all women will be safe and abuse will be no more.

We draw upon our healing texts and practices to help make our families and societies whole.

Our religious and spiritual traditions compel us to work for justice and the eradication of violence against women.

We call upon people of all religious and spiritual traditions to join us.[27]

For Jews experiencing or witnessing family violence, rabbis and Jewish Family Service can often be of help in finding shelters for battered women and children (Jewish Family Service of Los Angeles, for example, operates two such shelters), and they can also be of help in finding treatment programs for batterers. Similar resources exist for Christians. This is a scourge on the community that we must acknowledge as real as a first step to taking actions to stop it. Helping batterers confront why they batter and how to change their behavior, and protecting women, men, and children from physical, sexual, verbal, and psychological abuse is *tikkun olam* in a sorely needed and a most graphic sense.

6

CHILDREN'S DUTIES TO THEIR PARENTS

Tikkun olam involves regulating the relationships between parents and children such that parents can be taken care of in their old age and children can be taught the norms and skills of relating to others in their youth. If the former does not happen, society as a whole will bear the burden of aiding seniors who can no longer live independently; if the latter does not happen, children will grow into antisocial and perhaps even criminal adults without the skills to earn a living. Thus, society at large has serious stakes in both directions of the parent–child relationship. Jewish sources try to structure that relationship to assure—or at least to make it more probable—that these social ends are met.

Beyond these goals, proper parent–child relationships go to the very heart of the Jewish vision of what kinds of people we should be. That is, even if the pragmatic needs of parents and children could be met by others in society, the very nature of the parent–child relationship as conceived in the Jewish tradition requires that all parents fulfill parental duties to their children and that all children fulfill their filial duties to their parents. It is simply a matter of character, of the kind of person you should be and the kind of society you should help to create.

In describing filial and parental duties in this chapter and the next, we will be looking at *tikkun olam* in two separate senses. First, these Jewish norms seek to establish parent–child relations so that society's practical needs for the care of parents and the raising of children can be met at least in part by the parents and children themselves and not wholly by society. This will "fix" society in the sense of *ordering* it by distributing the responsibility of fulfilling its needs among its members. It will enable society to meet its members' needs more effectively and efficiently than social agencies alone could accomplish.

Second, these parental and filial norms will "fix" society in the sense of *improving* it by setting guidelines to inform and foster the character development of its members through educating them to recognize and fulfill their duties as proper parents or children. Thus society will hopefully be filled with people who not only carry out their minimal duties to their close family, but go beyond that to treat the members of their family in a noble and virtuous way.

THE TWO BASIC FILIAL DUTIES: HONOR AND RESPECT

Two of the Torah's commandments establish the foundation for the Jewish conception of parent–child relationships—the duties to honor your parents and to fear or respect them:

> Honor your father and your mother, that your days may be long upon the land which the Lord your God is giving you.
>
> —Exodus 20:12

> You shall fear every man his mother and his father, and you shall keep My sabbaths: I am the Lord your God.
>
> —Leviticus 19:3

In typical rabbinic fashion, the Rabbis immediately try to define what each of these commandments entails and how they differ from each other. As a boy, I always thought that the command to honor my parents applied to me and my young friends and that it commanded us to obey our parents. That, however, is not how the Rabbis define it. They instead determine that it applies to adult children who have positive duties (that is, things they must do) to care for their elderly parents when they cannot care for themselves. As long as the parents have financial resources, the children may use them to carry out this obligation, but once the parents' money runs out, the children must use their own resources to finance the services required by this commandment.

The duty to respect (or fear) your parents, on the other hand, involves negative duties to refrain from those actions that would reduce them psychologically and socially to the level of their children. They may therefore not sit in either parent's chair (assuming that the parent has a special one) or contradict the parent in public. The latter duty, however, does not mean that the children must always agree with the parent or may not challenge the parent in private; it is rather a matter of preserving the honor of the parent in public forums. As the Talmud makes clear, these duties apply to both sons and daughters and to both mothers and fathers, and so "he" and "father" in these sources refer also to "she" and "mother":

> Our Rabbis taught: What is "fear" and what is "honor"? "Fear" means that he [the son] must neither stand nor sit in his [the father's] place, nor contradict his words, nor tip the scales against him. "Honor" means that he must give him food and drink, clothe and cover him, lead him in and out. The Scholars propounded: At whose expense? Rav Judah said: The son's. Rabbi Nahman b. Oshaia said:

The father's. The Rabbis gave a ruling to Rabbi Jeremiah—others state to Rabbi Jeremiah's son—in accordance with the view that it may be at the father's expense. An objection is raised: The Bible says, "Honor your father and your mother," and it also says, "Honor the Lord with your substance" (Proverbs 3:9): just as the latter means at personal cost, so the former too. But if you say [that the son provides goods and services to his father] at the father's [expense], how does it affect him [the son such that it is a duty of his]?—Through loss of time.

—B. *Kiddushin* 31b–32a

The last line of this source indicates that the Rabbis presumed that adult children would personally carry out these duties of honor. This is made explicit in the following source, which compares the way we should honor our parents with the way we should honor God:

You are My children, and I am your Father.... It is an honor for children to dwell with their father, and it is an honor for the father to dwell with his children.... Therefore make a house for the Father in which He can dwell with His children.

—*Exodus Rabbah* 34:3

As we shall discuss in the next section of this chapter, this will raise questions in our day about placing elderly parents in nursing homes.

The connection between the honor of parents and the honor of God is a common theme among the Rabbis. It affects not only the way we should ideally honor our parents—that is, personally—but also the effects of honor of parents on their children—namely, that they honor God in the process. This is, in part, because the Rabbis maintained that along with your mother and father, God is one of your parents, and so honoring our earthly parents is a way to honor our heavenly parent as well:

> There are three partners in the production of a human being: the Holy One, blessed be He, the father, and the mother. The father provides the white matter from which are formed the bones, sinews, nails, brain, and the white part of the eye. [The Rabbis probably thought this because semen is white.] The mother provides the red matter from which are formed the skin, flesh, hair, and the pupil of the eye. [The Rabbis probably thought this because menstrual blood is red.] The Holy One, blessed be He, infuses into him/her breath, soul, features, vision, hearing, speech, power of motion, understanding, and intelligence.
>
> —B. *Niddah* 31a

> The Rabbis say: Three combine in the making of each person: God, the father, and the mother. If people honor their father and mother, God says, "I ascribe merit to them as if I dwelled among them and as if they honored Me."
>
> —B. *Kiddushin* 30b

Philo of Alexandria, a first-century thinker who is arguably the first Jewish philosopher, expands on the connection between honoring parents and honoring God by focusing on the placement of the command to honor parents in the Decalogue (the Ten Commandments). A common rabbinic theme is that the first five of those commandments govern the relationships between God and human beings and the second group of five regulates the relationships that human beings have with each other. Parents, of course, are human beings, and so the fact that the Torah places the command to honor them as the last of the first group of five indicates that it makes parents akin to God. Like God, our parents are responsible not only for our physical existence but also for our moral, theological, and professional education. Furthermore, parents function as a bridge from God to the human world and from the human world to God:

> After dealing with the seventh day [the Fourth of the Ten Commandments], He gives the Fifth Commandment on the honor due to parents. This commandment He placed on the borderline between the two sets of five: it is the last of the first set, in which the most sacred injunctions, those dealing with God, are given, and it adjoins the second set of five, which contain the duties of human beings to each other. The reason, I think, is this: we see that parents by their nature stand on the borderline between the mortal and the immortal sides of existence—the mortal, because of their kinship with people and with other animals through the perishableness of the body; the immortal, because the act of generation assimilates them to God, the progenitor of everything....
>
> Some bolder spirits, glorifying the name of parenthood, say that a father and mother are in fact gods revealed to sight, who copy the Uncreated in His work as the Framer of life.... How can reverence be rendered to the invisible God by those who show irreverence to the gods who are near at hand and seen by the eye?
>
> —Philo (first century, Alexandria),
> Treatise on the Decalogue

As we can see from the Talmud's definitions of "honor" and "fear" of parents, the Jewish tradition, as usual, translates

what looks like matters of feeling and attitude into demands
for concrete actions. It never takes lip service to be sufficient.
At the same time, it was certainly not blind to the importance
of the tenor and feelings with which a person fulfills commandments, especially ones as personal as these. Thus the
Talmud includes this remarkable passage in which the Rabbis
make clear that while proper feelings are not enough, proper
actions are not enough either; you need to do the right things
for your parents in the context of an attitude of honor and
respect:

> A man may feed his father on fattened chickens and
> inherit Hell as his reward, and another may put his father
> to work in a mill and inherit Paradise.
>
> How is it possible that a man might feed his father
> fattened chickens and inherit Hell? It once happened that
> a man used to feed his father fattened chickens. Once his
> father said to him: "My son, where did you get these?" He
> answered: "Old man, old man, eat and be silent, just as
> dogs eat and are silent." In such an instance, he feeds his
> father fattened chickens, but he inherits Hell.
>
> How is it possible that a man might put his father to
> work in a mill and inherit Paradise? It once happened that
> a man was working in a mill. The king decreed millers
> should be brought to work for him. The son said to his
> father: "Father, go and work in the mill in my place, (and
> I will go to work for the king). For it may be (that the
> workers will be) ill-treated, in which case let me be ill-
> treated instead of you. And it may be (that the workers
> will be) beaten, in which case let me be beaten instead of
> you." In such an instance, he puts his father to work in a
> mill, but he inherits Paradise.
>
> —B. *Kiddushin* 31a–31b

By comparison, notice three things about Pope John Paul II's interpretation of the commandment to honor your parents, reproduced below: (1) he sees it as the first of the commandments regarding our duties to people rather than the last of the Ten Commandments concerning our duties to God, as Philo and the Rabbis classify it; (2) he uses this commandment and that in Leviticus 19:32 to expand our care and concern not only to parents but to all elderly people, which the Jewish tradition likewise did but only on the basis of Leviticus 19:32[1]; and (3) he interprets it to require love of our parents, which, as we shall see, the Jewish tradition encouraged but did not require:

11. Why then should we not continue to give the elderly the respect which the sound traditions of many cultures on every continent have prized so highly? For peoples influenced by the Bible, the point of reference through the centuries has been the commandment of the Decalogue: "Honor your father and mother," a duty which, for that matter, is universally recognized. The full and consistent application of this commandment has not only been a source of the love of children for their parents, but it has also forged the strong link that exists between the generations. Where this commandment is accepted and faithfully observed, there is little danger that older people will be regarded as a useless and troublesome burden.

The same commandment also teaches respect for those who have gone before us and for all the good that they have done: the words "father and mother" point to the past, to the bond between generations that makes possible the very existence of a people. In the two versions found in the Bible (cf. Exod. 20:2–17;

Deut. 5:6–21), this divine commandment is the first of those inscribed on the second Tablet of the Law, which deals with the duties of human beings towards one another and towards society. Furthermore, it is the only commandment to which a promise is attached: "Honor your father and mother, so that your days in the land which the Lord your God gives you may be long" (Exod. 20:12; cf. Deut. 5:16).

12. "Rise in the presence of one with grey hair; honor the person of the older man" (Lev. 19:32). Honoring older people involves a threefold duty: welcoming them, helping them and making good use of their qualities. In many places this happens almost spontaneously, as the result of long-standing custom. Elsewhere, and especially in the more economically advanced nations, there needs to be a reversal of the current trend, to ensure that elderly people can grow old with dignity, without having to fear that they will end up no longer counting for anything. There must be a growing conviction that a fully human civilization shows respect and love for the elderly, so that despite their diminishing strength they feel a vital part of society. Cicero himself noted that "the burden of age is lighter for those who feel respected and loved by the young."[2]

LIMITS ON THE FILIAL DUTIES

In establishing duties of honor and respect for parents, the Jewish tradition also sets limits for these duties. These include obeying God's commandments rather than those of your parents when they conflict, protecting your own welfare, and exempting children from responding to parents' unreasonable demands.

God's Commandments

The tie between honoring parents and honoring God has direct implications for determining the hierarchy of our duties. For the Rabbis, the order was very clear: because all Jews, including our parents, are duty-bound to obey God, God's commands take precedence over those of our parents when they conflict:

> It was taught: One might think that the honor of father and mother supersedes the Sabbath, [but that is not so:] The Torah says, "You shall fear every man his mother and his father, and you shall keep My sabbaths; I am the Lord your God," [meaning] that all of you are obligated to honor Me.
>
> —B. *Yevamot* 5b
> (based on *Sifra Leviticus, Kedoshim* 1:10)

This aspect of Jewish law should not be an excuse for children to dishonor their parents in a kind of religious one-upmanship. If the children decide to become more religiously involved and observant than their parents, they must do it in a way that continues to show their parents honor in attitude, word, and deed. If the children are teenagers, they need to work out with their parents exactly how the new patterns of observance they want to adopt can fit in to the family structure. Sometimes, for example, the parents might be convinced to make the home kosher or to refrain from some of their customary activities on the Sabbath and instead do things appropriate to the Sabbath as they themselves grow in their Judaism along with their children. In other families, the parents and children have to negotiate a way in which each can live and let live in their own, distinct way while living under the same roof. The critical thing is not the ultimate agreement; it is rather that the conversations in which these negotiations take place remain calm and mutually respectful and that all family members then continue to interact with each other in the same manner.

If the children are adults living on their own and the issue is visits to each other's homes, the situation is somewhat easier, both because the time spent together is considerably shorter and because parents presume that college-age and older children will be making their own life decisions about religion and, indeed, about everything else. Still, if, say, the children keep kosher and the parents do not, then the parents and children need to work out some way to make it possible for them to see each another and socialize together. The situation is even worse on Passover, when Jewish dietary laws are even stricter. If both parents and children keep kosher, or kosher for Passover, but in different ways, it is usually best for each simply to give full faith and credit to the other without asking questions. Again, the tone in which these issues are negotiated is usually more important than the specific agreement.

Another increasingly common issue that falls under this category occurs when parents have made it clear that upon their death they want to be cremated. It is bad enough if only one adult child is involved in this decision, for when the child has the parent buried, he or she must bear the burden of acting against the express wishes of the parent after the parent has died and cannot protest or even argue. If the child acquiesces to the parent's wishes, he or she must suffer the guilt of violating Jewish law. The situation is yet worse when there are two or more children involved, one or more of whom wants to bury Mom or Dad according to traditional Jewish rites, despite the parent's instructions to the contrary, and one or more of whom want to carry out the parent's wishes, whether or not they agree with them. Jewish tradition is clear: neither the parent nor the children have the right to violate Jewish law, and so the children should bury, and not cremate, the parent. Putting this decision into practice, however, is often not simple, and the adult children would be well advised to get the help of their rabbi in working this out so that they can have reasonable relationships with each other thereafter.

Mutual respect among family members is even more important when the requirements of Jewish law are not clear. For example, adult children eventually face the decision of whether to remove life support systems from a parent when there is no reasonable hope for his or her recovery. While Jewish law is clear in its prohibition of cremation, rabbis differ on what Jewish law does and does not demand with regard to end-of-life care, especially the status of artificial nutrition and hydration.

On one end of the spectrum, some Orthodox rabbis demand that absolutely everything must be done to keep a body alive, even if that means the person will never regain consciousness and will forever have to be on machines. On the other end of the spectrum, some Reform rabbis maintain that individual family members should seek the advice of their rabbi but in the end should make their decisions however they think is best. In the middle are multiple positions that rabbis of all movements have taken on these issues. Some see artificial nutrition and hydration as food and liquids and therefore require that they be administered under all circumstances, while others maintain that artificial nutrition and hydration are medicine and therefore may be withheld or withdrawn.

All Jewish authorities would say that patients must be kept as comfortable as possible, for, unlike some forms of Christianity, Judaism does not regard pain as a good thing. Furthermore, each movement in Judaism has produced its distinctive form of advance directive, so that people can indicate what medical treatments they would choose at the end of life as framed by the choices open to them according to their movement's approach to Jewish law. Books on medical ethics and particularly on how adult children should understand their duty to feed their parents at the end of life have been published from the viewpoints of all movements in Judaism.[3] Jews may also consult with their rabbi in such circumstances for guidance in what is always an emotional, and often an unfamiliar, set of decisions to make.

The Jewish tradition demands honor and respect for parents even if you are not supposed to follow their directions to violate the other commandments. When Jewish law is clear on a given issue and the parents want the child to do something else, you must find a way to honor your parents even while disobeying them in the name of Jewish law, and it may even mean compromising your standards of observance in the name of such honor. After all, religion should strengthen families, not divide them. When Jewish law is not clear on a given issue, or when it permits several different options, your parents' wishes should play a stronger role in how you honor them. In the end, then, Jews must find a way to uphold *both* of these Jewish duties—to abide by Jewish law, on the one hand, and to honor parents, on the other—recognizing full well that this may be difficult for some families on at least some issues and that to do this may require us to be more creative and flexible than we would normally be.

Your Own Welfare

The Talmud establishes a principle that saving your own life takes precedence over saving anyone else's life, including that of your parents or teachers.[4] Does the same hierarchy apply to your property? The Talmud maintains that honor to parents extends to the point of allowing them to squander your property; but Rabbenu Yitzhak, one of the

Tosafists, important twelfth-century commentators on the Talmud, maintains that recovering your own property takes precedence over some act of honor for your parents:

> They asked Rabbi Eliezar, "What is the limit for honoring one's father and mother?" He said, "To the point where the parent takes [his or her child's] wallet or money and throws it into the ocean, and his child does not rebuke him."
>
> —B. *Kiddushin* 32a

> Rabbenu Yitzhak is of the opinion that one should defer parental honor as well as the return of a lost object to another in order to recover one's own lost object. For when the Talmud says that parental honor has precedence [over the property of the child], that is only in a case such as permitting one's parent full license with one's money, for that is honor *per se*. However, when it comes to recovering one's lost article, the son need not forgo its recovery on account of his father's honor.
>
> —*Tosafot* to B. *Kiddushin* 32a

In other words, if the parent is going to get some benefit from the child's property, even if it is an apparently irrational benefit, the parent has a right to use the child's property. But if the parent is not going to get any benefit from the child's loss of money and simply has to have the patience to wait while the child retrieves his property before doing something to honor the parent, then the child should first retrieve his or her property.

How should we draw the limit now between the child's right to retain his or her money and the parent's right to that money for, say, extended health care in old age? To what extent does it matter, for example, if the parents paid for the day school and/or college and graduate school tuition for the child long ago? What about all of the parents' expenses in simply providing the child with food, shelter, and clothing during childhood and through the many years of the child's education? (Remember that until the twentieth century, children began helping their families earn a living by age ten or so.) In other words, just as the factors warranting the child's control of his or her money have been enhanced in modern times by Enlightenment notions of an individual's right to the pursuit of happiness and property[5] and by the new technological world in which rapidly changing circumstances make our parents' experience less relevant for at least some things, so too have the factors justifying a greater financial duty to parents grown in our time. Only one thing is certain about all of this: drawing sensible and morally sensitive guidelines about this matter, with substantial input from the Jewish tradition's demand of honor and respect for parents, is definitely not easy!

Unreasonable Demands

Jewish sources demand a high degree of tolerance for our parents and their demands, interestingly learning this from the model of a non-Jew:

> Rabbi Eliezer the Great's disciples asked him, "How far does honor of father and mother extend?" He replied, "Go and see what Dama B. Netina [a non-Jew] did. He was president of the city council. One time she [his mother] came and slapped him in the presence of the whole assembly, and all he said was, 'May that be enough for you, my mother.' Our rabbis say that some of our wise men came to him to buy a precious stone in the place of one that had fallen out and been lost from the breastplate of the High Priest.... They agreed to give him a thousand

gold pieces for the stone. He went in, and he found his father asleep with his leg stretched out upon the box that contained the jewel. He would not disturb him and came back without it. When the wise men perceived this, they thought that he wanted more money, and they offered ten thousand gold pieces. When his father woke up, he went in and brought out the jewel. The wise men offered him the ten thousand pieces, but he replied, 'Far be it from me to make a profit from honoring my father; I will take only the thousand to which we had agreed.' And what reward did God give him? Our Rabbis say that in that very year his cow bore a red calf [which is extremely rare and whose ashes are necessary for a number of the Temple rites] that he sold for more than ten thousand gold pieces.

—*Deuteronomy Rabbah, Devarim* 1:15
(cf. B. *Kiddushin* 31a and J. *Pe'ah* 15c)

But Jewish sources also recognize limits to what parents may demand, although they do not spell out those limits with clarity. As you read the following passage, try to generalize a rule that defines when a parental demand is legitimate and the children must satisfy it, and when a demand is illegitimate, lacking any legal requirement to fulfill it. If you cannot devise such a general rule, this may be like the famous problem Justice Potter Stewart of the U.S. Supreme Court had in defining pornography, finally giving up and saying, "I cannot define it, but I know it when we see it!"[6] Are honor and respect for parents similarly indefinable in general principle but recognizable in practice?

If one's father or mother becomes mentally disturbed, he should try to treat them as their mental state demands, until they are pitied by God. But if he finds that he cannot endure the situation because of their extreme

madness, he may leave and go away, appointing others to
care for them properly.

> —Maimonides, *M. T. Laws of Rebels* 6:10; *S. A.*
> *Yoreh De'ah* 240:10

In our day, this source has a broader application than it
did in the past. Although it is still true that children may not
be psychologically able to care for parents who have
Alzheimer's disease or some other form of dementia, it is also
true that many adult children cannot care for parents who are
perfectly sane and even warm and loving. With both the husband and wife often working to support their family, giving
personal care to their elderly parents, which the tradition sees
as the ideal, may not be possible because of the long stretches
of time during which neither member of the couple is home
to tend to the parents. Furthermore, as much as they might
love their children and grandchildren, some elderly people
may prefer to have the companionship of people their own
age on a regular basis, thus making living with their children,
even if possible, less than desirable. Because many families
now face this situation, assisted living facilities and nursing
homes have been developed to care for those who can no
longer care for themselves.

In light of these new circumstances, we can imagine an
argument, consistent with the Jewish values of honor and
respect for parents, to place a parent in such a home. Still, the
following testimony by Mother Teresa to the U.S. Senate and
House of Representatives sounds a cautionary note for us all
and reinforces the Jewish ideal of personal care for our parents:

> I can never forget the experience I had in visiting a
> (retirement) home where they kept all these old parents of
> sons and daughters who had just put them into an insti-

tution and forgotten them—maybe. I saw that in that home these old people had everything—good food, comfortable place, television, everything, but everyone was looking toward the door. And I did not see a single one with a smile on the face. I turned to Sister and I asked: "Why do these people who have every comfort here, why are they all looking toward the door? Why are they not smiling?" I am so used to seeing the smiles on our people, even the dying ones smile. And Sister said: "This is the way it is nearly everyday. They are expecting, they are hoping that a son or daughter will come to visit them. They are hurt because they are forgotten." And see, this neglect to love brings spiritual poverty. Maybe in our own family we have somebody who is feeling lonely, who is feeling sick, who is feeling worried. Are we there? Are we willing to give until it hurts in order to be with our families, or do we put our own interests first? ... We must remember that love begins at home, and we must also remember that 'the future of humanity passes through the family.'[7]

Thus even if placing parents in an assisted living facility or a nursing home is the best possible option, children need to ensure that the facility meets the parents' needs honorably and they should phone and visit often.

Love and Its Opposites: Abuse and Neglect

Finally, although it certainly is ideal not only to honor and respect your parents but also to love them, Jewish law does not require love. Perhaps this stems from the tradition's recognition that love of parents cannot be legally demanded, that it can only flow naturally out of the personal relationship between parents and children:

> We were commanded to honor and revere our parents,
> and to obey the prophets, and it is possible for a person to
> honor and revere and obey those whom s/he does not
> love. But with regard to the proselyte, there is a command
> to love him/her with a great, heartfelt love ... much as we
> are commanded to love God.
>
> —Maimonides, *Responsa*, #448

This is especially relevant to two special contexts. First, if
your parents were not only demanding but downright abusive,
then most Jewish authorities would exempt children of such
parents from the duties of honor and respect. On the contrary,
because self-preservation takes precedence over all other duties
except the bans against murder, idolatry, and adultery or
incest,[8] you must seek to extricate yourself from abusive situations. How you do that depends on your age, but teachers and
relatives who suspect child abuse are required by law in most
jurisdictions to report such suspicions to governmental authorities. Like adults who are exposed to spousal abuse, children
whose parents abuse them should be removed from the house
for their own safety.

Conversely, adult children do not have the right to abuse
their elderly parents, whether physically or verbally. If they
find themselves unable to control themselves, they should distance themselves from their parents and pay for others to care
for them. For further discussion of Jewish law on family violence, see the chapter on that subject in my book, *Love Your
Neighbor and Yourself*,[9] which is my rabbinic ruling on that
topic approved by the Conservative movement's Committee
on Jewish Law and Standards.

The other context that excuses children from the duties
of honor and respect is abandonment. Sometimes people give
up their children for adoption for the best of reasons, but when

they do so, they also give up their right to their children's honor and respect unless it is an open adoption and they play at least some part in raising the children. Adopted children do have the full duties of honor and respect, however, toward their adoptive parents.

APPLYING FILIAL DUTIES TO TODAY

Much of what the Torah and rabbinic tradition say about filial duties of honor and respect is immediately relevant and instructive for our times. Even though parents and children have been around since the dawn of the human species, we cannot mechanically apply all of what the tradition says to our modern context. Far-flung families, people living to much older ages, and the advent of assisted living facilities and nursing homes all require that we use sensitivity and judgment in applying the tradition's mandates to our own relationships with our parents. Still, the attitudes and values that the tradition articulates in shaping the contours of that relationship are as relevant and important today as they ever were.

7

PARENTS' DUTIES TO
THEIR CHILDREN

As conceived in Jewish sources, the parent–child relationship is a two-way street. Just as children have duties to parents, so too do parents have obligations to their children. Thus what we hope will be a loving, supportive relationship, where parents and children will be there for each other throughout life both materially and emotionally, is not left to the realm of hopes in the Jewish tradition but is rather made the subject of legal duties.

Interestingly, American law says little about children's duties but does prescribe some parental duties. In contrast to the Jewish tradition, American law does not make adult children responsible for the care or financial support of their elderly parents, let alone prescribe duties of honor and respect in attitude. It does, however, hold parents liable for abandonment and neglect and punishes them even more severely for child abuse.

Judaism's specification of legal duties for both parents and children certainly does not preclude warm, supportive relationships between the two parties; it just ensures that at least some of the practical results of such a relationship in fact take place, whether the family has such emotional ties or not. The guidelines minimally serve the practical need of saving society as a whole from having to care for the children and parents in these ways. They also serve the moral end of establishing a standard for what Judaism asserts are minimal requirements of character for both parents and children in their relationships with each other.

THE PRIMARY RABBINIC SOURCE FOR PARENTAL DUTIES

The Rabbis summarize parental duties in the following passage:

> Our Rabbis taught: A man is responsible to circumcise his son, to redeem him [from Temple service if he is the first born, "*pidyon ha-ben*"], to teach him Torah, to marry him off to a woman, and to teach him a trade, and there are some who say that he must also teach him to swim. Rabbi Judah says: Anyone who fails to teach his son a trade teaches him to steal.
>
> —B. *Kiddushin* 29a

After discussing the degree to which this source applies to daughters, this chapter examines three of these duties: Jewish education, professional education, and finding a marriage partner. Despite the order of this rabbinic source, the discussion of what is involved in the duty to "teach him Torah" will be followed by a description of the parameters of the duty to "teach him a trade" because both involve forms of education that the parents are obliged to provide.

Mothers and Daughters

Because the above passage includes circumcision and redemption from Temple service, both clearly understood to apply only to sons, the immediate question arises as to whether the other duties apply to mothers and daughters as well. Surprisingly, the general answer is no. Mothers did not have the

163

duties enumerated in the source above, undoubtedly because they did not control the family's economic resources, and, except for the father's duty to marry off his children of both genders, he did not have to educate his daughters in Torah or a trade.[1] There was real controversy as to whether a man, although not obligated to teach his daughters Torah, should nevertheless do so.[2]

In our own day, however, few Jewish communities, even among the Orthodox, refuse to teach their daughters Torah. Indeed, in the Conservative, Reconstructionist, and Reform movements, women can even become rabbis. Similarly, although parents are not required by Jewish law to teach their daughters a trade, the Mishnah speaks of women learning and doing household chores and spinning wool,[3] and especially before or after their childbearing years, they would often help their fathers or husbands in the family business, sometimes even running it.[4]

At the same time, fathers had duties toward their daughters that they did not have toward their sons. Specifically, the Rabbis of the Mishnah and Talmud interpreted the Torah to require a man to support his children to age six. Beyond that, the Rabbis enacted a requirement on their own authority that a man must support his children until they reached the age of puberty.[5] If he was poor, however, he should send out his sons to beg and support his daughters, for girls who begged would be more likely to be physically abused.[6] Furthermore, the Rabbis had transformed the bride price that a groom traditionally had to pay at the time of marriage to a lien against his property that was payable only in the event of his divorcing or predeceasing her in order to encourage marriage and discourage divorce,[7] but the groom still faced the financial burden of supporting his new wife. The Rabbis ruled, however, that if the family was poor, the charity fund would support orphan girls with money for their dowry so that they could be married and not orphan boys, unless the money in the fund was sufficient to help both.[8]

"TO TEACH HIM TORAH"

This duty began with Abraham and is articulated in verses made famous through their inclusion as the first and second paragraphs of the *Shema*:

> For I [God] have singled him [Abraham] out, that he may instruct his children and his posterity to keep the way of the Lord by doing what is just and right, in order that the Lord may bring about for Abraham what He has promised him.
>
> —Genesis 18:19

> Hear, O Israel! The Lord is our God, the Lord alone [or, is one]. You shall love the Lord your God with all your heart and with all your soul and with all your might. Take to heart these instructions with which I charge you this day. Impress them [teach them diligently] upon your children. Recite them when you stay at home and when you are away, when you lie down and when you get up. Bind them as a sign on your hand and let them serve as a symbol on your forehead; inscribe them on the doorposts of your house and on your gates.
>
> —Deuteronomy 6:4–9 (the first paragraph of the *Shema;* see also Deuteronomy 11:18–21)

Furthermore, this duty applies to grandparents as well as to parents:

> Take utmost care and watch yourselves scrupulously, so that you do not forget the things that you saw with your

own eyes and so that they do not fade from your mind as long as you live. And make them known to your children and to your children's children.

—Deuteronomy 4:9

Are grandparents responsible for teaching their grandchildren? ... "And you shall teach your children" (Deuteronomy 11:19), from that I only know that I must teach my children; how do I know that I must also teach my grandchildren? Because the Torah says, "and make them known to your children and to your children's children" (Deuteronomy 4:9).

—B. *Kiddushin* 30a

In our own day, this implies that grandparents have a duty to help their children provide a Jewish education for their grandchildren. That includes providing a Jewish model for their grandchildren, especially if they are the product of an interfaith marriage. For those grandparents who have greater financial resources than their adult children as well as fewer economic responsibilities, this duty also includes paying the tuition (or part of it) for their grandchildren's Jewish day school or religious school education, camp, or youth group. Grandparents may feel good about themselves in doing this, but not too good: after all, they are simply fulfilling their Jewish legal duty!

In a manner typical of them, the Rabbis then sought to define the scope of this obligation:

To what extent is a man obliged to teach his son Torah? Rav Judah said in Samuel's name: For example, Zevulun, the son of Dan, whom his grandfather taught Scripture, Mishnah, Talmud, laws and legends. An objection was raised: [We have a tradition that] If he [his father] taught

him Scripture, he need not teach him Mishnah ... [The
law, then, is] like Zevulun, son of Dan, yet not altogether
so.... for whereas there [he was taught] Scripture,
Mishnah, Talmud, laws, and legends, here [i.e., as a general
rule] Scripture alone [suffices].

—B. *Kiddushin* 30a

That is, the father must teach his son minimally the Torah,
but ideally he should teach him all the things that Zevulun, son
of Dan, learned. The obligation to teach your children and
grandchildren begins when the child reaches age five, and the
curriculum increases in difficulty as the child ages:

He [Yehudah ben Tema] used to say: At five years of
age—the study of Bible; at ten—the study of Mishnah; at
thirteen—responsibility for the commandments; at fifteen—the study of Talmud; at eighteen—marriage; at
twenty—pursuit of a livelihood; at thirty—the peak of
one's powers; at forty—the age of understanding; at
fifty—the age of giving counsel; at sixty—old age; at seventy—the hoary head [or, white old age]; at eighty—the
age of strength [or, rare old age]; at ninety—the bent back;
at one hundred—as one dead and out of this world.

—M. *Avot* 5:23 (5:24 in some editions)

The Rabbis were keenly aware, however, that the curriculum of teaching Judaism should not consist of text knowledge
and skills alone; character education is a critical part of learning Torah as well. This obviously includes teaching children
values like respect for persons, respect for property, honesty,
responsibility, and the like. It also includes negative demands
like avoiding assault and battery, stealing, and the like. One
graphic example of moral education affects parents and children.

Because striking a parent or even cursing a parent are, according to the Torah, capital offenses (Exod. 23:15, 17), the Rabbis instructed parents not to strike their grown children lest their children curse them or strike them back, making the parents, in turn, liable for leading the children to sin ("placing a [moral and legal] stumbling block before the blind").[9] Along these lines, a nineteenth-century moralist applied this to both children and parents:

> If a man cannot honor his parents as they should be honored, then ... it is best that he no longer share his father's board, provided his father agrees to this. It is also best that a man [who gets angry]—if he can—send his children from his table, lest he be guilty of placing a stumbling block before them [by provoking them to speak dishonorably to him and thus violating Leviticus 19:14] ... and thus there shall be peace in your home.
>
> —Rabbi Eliezer Pappo, *Pele Yo'etz,*
> part I, *Kaph,* pp. 170–72

Because parents were often not very well educated themselves, the Rabbis were concerned that they may not be able to fulfill this commandment even if they wanted to do so. That would not only fail to fulfill a commandment of the Torah but also deprive children of their heritage. Therefore, while the duty to educate your children in Judaism falls primarily on the parents, they may delegate it to a Jewish school. In fact, Jews were among the first to establish schools, dating from the second century:

> He who denies a child religious knowledge robs him of his heritage.
>
> —B. *Sanhedrin* 91b

Rabbi Judah said in the name of Rav: Rabbi Joshua ben
Gamla should be remembered for good, for had it not
been for him the Torah would have been forgotten in
Israel. For at first, the boy who had a father was taught
Torah by him, while the boy who had no father did not
learn. Later, they appointed teachers of boys in
Jerusalem, and the boys who had fathers were brought
by them [to the teachers] and were taught; those who
had no fathers were still not brought. So then they
ordered that teachers should be appointed in every district, and they brought to them lads of the age of sixteen
or seventeen. And when the teacher was cross with any
of the lads, the lad would kick at him and run away. So
then Rabbi Joshua ben Gamla ordered that teachers
should be appointed in every district and in every city
and that the boys should be sent to them at the age of
six or seven years.

—B. *Bava Batra* 21a

Even though the parents may delegate the duty to
educate their children to a school, the parents themselves
retain the ultimate duty. They therefore must check periodi-
cally that the teachers are effectively doing their job. This
led to the common practice around the Sabbath table for
parents to ask their children about what they learned in
their Jewish schooling that week and to discuss it further
with them. It has also led the Conservative movement, for
example, to establish the Parent Education Program in
which the parents are taught what the students are learning
so that they can interact with their children on Jewish
matters and reinforce what they are learning in school. That
way both generations fulfill Judaism's lifelong duty to study
the tradition.

"TO TEACH HIM A TRADE"

Until very recently in Jewish history, very few Jews had a formal education in anything. Parents simply could not afford to let their children stay in school very long, for they were needed to help earn a living. Girls got almost no formal education, and even the one that boys got was short, ending usually by age ten or so. And when boys learned a trade, it was as an apprentice: their father and possibly their uncles taught them how to do what men in the family for generations had done to earn a living.

Much has changed in the last century. In the United States, in 1910, only 13 percent of the population graduated from high school and only 3 percent from college; in 1999, 83 percent of Americans had graduated from high school and 25 percent from college.[10] Because Jews and Judaism treasure education so deeply, and because Jews in the early and middle of the twentieth century found education to be their path into America's middle and upper classes, Jews have tended to be ahead of the curve, and to this day much higher percentages of Jews complete college and professional schools than is true of the general American population.[11]

On the one hand, Jews can rightfully be proud, for these numbers graphically illustrate the strong Jewish commitment to education. Furthermore, as more and more jobs require more and more education, Jews spending a considerable amount of time and money for college and graduate school are putting themselves in a position to do well economically in the time to come.

On the other hand, though, our ancestors spent all the money they could on enabling at least their sons to get a Jewish education. In our time, some Jewish families are spending equivalent or greater percentages of their incomes on Jewish day schools, camps, and youth groups, but a frightening percentage are giving their children only a perfunctory Jewish education or none at all. That is, many contemporary Jews have completely upended traditional Jewish values of education, with "teaching him a trade" taking ever more time and resources and "teaching him Torah" taking ever fewer.

Christians who recognize the importance of religious education for the religious formation of their own children will understand that this situation does not bode well for the future Jewish identity or depth of conviction of Jews. It suggests that Jews must engage in considerable *tikkun olam* in making Jewish formal and informal education once again a serious priority among American Jews, one that parallels their commitment to general and professional education. In addition, Jews of all ages and economic resources must do everything possible to enable Jewish parents who do take the Jewish future of their children and of the Jewish people seriously to afford a meaningful form of it for their children. Further, through what they do in their own lives, Jews must themselves resume the traditional responsibility of ensuring that they deepen their own knowledge of Judaism, both because in Judaism learning is lifelong and also to model for their children a commitment to Judaism's skills, concepts, and values as well as a love of practicing Judaism and being part of the Jewish People. In the end, children will take religion seriously only if their parents do as well—a maxim for Christians as much as it is for Jews.

"To Marry Him Off"

The Talmud clearly assumes that the marriages would be arranged by parents of both the bride and groom. This system lasted a very long time; my own grandparents had an arranged

171

marriage. They did not know each other until they stood under the *huppah* (wedding canopy). When my mother asked her mother why she had agreed to marry my grandfather, she said, "Because I had heard that he was a kind man, and that was enough for me." From everything I could observe and from everything my mother told me, they had an idyllic marriage—in no small measure, I think, because they had begun with much more realistic assumptions about the nature and aims of marriage than the American ideal of romantic love presents us. Not all arranged marriages worked out that well, of course, but our current system of dating does no better and probably worse in producing long and happy marriages.

Although the system of arranged marriages put the decision of whom to marry in parents' hands, it did not do so completely. Rabbi Solomon ben Adret ("Rashba," c. 1235–c. 1310, Spain) uses the talmudic principle that divine commands supercede parental ones to permit a man to violate his parents' wishes in marrying the woman he loves, even if this means that the son would live at some distance from his parents and thus be precluded from providing the range of services prescribed as part of the honor and respect due to parents. (This does not apply to a marriage that would violate the norms of Jewish law, such as an incestuous marriage or a marriage to a non-Jew; he is addressing the case where a Jewish man and woman who are eligible to marry each other want to do so over their parents' objections.) The man has the right to do this, according to Rashba, to fulfill the commandment "Be fruitful and multiply," for which marriage is a legal prerequisite.[12] Although some Rabbis disagree,[13] ultimately Rabbi Moses Isserles, in his authoritative additions ("glosses") to the important code, the *Shulhan Arukh*, states that "If a father opposes the marriage of his son to a woman of his son's desire, the son need not accede to the father."[14]

By and large, though, parental matchmaking, sometimes with the assistance of a professional matchmaker, was the mechanism that paired off people in marriage. This system had the distinct advantage of guaranteeing a marriage for virtually everyone, usually in their teens. In fact, even though the Mishnah quoted earlier indicates that eighteen was the appropriate age for a man to marry, presumably a woman of sixteen or seventeen, it was often common for marriages to take place in the early teens, thus ensuring that both members of the couple would satisfy their sexual urges in a legal context.[15] The system of matchmaking took away much of the pressure and uncertainty that our contemporary high school and college students have about whom they will marry. It also assured marriage at the time when both the man and woman were biologically at the most fertile stages of their lives, thus avoiding some of the infertility problems that today's couples face when they get married in their late twenties and do not even begin to try to have children until their thirties.

For better or worse, though, the old way is not coming back. This leaves current adult children and their parents with a real problem. High school and college provide a natural environment in which people can meet each other, and for some people graduate school lengthens yet further the time in which school can be the venue for meeting their mate. Once schooling is over, though, there is no obvious place for people to meet each other.

People in their early and mid-twenties—the first generation to pass through adolescence in a world with e-mail—are using the Internet for this purpose to an extent that older generations find intimidating. This has changed the assumptions of getting to know a potential spouse. Dating once implied "a very long process where you disclose things over time," according to Robert Rosenwein, a professor of social psychology at Lehigh

University in Bethlehem, Pennsylvania. "The Internet speeds that up considerably. There's a renegotiation of the concept of intimacy," adds *New York Times* reporter Warren St. John. Moreover, even with pictures, which young people usually demand before they will respond to an ad, there is always the problem of leaving out pertinent information, for the ads often represent "the author's aspirations, more than the reality,"[16] says St. John.

While the Internet can surely help people meet each other, especially those who no longer have school as a venue to make connections, it is not a panacea. Some people will not find a suitable spouse in the traditional places—work or the synagogue or parties of mutual friends. Parents must not hesitate, then, to help their children find someone, even if the children first object to any parental interventions. Parents can suggest, for example, that their children attend services or a family wedding or some other activities at the synagogue for the express motive of trying to meet someone. After all, the synagogue is not only a *bet tefillah* (house of prayer) and *bet midrash* (house of study); it is most commonly called a *bet k'nesset* (house of meeting—although not usually intended in quite this way!). They can also suggest that their children get involved as volunteers in various Jewish communal activities through Jewish social service groups forming young adult divisions. I know of two families—the Salters and the Wagners—who formed the S&W Good Company when their children were reaching their mid-twenties with no marital prospects on the horizon. The parents simply had their children invite all of their friends and friends' friends to their homes once a month for some kind of program—social, social action, intellectual, or religious (like a holiday celebration)—and lo and behold, all of them found their spouses that way. The method particular parents will use may be different, but the message is the same: parents need not stand idly by if their children are having trouble meeting potential spouses.

The problem in fulfilling this talmudic duty for parents in our own day, though, goes beyond finding someone to marry; it also involves their *intention* to marry at a young enough age to have a reasonable chance of having children without difficulty. Given young Jews' extensive educational programs, which in itself is an expression of their commitment to the value of education and professional achievement, they rarely plan to marry before their late twenties. Because of the modern techniques that have been developed to overcome infertility, young adult Jews often wrongly assume that they can have children into their forties, and so there is no rush to get married and procreate.

In fact, the younger the couple is, the more likely doctors will be able to assist them through currently available technology. Furthermore, although men do not go through menopause as clearly as women do, aging affects men's fertility, too, with the result that couples experiencing infertility are just as likely to find the problem is with the man as with the woman.

Most importantly, fertility problems impose immense strains on the marriage. It causes the couple to wonder about some deeply personal things: Who am I as a man? Who am I as a woman? Who are we as a couple? Do we have a future together without the children we dreamed of having? If so, what is our future together supposed to be like? All too many marriages break up over these issues.[17]

Marrying and beginning the process of procreation earlier does not guarantee freedom from fertility problems, but it certainly increases the likelihood of reproductive success. This, then, suggests several modern and personal forms of *tikkun olam* for parents in this area as a kind of modern interpolation of their talmudic duty to marry off their children.

Studies have shown that only a small minority of inter-faith couples raise their children as Jews, and the Jewish people, who are already 0.2 percent of the world's population, cannot afford to lose its demographic future. This makes endogamy (marrying someone from within your own religion) a major goal for the Jewish community in a way that it may not be for the Christian community who populate a full third of the world population.[18]

To raise the probability that Jews will marry born Jews or Jews by Choice, recent research suggests that Jewish camping and youth groups are the most critical factors.[19] Parents should therefore enroll their children in such programs, and communities should make that financially possible for those who cannot afford this on their own. For the same demographic reasons, parents should make sure their children attend a college with a large number of Jewish students. We need to get across to our young people that while college is not a failure if you do not emerge married, it is not too early to look for a mate while in college and to get married and begin to have children while in graduate school. The pressures of graduate school are no greater and usually less than the pressures of the first years in one's job or profession.

At the same time, all Jews and Jewish communal institutions need to recognize that there are many single Jews who would like nothing better than to get married (or remarried) but cannot find a suitable spouse. We must walk a delicate tightrope here. On the one hand, we must respect the inherent divine dignity of singles, as we must do for all people, and we must make our institutions as welcoming for them as they are for married couples. On the other, as part of our empathy and compassion for our singles, we need to take active steps to help them find the mates they seek. Internet dating services like JDate have been remarkably effective in this effort for many people, but we dare not rest with them alone. Instead, individual Jews and Jewish institutions must create programs where Jewish singles can meet in a supportive and respectful context.

Then we older Jews beyond child-bearing years must put our money where our mouths are by ensuring that Jewish venues are available and affordable for day care for young children and that formal and informal Jewish schooling is affordable as well. Since charity begins at home, it is important to note that, as quoted above, Jewish law imposes a duty to educate children in Torah not only on parents, but also on grandparents.[20] Thus grandparents, who often have more money than young parents do, have a special duty to contribute to their grandchildren's care and Jewish education.

Thus even though parents no longer "marry off" their children by choosing a mate for them, parents still have a major role to play in carrying out this talmudic duty, this form of *tikkun olam*.

PART FOUR

Envisioning a World Shaped by *Tikkun Olam*

8

ELEMENTS OF THE TRADITIONAL JEWISH VISION OF THE IDEAL WORLD

What are the goals of repairing the world (*tikkun olam*)? We have described some of the specific elements that are critical in shaping a better world as Judaism envisions it, but what does the ideal look like? What kind of world do Jews seek to create?

Clearly, the Jewish ideal world is characterized by the success of all of our efforts to fix the world in the ways described in the chapters above. In such a world, on a social level people:

- talk to each other with respect and avoid all forms of defamation and gossip.
- help others learn how to make a living and aid the poor directly in the meantime.
- provide the means to all people and societies to prevent diseases whenever possible, cure them when they occur, attend to the sick through visits and physical and emotional support, and engage in research to avoid or cure those maladies we cannot yet treat.

On a personal level, in the ideal world, people:

- prepare for marriage so that couples can learn how to care for each other, deepen and broaden their relationship over the years, and avoid divorce.

- honor and respect their parents, especially as they age, in the ways that Jewish law prescribes, ideally as an act of love but at least in fulfillment of their duties under Jewish law.
- care for their children in the ways that Jewish law prescribes, ideally in the context of a close, loving relationship but minimally in response to the parents' duties under Jewish law.

In addition to these elements, Jewish sources describe other factors that characterize the world toward which we all should be striving. There is no one official depiction of the Jewish ideal world; in this matter, as on virtually every other topic, Jewish sources include many voices. This is not to say that Judaism is incoherent in its ideals, though, for many of the factors described in some sources complement those in others. There are differences in emphasis, however, and it is important to understand this pluralism in assessing the most important aspects of Judaism's ideal world.

Two other factors need to be mentioned at the outset. First, Judaism portrays all human efforts as being in partnership with God. Sometimes God is the dominant partner, as in the Exodus from Egypt. But even there, Moses, Aaron, Miriam, and, according to rabbinic legend, Nahshon ben Aminadav played crucial roles in enabling the Exodus to happen. At other times, human beings must take the initiative, as in our efforts to create a society devoid of gossip and defamatory speech. Most of the time, *tikkun olam* happens as a result of a partnership between God and us, as is illustrated in the case of finding cures for illness and then ensuring that all of the world's people benefit from them. Thus, as we consider Jewish visions of the ideal, we should take note of the varying roles played by God and by human beings in enabling the ideal to become more and more real.

Second, Jewish visions of the ideal did not end with the Bible and Talmud. Jews in the Middle Ages and in the modern period added their own depictions of the ideal world. This chapter addresses some of the primary features of the visions we find in Jewish classical literature—the Bible and rabbinic literature (Mishnah, Talmud, Midrash, and later summaries of that material in Maimonides's code).

CHILDREN

God's very first blessing of Abraham (when he was still called Abram) is children, and it is the promise of many offspring that changes his name from Abram to Abraham, "father of many nations":

> Some time later, the word of the Lord came to Abram in a vision. He said: "Fear not, Abram, I am a shield to you; your reward shall be very great." But Abram said, "O Lord, God, what can You give me, seeing that I shall die childless.... The word of the Lord came to him in reply: "None but your very own issue shall be your heir." He took him outside and said, "Look toward heaven and count the stars, if you are able to count them." And He added, "So shall your offspring be."
> —Genesis 15:1–7

> Happy are all who fear the Lord, who follow His ways....
> Your wife shall be like a fruitful vine within your house;
>   your children, like olive saplings around your table.
> So shall the man who fears the Lord be blessed....
> May you live to see your children's children. May all be well
>   with Israel!
> —Psalms 128:1, 3, 6

Although this is a wonderful promise for those who are able to have children, it feels like a harsh curse for those who cannot. Efforts to help Jews meet, marry, and procreate in their twenties so as to avoid the major factor in infertility (age) and efforts to assist infertile couples medically are very much a part of *tikkun olam* so that we can all attain the great blessing of children. In addition, sensitivity to both the many singles who would love to get married and have children but cannot find a suitable mate and to the many couples who badly want children but cannot have them will make our community a much more ideal one, as we support them emotionally as well as help them in practical ways to attain these goals.

THE LAND OF ISRAEL

The other part of God's very first blessing to Abram is the Land of Israel (Gen. 15:7–21), a blessing repeated, as is the blessing of children, to Abraham (Gen. 17:8), Isaac (Gen. 26:2–5), Jacob (Gen. 28:13–15), and the People Israel as a whole (e.g., Deut. 28:1–12). To make this promise real, God will help you "dislodge those peoples [of Canaan] little by little; you will not be able to put an end to them at once, else the wild beasts would multiply to your hurt" (Deut. 7:22). Eventually, however, Israel would rule the Land of Israel.

Israel's hold on the land, however, was, from the very first promise to Abram, dependent on obeying God's will. Thus, as the Bible and Rabbis present it, it was Israel's failure to obey God that prompted God to allow other nations (Assyria, Babylonia, and Rome) to conquer Israel and drive the People Israel from the land. Part of the promise of the Land of Israel, then, is a war to regain the land from Israel's oppressors. Elijah would herald the coming of the Messiah, the one anointed to lead the Israelites in battle against their oppressors (Zech. 14:12–15). Religious Zionists understand the Jews' claim to the Land of Israel in these biblical terms to this day. Other Jews, and many religious Jews as well, also root the Jewish claim to Israel in historical considerations: arguably from the time of Abraham and certainly from the time of Joshua, Israel was the Jewish homeland, and even though it has been ruled by others, some Jews have always lived there. Modern Israelis' fascination with archeology is one manifestation of this historical tie to the land. Others—again including some who assert religious and historical links to the land—are "cultural Zionists." They see Israel as the hothouse of Jewish culture, the place where Hebrew has been revived as a spoken language; where the Jewish calendar determines days off; and where Jewish art, music, dance, literature, and philosophy are most likely to flourish. Still others point to political considerations—namely, that the 1947 United Nations Declaration establishing a Jewish State in Israel. This makes the Jews' claim to Israel stronger than that of most other nations, for, as Mark Twain noted, most nations came to be through stealing their land from someone else:

> All the territorial possessions of all the political establishments on earth—including America, of course—consist of pilferings from other people's wash. No tribe, howsoever insignificant, and no nation, howsoever mighty, occupies a foot of land that was not stolen. When the English, the French, and the Spaniards reached America, the Indian tribes had been raiding each other's territorial clotheslines for ages, and every acre of ground in the continent had been stolen and restolen 500 times.[1]

Although these historical, cultural, and political factors buttress the Jewish connection to the Land of Israel, the Jewish religious vision of the ideal world includes the return of Jews to Israel under circumstances in which they rule themselves. One source, in fact, asserts that the only difference between current, historical times and the Messianic era is that in the latter, Jews will be freed of foreign rule and enjoy political independence (B. *Berakhot* 34b). It is this source that led the Chief Rabbinate of the State of Israel to declare in its prayer for the state that its very existence is "the beginning of the flowering of our redemption," for even though the other factors described in this chapter have yet to come, Jewish political independence in the modern State of Israel foreshadows the advent of the other elements in the Jewish messianic vision.

The Ingathering of the Exiles

As part of the dream of political independence in the Land of Israel, both the Bible and the Rabbis asserted that Messianic times would see the ingathering of Jewish exiles from all over the world to Israel. It is this part of the ideal world of classical Judaism that motivates some religious forms of Zionism.

> And in that day, a great ram's horn shall be sounded; and the strayed who are in the land of Assyria and the expelled who are in the land of Egypt shall come and worship the Lord on the holy mount, in Jerusalem.
> —Isaiah 27:13; see also 43:3–6 and Jeremiah 3:14

Prosperity

Prosperity is part of the Torah's promises for obeying God's commandments, and the Rabbis imagine even greater prosperity in Messianic times:

> Blessed shall you be in the city, and blessed shall you be in the country. Blessed shall be the issue of your womb, the produce of your soil, and the offspring of your cattle, the calving of your herd, and the lambing of your flock. Blessed shall be your basket and your kneading bowl....

The Lord will ordain blessings for you upon your barns and upon all your undertakings. He will bless you in the land that the Lord is giving you.... The Lord will open for you His bounteous store, the heavens, to provide rain for your land in season and to bless your undertakings. You will be creditor to many nations, but debtor to none.

—Deuteronomy 28:3–5, 8, 12

The World to Come [the Messianic era] will not be like this world. In this world one has the trouble to harvest the grapes and press them [to get wine], but in the World to Come a person will bring a single grape in a wagon or ship, store it in the corner of his house, and draw from it enough wine to fill a large flagon, and its stalk will be used as fuel under the pot. There will not be a grape that will not yield thirty measures of wine.... In the Hereafter the land of Israel will grow loaves of the finest flour and garments of the finest wool; and the soil will produce wheat, the ears of which will be the size of two kidneys of a large ox.

—B. *Ketubbot* 111b

Although loaves growing fully made from the ground is clearly fanciful, it indicates the depth of the Jewish dream for prosperity.

While there are some expressions of asceticism in the Jewish tradition,[2] the vast majority of Jewish sources do not see wealth alone as a sin or even a necessary cause of sin. Wealth, like everything else in life, gets its moral character from how we use it.

Still, wealth imposes a special duty on the rich to use their riches to help those less fortunate. All of us must certainly recognize that our world is filled with such people. Millions die each year from starvation and homelessness. The Jewish vision of the ideal world, then, provides yet another reason to those described in Chapter 2 for working to ensure that no human being goes hungry or naked, and that everyone has a roof over his or her head at night.

HEALTH

Often associated with the promise of prosperity is God's pledge to prevent disease altogether, as is evident from this passage below.

> You shall be blessed above all other peoples; there shall be no sterile male or female among you or among your flock. The Lord will ward off from you all sickness; He will not bring upon you any of the dreadful diseases of Egypt, about which you know, but will inflict them upon all your enemies.
>
> —Deuteronomy 7:14–15

If God does allow people to be stricken with diseases, God will heal them (Exod. 15:26):

Although the Torah sees freedom from illness as one advantage of God's covenant with Israel specifically, we now recognize that diseases rarely honor national boundaries, that they spread across the world. Therefore, our hope and efforts in our time must be for global measures to prevent and cure diseases.

This vision of a world free of disease imposes a duty on us to work toward that end as individuals. Some of us will work in health care directly, as doctors, nurses, medical social workers, chaplains, and volunteers. All of us have the duty to visit the sick, however distasteful we may find it, and, as we have seen in Chapter 4, the Jewish tradition even provides some advice about how to overcome that discomfort and make your visit effective for both the patient and the visitor.[3] We all must get actively involved in political and economic efforts to provide clean water, food, and health care to those without them, both in our own country and abroad.

JUSTICE

As indicated in the introduction (p. xiii), a majority of contemporary Jews responding to polls assert that in their view social justice is the core commitment of the Jewish tradition. Such responses are not far off the mark, as the demand for justice is indeed a persistent part of Jewish sources, from the Bible to our own day, and a significant element in Jewish visions of the future.

This includes both procedural justice and substantive justice. Procedural justice demands that people be treated fairly in court and in society generally, with distinctions drawn among persons only for reasons having to do with their own actions or skills. For example, a just society is one in which people are not judged as to their guilt or innocence or as to their fitness for a job according to the color of their skin or how much money they currently have. Substantive justice, in contrast, demands that society be so structured that people have basic food, clothing, and shelter—and, in our own day, health care and access to transportation. Biblical sources on this include (but are certainly not limited to) the following, many of which tie justice to other aspects of the Jewish dream of the ideal society discussed earlier:

Procedural Justice

You shall appoint magistrates and officials for your tribes, in all the settlements that the Lord your God is giving you, and they shall govern the people with due justice. You shall not judge unfairly; you shall show no partiality; you shall not take bribes, for bribes blind the eyes of the discerning and upset the plea of the just. Justice, justice shall you pursue, that you may thrive and occupy the land that the Lord, your God, is giving to you.

—Deuteronomy 16:18–20; see also Leviticus 19:15

Parents shall not be put to death for children, nor children be put to death for parents: a person shall be put to death only for his own crime.

—Deuteronomy 24:16

[1]It is a positive commandment for the judge to judge fairly, as Scripture says, "Judge your neighbor fairly" (Leviticus 19:15). What is fair judgment? It is equalizing the two litigants in every respect. One should not let one litigant speak as long as he wants and tell the other to be brief; and one should not be friendly to one litigant, speaking to him softly, while frowning upon the other and speaking to him harshly.

[2]If one of the litigants is richly dressed and the other poorly dressed, the judge must say to the former, "Either dress him like yourself before you come to trial against him, or dress like him such that you are equal; then the two of you may stand in judgment."

[3]It must not be that one litigant sits and the other stands, but rather both should stand. If the court wanted to permit both to be seated, it may do so. However, one must not sit on a seat higher than the other; they must be seated side by side.

—Maimonides, *M. T. Laws of Courts*
[*Sanhedrin*] 21:1–3

Although some of this may seem obvious to us now, much of it took quite a long time to become adopted in Anglo-American law. The guarantee that parents and children not be held liable for each other's offenses, although articulated in Deuteronomy 24:16, which scholars date at the end of the seventh century BCE, was not part of British law until about 1830. Until then, descendants would suffer for their ancestors' treason, a process known as "attaint." Not surprisingly, the founding fathers of the United States banned that explicitly in Article 3, Section 3 of the U.S. Constitution in 1789. More pervasively, the kind of fairness envisioned in the Torah and by Maimonides was not common practice in the United States until very recently, for the poor and blacks were commonly treated unfairly just because they were poor or black. It is still the case in the United States, in fact, that blacks are much more likely to be executed for killing whites than whites are for killing blacks. Furthermore, American law does not insist on the formal requirements that Maimonides articulates to make both litigants look alike in social status. Thus the Jewish vision of an ideal world should prompt us to work toward refining the American sense of procedural justice.

If this is true for the United States, which in our day has a relatively advanced sense of procedural justice in comparison to its own past and to many other nations of the past and present, the Jewish vision of procedural justice in the ideal society is even further from reality in most other countries of the world—in Asia, Africa, South America, and in Arab lands. Thus biblical and rabbinic standards of procedural justice still have a lot to teach contemporary humanity.

Substantive Justice

Western concepts of substantive justice—the claim that society must provide a basic minimum of food, clothing, shelter, and health care for all people everywhere—have their roots in the Torah. Contrary to Mesopotamia, Egypt, Persia, Greece, Rome, and most other nations of the ancient world, the Torah demands that such basic care be supplied not only for citizens but even for strangers:

> For the Lord your God is God supreme and Lord supreme,
> the great, the mighty, and the awesome God, who shows
> no favor and takes no bribe, but upholds the cause of the
> fatherless and the widow, and befriends the stranger, pro-
> viding him with food and clothing. You too must befriend
> the stranger, for you were strangers in the land of Egypt.
> —Deuteronomy 10:17–19

The biblical prophets are perhaps best known for their
scathing criticism of the people—Jews as well as people of
other nations—who fail to care for the downtrodden and destitute. For example, Amos (5:7, 10–15, 24), Isaiah (1:16–17,
21–26), and Jeremiah (22:1:1–5) all chastise the Israelites for
failing to care for the downtrodden, and both Amos (chapters
1 and 2) and Jeremiah (chaps. 46–51) castigate other nations for
the same thing. Ultimately, though, as we shall see shortly, the
prophets look forward to a time when both procedural and
substantive justice will prevail, and the message to us is clearly
that we must work to make that happen as part of our repairing the world (*tikkun olam*).

KNOWLEDGE OF GOD'S WORD

The biblical dream of the ideal world is that not only Jews
would know how to be just and act on this knowledge, but
that all peoples of the world would know what to do and act
accordingly. This is because in the ideal world, all peoples
would learn what God wants of them by learning the Torah.
This makes Judaism the exact opposite of those traditions
that would keep the convictions of the faith in the hands of
a few elite. On the contrary, the Torah demands that parents
teach the tradition to their children (Deut. 6:1–2, 7; 11:19),
and it requires that every seven years the entire Torah be
read and explained to the entire people, "men, women, and

children" (Deut. 31:9–13). The Rabbis later expanded this to a yearly reading of the Torah, one section each week on Saturday mornings, with shorter readings three other times during the week. Isaiah and Micah look forward to a time when not only all Jews but all the nations of the world know Israel's God and follow the Divine's ways:

> The word that Isaiah, son of Amoz, prophesied con-
> cerning Judah and Jerusalem:
> In the days to come,...
> The many peoples shall go and say:
> "Come, let us go up to the Mount of the Lord,
> To the House of the God of Jacob;
> That He may instruct us in His ways,
> And that we may walk in His paths."
> For instruction shall come forth from Zion,
> The word of the Lord from Jerusalem.
> Thus He will judge among the many peoples,
> And arbitrate for the multitude of nations, however distant;
> And they shall beat their swords into plowshares
> And their spears into pruning hooks.
> Nation shall not take up sword against nation;
> They shall never again know war.
>
> —Isaiah 2:1–4

> But every man shall sit under his grapevine or fig tree
> With no one to disturb him.
> For it was the Lord of Hosts who spoke.
> Though all the peoples will walk
> Each in the names of its gods,
> We will walk
> In the name of the Lord our God
> Forever and ever.
>
> —Micah 4:4–5

Isaiah imagines a world in which everyone follows one God and one set of rules. Similarly, in a verse made famous by its inclusion at the end of *Alenu*, the prayer that ends every Jewish worship service, the prophet Zechariah proclaims, "And the Lord shall be king over all the earth; in that day there shall be one Lord with one name" (Zech. 14:9). Micah, however, conceives of a world in which all people learn from Israel's Torah but act according to their own understanding of what is right in a pluralistic world. In our time, these sources summon us to work for a world that may include pluralistic beliefs but also manifests a universal commitment to the values Jews learn from the Torah—children, education, family, community, care for those less fortunate, procedural and substantive justice, and, finally, peace.

PEACE

Unlike some other traditions, war is not valorized in Judaism. Jewish heroes—with the possible exception of the Maccabees—are not warriors; they are instead people who study and practice the values of the Torah and work toward a better world:

> Hillel says: Be a disciple of Aaron, loving peace and pursuing peace, loving your fellow creatures and attracting them to [the study and practice of] the Torah.
>
> —M. *Avot* 1:12

Judaism is not pacifistic—the Talmud says that "If one comes to kill you, rise up early in the morning to kill him first,"[4] and Jewish law permits defensive wars[5]—but it nevertheless urges us to work for peace. Thus every *Amidah*—the prayer said while standing three times each day, four times on Sabbaths, Rosh Hashanah, and festivals, and five times on Yom Kippur—ends with an entreaty to God for peace. But we may not rest with asking God to bring peace; we must do what we can as well. In fact, based on the verse from Psalms, "Seek peace and pursue it" (Ps. 34:15), the Rabbis declare that the commandment to seek peace is unlike any other in that we do not do it only when the occasion arises but must rather go out of our way to find ways to make peace (J. *Pe'ah* 1:1 [4a]). Finally, the Rabbis maintain that peace is an underlying condition for all other blessings and that God's name is thus associated with peace: "Great is peace, for all blessings are contained in it.... Great is peace, for God's name is peace" (*Numbers Rabbah* 11:7).

It is not surprising, then, that both Isaiah's and Micah's vision of the ideal society, includes a cessation of war. In a later prophecy, Isaiah goes yet further, combining many of the elements we have seen in Judaism's vision of an ideal society and asserting that in such a time and place even animals that are normally at war with each other will be at peace:

> But a shoot shall grow out of the stump of Jesse [David's
>   father],
> A twig shall sprout from his stock.
> The spirit of the Lord will alight upon him:
> A spirit of wisdom and insight,
> A spirit of counsel and valor,
> A spirit of devotion and reverence for the Lord.
> He shall sense the truth by his reverence for the Lord:
> He shall not judge by what his eyes behold,
> Nor decide by what his ears perceive.
> Thus he shall judge the poor with equity
> And decide with justice for the lowly of the land.
> He shall strike down the ruthless with the rod of his
>   mouth
> And slay the wicked with the breath of his lips.
> Justice shall be the girdle of his loins,
> And faithfulness the girdle of his waist.
> The wolf shall dwell with the lamb,
> The leopard lie down with the kid;
> The calf, the beast of prey, and the fatling together,

With a little boy to herd them.
The cow and the bear shall graze,
Their young shall lie down together;
And the lion, like the ox, shall eat straw.
A babe shall play over a viper's hole,
And an infant pass his hand over an adder's den.
In all of My sacred mountain
Nothing evil or vile shall be done;
For the land shall be filled with devotion to the Lord
As water covers the sea.
In that day,
The stock of Jesse that has remained standing
Shall become a standard to the peoples—
Nations shall seek his counsel
And his abode shall be honored.
In that day, My Lord will apply His hand again to
    redeeming the other part of His people from Assyria—
    as also from Egypt, Pathros, Nubia, Elam, Shinar,
    Hamath, and the coastlands.
He will hold up a signal to the nations
And assemble the banished of Israel,
And gather the dispersed of Judah
From the four corners of the earth....

—Isaiah 11:1–12

Our ultimate goal in *tikkun olam*, then, is a world at peace. This, as we have seen, does not mean just cessation of hostilities. It means also a world in which we have the blessings of children, a Jewish state in the Land of Israel to which Jewish exiles can and do come to live, prosperity, health, procedural and substantive justice, recognition of Israel's God and of Torah values as authoritative, and peace. May we all work toward these ends in our lives, not only for the sense of meaning and purpose that such efforts give us but also for the good we thereby do in the world. And with God's help, may we succeed!

NOTES

Key to abbreviations:

M. = Mishnah, edited c. 200 CE by Rabbi Judah, president of the Sanhedrin.

T. = Tosefta, edited c. 200 CE by Rabbis Hiyya and Oshaya.

J. = Jerusalem (Palestinian or Western) Talmud, edited c. 400 CE.

B. = Babylonian Talmud, edited c. 500 CE by Ravina and Rav Ashi.

M.T. = *Mishneh Torah* by Maimonides, completed in 1180 CE.

S.A. = *Shulhan Arukh* by Joseph Karo, completed in 1563 CE, with additions ("glosses") by Rabbi Moses Issserles indicating where the practices of Ashkenazic (northern European) Jews differed from those of Sephardic (Mediterranean) Jews.

INTRODUCTION

1. *Los Angeles Times*, April 13, 1988, A1, 14–15.

2. The study, "American Jews and Their Social Justice Involvement: Evidence from a National Survey," was released in 2000 and used to launch Amos: The National Jewish Partnership for Social Justice. Amos got some initial foundation support and functioned for a few years with a board and small staff until its funding ran out. See Sidney Schwarz, *Judaism and Justice: The Jewish Passion to Repair the World* (Woodstock, VT: Jewish Lights, 2006), 247, 298 n. 12.

3. *Los Angeles Times*, February 1, 2003, part 2, 23.

4. Throughout the book I use "Rabbis" (with a capital R) to refer to the classical Rabbis of the Mishnah, Talmud, and Midrash, while "rabbis" refers to rabbis from medieval and modern times. In adherence to standard English form, though, the adjectival form, "rabbinic," is spelled with a lowercase r even when it refers to the classical rabbis.

1 The Meaning and Significance of *Tikkun Olam*

1. Elliot N. Dorff, *The Way Into* Tikkun Olam *(Repairing the World)* (Woodstock, VT: Jewish Lights, 2007), chap. 1.
2. We will explore some of the more important aspects of the substantive meaning of the term in chap. 2; for more on that and for the procedural meaning of the term, see my book, *To Do the Right and the Good: A Jewish Approach to Modern Social Ethics* (Philadelphia: Jewish Publication Society, 2002), chaps. 5–6.
3. See, for example, Umberto Cassuto, *A Commentary on the Book of Exodus* (Jerusalem: Magnes Press [Hebrew University], 1967), 260–64, who points out that if Exodus 21–24 were really a law code, it should have clear rules about normal activities in life, such as completing a business deal and getting married. The fact that those chapters do not address such common things indicates that they are simply a collection of judicial precedents.
4. The term is also used this way and translated as "rules" in Deuteronomy 4:8, 14; Ezekiel 20:25; and Malachi 3:22.
5. The term possibly also has the meaning of justice (as well as judgment) in Psalm 103:6: "The Lord executes righteous acts and judgments [*u'mishpatim*, justice?] for all who are wronged."
6. It is possible that the original meaning of this verse is different, namely, that both *tzadik* and *hasid* are synonyms for faithful, or trustworthy. That would preserve the parallelism common to biblical poetry. The Rabbis, however, understood these words as I have translated them here, and so at least in rabbinic theology, if not in biblical thought, justice and kindness are put in balance.
7. For a description of Jewish demands of procedural justice—that is, that judgments be fair and that rules be followed for making them so—see my book, *To Do the Right and the Good* (at n. 2 above), chap. 5.
8. See Elliot N. Dorff, *Love Your Neighbor and Yourself: A Jewish Approach to Modern Personal Ethics* (Philadelphia: Jewish Publication Society, 2003), appendix, and Dorff, *The Way Into* Tikkun Olam *(Repairing the World)* (at n. 1 above), chap. 3.

2 Why Should I Care?

1. See also Genesis 14:19; Exodus 20:11; Leviticus 25:23, 42, 55; and Deuteronomy 4:35, 39; 32:6. I discuss the medical implications of this

belief in *Matters of Life and Death: A Jewish Approach to Modern Medical Ethics* (Philadelphia: Jewish Publication Society, 1998), 15–18 and throughout, and its implications for social ethics in *To Do the Right and the Good: A Jewish Approach to Modern Social Ethics* (Philadelphia: Jewish Publication Society, 2002), chap. 6.

2. This appears in the paragraph after the call to prayer, the *Barkhu* and the first blessing of the core of the service. In *Siddur Sim Shalom*, Jules Harlow, ed. (New York: Rabbinical Assembly, 1985), 96, 98.

3. T. *Pe'ah* 4:20.

4. National Conference of Catholic Bishops, *Economic Justice for All: Pastoral Letter on Catholic Social Teaching and the U.S. Economy* (Washington, DC: United States Catholic Conference, 1983), 18–19. The footnote to the quotation at the end of this excerpt is the following: St. Cyprian, *On Works and Almsgiving*, 25, trans. R. J. Defarrari, *St. Cyprian: Treatises*, 36 (New York: Fathers of the Church, 1958), 251. Original text in Migne, *Patrologa Latina*, vol. 4, 620. On the Patristic teaching, see C. Avila, *Ownership: Early Christian Teaching* (Maryknoll, NY: Orbis Books, 1983). Collection of original texts and translation.

5. For Jewish sources that articulate this duty, see Dorff, *Matters of Life and Death* (at n. 1 above), chap. 2.

6. Jeremy Bernstein, *The Way Into Judaism and the Environment* (Woodstock, VT: Jewish Lights, 2006). See also Arthur Waskow, ed., *Torah of the Earth: Exploring 4,000 Years of Ecology in Jewish Thought* (Woodstock, VT: Jewish Lights, 2000), 2 vols.; and Ellen Bernstein, ed., *Ecology and the Jewish Spirit: Where Nature and the Sacred Meet* (Woodstock, VT: Jewish Lights, 1998).

7. See B. *Ketubbot* 50a; B. *Ta'anit* 24a; M. T. *Laws of Gifts to the Poor* 7:5; and, in general, the section of this chapter on "Limits on Giving" (pp. 42–46).

8. Dallas Willard, *The Spirit of the Disciplines: Understanding How God Changes Lives* (New York: HarperCollins, 1991), 194.

9. National Conference of Catholic Bishops, *Economic Justice for All* (at n. 4 above), 92.

10. Ronald J. Sider and Heidi Unruh, "Why and How Christians Should Care for Poor Children," *Evangelicals for Social Action*, www.esa-online.org/Article.asp?RecordKey=7450B67E-5A41-47E9-A345-D0EAC8D33FE0 (accessed October 10, 2007). American theologian Jonathan Edwards made a similar point: see "Charity Explained and

Enforced," in *The Works of Jonathan Edwards Vol. 2* (Peabody, MA: Hendrickson Publishers, 2003), 164.

11. Richard Mouw, *The God Who Commands* (Notre Dame, IN: Notre Dame Press, 1990).

12. Sider and Unruh, *Evangelicals for Social Action* (at n. 10 above).

13. For a more thorough discussion of the motivations included in this chapter, see Elliot N. Dorff and Arthur Rosett, *A Living Tree: The Roots and Growth of Jewish Law* (Albany: State University of New York Press, 1988), 82–123, 246–257, and even more extensively, Elliot N. Dorff, *Mitzvah Means Commandment* (New York: United Synagogue of America, 1989) and Elliot N. Dorff, *For the Love of God and People: A Philosophy of Jewish Law* (Philadelphia: Jewish Publication Society, 2007), chap. 4.

14. See Genesis 1:26–27; 3:1–7, 22–24.

15. See Genesis 2:18–24; Numbers 12:1–16; Deuteronomy 22:13–19. Note also that *ha-middaber*, "the speaker," is a synonym for the human being (in comparison to animals) in medieval Jewish philosophy.

16. Maimonides, *Guide for the Perplexed*, part I, chap. 1.

17. See Deuteronomy 6:5 and Leviticus 19:18, 33–4, and note that the traditional prayer book juxtaposes the paragraph just before the *Shema*, which speaks of God's love for us, with the first paragraph of the *Shema*, which commands us to love God.

18. Consider the prayer in the traditional, early-morning weekday service, "*Elohai neshamah she-natata bi*," "My God, the soul (or life-breath) which you have imparted to me is pure. You created it, You formed it, You breathed it into me; You guard it within me." Harlow, *Siddur Sim Shalom* (at n. 2 above), 8–11. Similarly, the Rabbis describe human beings as part divine and part animal, the latter consisting of the material aspects of the human being and the former consisting of that which we share with God; see *Sifre Deuteronomy*, par. 306; 132a. Or consider this rabbinic statement in *Genesis Rabbah* 8:11: "In four respects man resembles the creatures above, and in four respects the creatures below. Like the animals he eats and drinks, propagates his species, relieves himself, and dies. Like the ministering angels he stands erect, speaks, possesses intellect, and sees [in front of him and not on the side like an animal]."

19. *Genesis Rabbah* 24:7.

20. J. *Eruvin* 5:1. Barukh Halevi Epstein suggests that this is a scribal error, that because the previous aphorisms in this section of the Talmud refer

to welcoming scholars, here too the Talmud meant to say that a person who welcomes a scholar is like someone who welcomes the divine presence: Barukh Halevi Epstein, *Torah Temimah* (Tel Aviv: Am Olam, 1969), 182 (commentary on Exodus 18:12, n. 19). He may well be right contextually, but the version we have states an important, broader lesson that expresses the divine image in every person, regardless of their level of scholarship. Along the same lines, Shammai, who was not known for his friendliness and who in the immediately previous phrase warns us to "say little and do much," nevertheless admonishes, "Greet every person with a cheerful face" (M. *Avot* 1:15), undoubtedly in recognition of the divine image in each of us.

21. For a thorough discussion of this blessing and concept in the Jewish tradition, see Carl Astor, *Who Makes People Different: Jewish Perspectives on the Disabled* (New York: United Synagogue of America, 1985).

22. *Genesis Rabbah* 24:7; J. *Terumot* 47a. The various positions in this ruling are complex, and I discuss them in *Matters of Life and Death* (at n. 1 above), 291–99. See also Elijah J. Schochet, *A Responsum of Surrender* (Los Angeles: University of Judaism, 1973).

23. B. *Bava Kamma* 119a.

24. The Lausanne Covenant can be viewed at: www.lausanne.org/lausanne-1974/lausanne-covenant.html (accessed October 18, 2007). For an overview of the history of the Lausanne Movement, visit: www.lausanne.org (accessed November 6, 2007).

25. Dorff, *To Do the Right and the Good* (at n. 1 above), chap. 1, especially 16–26.

26. This was certainly the practice of all governments in the pre-Enlightenment world, and the political theories of pre-Enlightenment societies supported this practice. Christianity is one possible exception here, but even that is not clear. On the one hand, it focuses on the salvation of the individual, regardless of his or her social affiliation, and that would seem to lend at least some support to thinking of people as individuals rather than as members of groups that they cannot ignore or leave. On the other hand, though, based on a passage in the New Testament (Matthew 22:21) in which Christians are told to "give back to Caesar what belongs to Caesar, and to God what belongs to God," Christians in practice have made a sharp dichotomy between the City of God and the City of Man, as Augustine put it, reserving individualistic thinking for the City of God and ruling

earthly societies in accordance with the corporate theories prevalent before the Enlightenment.

27. See also B. *Rosh Hashanah* 17a; *M. T. Laws of Repentance* 3:4.
28. This was a 2003 American Jewish Committee poll asking 1,008 adult Jews which element of Judaism was most important in their identification as Jews. The results: 41 percent valued Jewish community most, followed by 21 percent valuing Jewish commitment to social justice, followed by only 13 percent who chose religious observance. As reported in the *Los Angeles Times*, February 1, 2003, part 2, p. 23. For the results of other such polls, see Elliot N. Dorff, *The Way Into Tikkun Olam (Repairing the World)* (Woodstock, VT: Jewish Lights, 2007), 1.
29. Jacob Neusner, *Tzedakah: Can Jewish Philanthropy Buy Jewish Survival?* (Chappaqua, NY: Rossel Books, 1982), 32, 67ff.
30. *Sifra*, Kedoshim 4:12.
31. Marry a fitting woman: T. *Sotah* 5:6; B. *Kiddushin* 41a. That a man should not have sexual intercourse with his wife during the day lest he see something he finds loathsome: B. *Niddah* 17a. That a child may draw blood from his or her parent in an effort to heal him or her despite the Torah's prohibition on injuring your parents, carrying the death penalty for doing so (Exod. 21:15): B. *Sanhedrin* 84b. The duty to choose "a beautiful death" for those condemned to die: T. *Sanhedrin* 9:3; B. *Pesahim* 75a; J. *Sotah* 1:5 (6a); J. *Sanhedrin* 6:4 (28a).
32. *M. T. Laws of Ethics (Hilkhot De'ot)* 6:3.
33. *M. T. Laws of Gifts to the Poor* 8:10.
34. *M. T. Laws of Mourning* 14:1.
35. B. *Bava Metzia* 59b.
36. Martin Luther King Jr., *Strength to Love* (Philidelphia: Fortress Press, 1981), 30–31.
37. B. *Pesahim* 50b, and in other places.
38. C. S. Lewis, *Mere Christianity* (Nashville, TN: Broadman and Holman Publishers, 1996), 115–17.
39. Jonathan Edwards, "Charity Explained and Enforced," in *The Works of Jonathan Edwards Vol. 2* (Peabody, MA: Hendrickson Publishers, 2003), 171.
40. The Rabbis go so far as to say, "If someone comes to kill you, get up early in the morning to kill him first!" B. *Berakhot* 58a, 62b; B. *Yoma* 85b.
41. Robert Murray M'Cheyne's sermon, based on this New Testament passage, is quoted in Timothy Keller, *Ministries of Mercies: The Call of the Jericho Road* (Phillipsburg, NJ: P&R Publishing, 1997), 40.

42. The Manila Manifesto, http://lausanne.gospelcom.net/statements/manila.html (accessed October 10, 2007).

43. Rick Warren's advocacy letter can be viewed at *Beliefnet*: www.beliefnet.com/story/168/story_16821_1.html (accessed October 10, 2007).

44. www.cristusrex.org/www1/CDHN/prologue.html charity (accessed August 7, 2008). The Church focused attention on this concern by ending the prologue of the Catholic catechism with this paragraph.

45. Keller, *Ministries of Mercies* (at n. 41 above), 93.

46. Ronald Sider, "Why and How Christians Should Care for Poor Children," *Evangelicals for Social Action*, www.esa-online.org/Article.asp?RecordKey=7450B67E-5A41-47E9-A345-D0EAC8D33FE0 (accessed October 10, 2007). Readers are encouraged to consult his essay for a more detailed description of what he means by these principles and how he applies them.

47. National Conference of Catholic Bishops, *Economic Justice for All* (at n. 4 above), 97–103 (italics in the original).

48. Online at www.usccb.org/cchd (accessed February 20, 2008).

49. See also *Sifre* on Deuteronomy 15:7; *M. T., Laws of Gifts to the Poor* 7:13; *S. A., Yoreh De'ah* 251:3.

50. *T. Pe'ah* 4:10-11.

51. B. *Ketubbot* 67b. *M. T. Laws of Gifts to the Poor* 7:3, 4; *S. A. Yoreh De'ah* 250:1.

52. *M. T. Laws of Gifts to the Poor* 7:3, 4; *S. A. Yoreh De'ah* 250:1.

53. B. *Shabbat* 118a.

54. Tony Campolo, *20 Hot Potatoes Christians Are Afraid to Touch* (Nashville, TN: Thomas Nelson, 1993), 102.

55. This clause appears in the Babylonian Talmud's version of the Tosefta but not in the printed version of the Tosefta itself. *Tosefta* means "additional." It is another collection, in addition to the Mishnah, of the oral traditions to approximately 200 CE.

56. A brief biographical sketch of Walter Rauschenbusch can be viewed at www.rauschenbusch.org/rauschenbusch.php (accessed November 7, 2007).

57. Online at www.wcc-coe.org/wcc/assembly/fprc2c-e.html (accessed February 15, 2008). For more information on the World Council of Churches, see www.oikoumene.org/en/who-are-we.html (accessed February 18, 2008).

3 THE POWER OF WORDS

1. Gerard S. Sloyan, *Catholic Morality Revisited: Origins and Contemporary Challenges* (Mystic, CT: Twenty-Third Publications, 1990), 127.

2. Joseph Telushkin, *Words That Hurt, Words That Heal: How to Choose Words Wisely and Well* (New York: William Morrow, 1996), 18–21.

3. Stephen Bates, *If No News, Send Rumors: Anecdotes of American Journalism* (New York: Henry Holt, 1989), 142–43.

4. Sloyan, *Catholic Morality Revisited* (at n. 1 above), 136.

5. Ibid.

6. B., *Bava Metzia* 58b.

7. For more on the process of return (*teshuvah*), see my book *Love Your Neighbor and Yourself: A Jewish Approach to Modern Personal Ethics* (Philadelphia: Jewish Publication Society, 2003), chap. 6. For a discussion of how these norms might apply to one community forgiving another for past or present wrongs (the case discussed is Catholics asking Jews for forgiveness for what the Church did and failed to do during the Holocaust), see my book *To Do the Right and the Good: A Jewish Approach to Modern Social Ethics* (Philadelphia: Jewish Publication Society, 2002), chap. 8.

8. B. *Pesahim* 22b; B. *Mo'ed Katan* 17a; B. *Bava Metzia* 75b.

9. For more on this, see the chapter on family violence in my book *Love Your Neighbor and Yourself* (at n. 7 above), chap. 5, especially 192–200 and 300 n. 132.

10. Augustine, "On Lying" and "Against Lying," in Roy Joseph Defarrari, ed., *Treatises on Various Subjects* (New York: Fathers of the Church, 1952), translated by Mary Sarah Muldowney. Both of these treatises, translated by Rev. H. Browne, are also available online at www.newadvent .org/fathers/1312.htm and www.newadvent.org/fathers/1313.htm (accessed February 24, 2008). See also St. Thomas Aquinas, "Question 110: Lying," in *Summa Theologiae* (New York: McGraw-Hill, 1964–1969), vol. 41, "Virtues of Justice in the Human Community," 2a, 2ae, 101–22.

11. J. David Bleich cites such studies in his book *Judaism and Healing: Halakhic Perspectives* (New York: Ktav, 1981), 31–32.

12. For more on hospice and the Jewish tradition, see Elliot N. Dorff, *Matters of Life and Death: A Jewish Approach to Modern Medical Ethics* (Philadelphia: Jewish Publication Society, 1998), 218–20 and chap. 8. For more on hope in the process of dying, see Maurice Lamm, *The*

Power of Hope: The One Essential of Life and Love (New York: Rawson Associates, 1995), 132–133.

13. Examples of "Speak to the Children of Israel": Exodus 25:2, 31:13; Leviticus 1:2, 4:2; 7:23, 29; 12:2; 18:2; 23:2, 10, 24, 34; 25:2; 27:2; Numbers 5:6, 12; 6:2; 9:10; 15:2, 18, 38. The commandment to read the Torah to "men, women, and children and the stranger within your midst" every seven years: Deuteronomy 31:10–13.

14. B. *Menahot* 43b.

4 THE MINISTRY OF PRESENCE

1. B. *Sanhedrin* 84b and Rashi there, s.v. *ve'ahavta*.

2. B. *Bava Kamma* 81b.

3. Thane Rosenbaum, *The Myth of Moral Justice* (New York: HarperCollins, 2004), 247–48; Steven J. Heyman, "The Duty to Rescue in Tort and Criminal Law," in *The Philosophy of Law: An Encyclopedia*, Christopher Berry Gray, ed. (New York: Garland, 1999); and Steven J. Heyman, "The Duty to Rescue: A Liberal-Communitarian Approach," in *The Communitarian Reader: Beyond the Essentials*, A. Etzioni, Andrew Volmert, and Elanit Rothschild, eds. (Lanham, MD: Rowman & Littlefield, 2004). Contrary to common law, eight states have laws requiring people to help strangers in peril: Florida, Massachusetts, Minnesota, Ohio, Rhode Island, Vermont, Washington, and Wisconsin. As Rosenbaum asserts, these laws are rarely applied and are generally ignored by citizens and lawmakers. Further, David A. Hyman demonstrates that there is no correlation between laws requiring citizens to rescue others and the actual behavior of people to do so; see David A. Hyman, "Rescue Without Law: An Empirical Perspective on the Duty to Rescue," *Texas Law Review* 84:3 (February 2006), 653–738.

4. B. *Shabbat* 10a, 119b. In the first of those passages, it is the judge who judges justly who is called God's partner; in the second, it is anyone who recites Genesis 2:1–3 (about God resting on the seventh day) on Friday night who thereby participates in God's ongoing act of creation.

5. On Judaism and mental health, see Moshe Halevi Spero, *Judaism and Psychology: Halakhic Perspectives* (New York: Ktav and Yeshiva University Press, 1980) and Levi Meier, *Jewish Values in Psychotherapy: Essays on Vital Issues on the Search for Meaning* (Lanham, MD: University Press of America, 1988). On Judaism and disabilities, see Carl Astor,

...*Who Makes People Different: Jewish Perspectives on the Disabled* (New York: United Synagogue of America, 1985).

6. On Christianity and disabilities, see the Charter of L'Arche, now 120 communities in eighteen countries of individuals who are physically or mentally handicapped; online at www.larcheusa.org; www.larcheusa.org/mission.html; and http://speakingoffaith.publicradio.org/programs/larche/larchecharter.shtml (accessed December 19, 2007). See also the National Council of Churches' Committee on Disabilities mission statement at www.ncccusa.org/elmc/disabilities.htm (accessed on December 18, 2007).

7. For more on ethical wills, see Israel Abrahams, *Hebrew Ethical Wills* (Philadelphia: Jewish Publication Society, 1926), 2 vols; and two books by Jack Riemer and Nathaniel Stampfer: *Ethical Wills: A Modern Treasury* (New York: Schocken, 1983) and *So That Your Values Live On: Ethical Wills and How to Prepare Them* (Woodstock, VT: Jewish Lights, 1991).

8. Rodney Stark, *The Rise of Christianity: How the Obscure, Marginal Jesus Movement Became the Dominant Religious Force in the Western World in a Few Centuries* (San Francisco: HarperCollins Publishers, 1997), 83–84; see also 76–83. The quotations of Julian's words are taken from Samuel Johnson, *Julian's Acts to Undermine and Extirpate Christianity* (London: Chiswell and Robinson, 1689; repr. 1976), 75, and *Records of Christianity*, David Ayerst and A.S.T. Fisher, eds. (Oxford, England: Blackwell, 1971), 179–81.

9. An especially helpful book for both mourners and those who visit them is Ron Wolfson's *A Time to Mourn, a Time to Comfort: A Guide to Jewish Bereavement*, 2nd ed. (Woodstock, VT: Jewish Lights, 2005), which not only explains Jewish mourning laws, rituals, and customs, but also gives people helpful suggestions as to how to make the experience of death and mourning meaningful for all concerned, including some vignettes of people actually engaging in the mourning practices or visiting mourners. Standard works on this topic from a Conservative perspective are Isaac Klein's *A Guide to Jewish Religious Practice* (New York: Jewish Theological Seminary of America, 1979), chaps. 19–20, and Isaac Klein's *A Time to Be Born, A Time to Die* (New York: United Synagogue of America, 1976). Two Orthodox works on issues of death and mourning are Maurice Lamm's *The Jewish Way in Death and Mourning* (New York: Jonathan David, 1969) and Abner Weiss's *Death and Bereavement: A*

Halakhic Guide (Hoboken, NJ: Ktav, and New York: The Union of Orthodox Jewish Congregations, 1991). A Reconstructionist manual on these matters by Richard Hirsch, "A Reconstructionist Guide to Mourning," is included in the new prayer book, *Tefilot Leveyt Ha'evel: Prayers for a House of Mourning*, David Teutsch, ed. (New York: Reconstructionist Foundation, 2003). For a Reform approach to these matters, see Mark Washofsky, *Jewish Living: A Guide to Contemporary Reform Practice* (New York: UAHC Press, 2000), 184–204.

10. Nicholas Wolterstorff, *Lament for a Son* (Grand Rapids, MI: Eerdmans Publishing, 1987), 34.

11. *S. A. Yoreh De'ah* 265:12 gloss.

5 DUTIES OF SPOUSES TO EACH OTHER

1. Elliot N. Dorff and Arthur Rosett, *A Living Tree: The Roots and Growth of Jewish Law* (Albany: State University of New York Press, 1988), 442–511.

2. During biblical times, the consent of the woman to the marriage was sought, but only in a perfunctory way (for example, compare Genesis 24:51 with Rebekah's belated consent in Genesis 24:57–58). The Talmud makes it clear that, in accord with Deuteronomy 24:1, the man must "take" the woman (and therefore presumably consent to the marriage) but that the marriage is valid only if the woman consents as well: B. *Kiddushin* 2a. The strength of this consent, though, must be understood in the context of the fact that until recently in Jewish history, it was really the woman's father who made the arrangement with the husband, and so her consent was really acquiescence.

3. M. *Gittin* 9:10. Procedurally, the man must institute divorce, but rabbis have found ways to enable a woman to remarry if there has been a divorce in civil law and her husband refuses to give her a Jewish writ of divorce. See Dorff and Rosett, *A Living Tree* (at n. 1 above), 523–45.

4. That there can be conditions to a betrothal (*t'nai b'kiddushin*): M. *Kiddushin* 3:2–6; M. T. *Laws of Marriage* chap. 6—except for those things that are out of his control to effect (M. *Kiddushin* 3:5) and except for conditions that would free him from having sex with her: B. *Kiddushin* 19b. For much more on valid and invalid conditions on a marriage, see Committee on Jewish Law and Standards, "T'nai B'kiddushin," *Proceedings of the Rabbinical Assembly* [1968], 229–41; reprinted in Dorff and Rosett, *A Living Tree* (at n. 1 above), 529–38.

5. A minyan (a qorum of ten adult Jews) is necessary for seven blessings: B. *Ketubbot* 7a; *M. T. Laws of Marriage* 10:5; *S. A. Even Ha'ezer* 34:4.

6. California Civil Code, sect. 5100.

7. California Civil Code, sect. 5102-5, 5131-2.

8. M. *Ketubbot* 4:7–12; 5:2, 6, 9; 7:3–10. These passages are translated in Dorff and Rosett, *A Living Tree* (at n. 1 above), 471–72, 474–76.

9. M. *Ketubbot* 5:5, 7, 9; 7:6. These passages are also translated in Dorff and Rosett, *A Living Tree* (at n. 1 above), 474–76. That the woman must work to avoid "idleness" and "lightmindedness" is stated in 5:5.

10. A man may not force himself on his wife: B. *Eruvin* 100b; *Leviticus Rabbah* 9:6; *Numbers Rabbah* 13:2; *M. T. Laws of Ethics (De'ot)* 5:4; *M. T. Laws of Forbidden Intercourse* 21:11; *S. A. Orah Hayyim* 240:10; *S. A. Even Ha'ezer* 25:2.

11. South Dakota was the first American state to prohibit marital rape in 1975, and it was not until July 5, 1993, that all fifty states banned it. Thirty states, however, retain some exemptions for the husband from prosecution for marital rape based on the presumption that all sex within marriage is consensual, which is the presumption that altogether excluded married men from prosecution for rape of their wives until these new laws were enacted. See Raquel Kennedy Bergen, "Marital Rape: New Research and Directions," online at Applied Research Forum, National Electronic Network on Violence Against Women, www.vawnet.org/Assoc_Files_VAWnet/AR_MaritalRape Revised.pdf, article dated February 2006 (retrieved March 22, 2008.)

12. Pope John Paul II, *Responsible Fatherhood and Motherhood*, published February 2, 1994; www.vatican.va/holy_father/john_paul_ii/letters/ documents/hf_jp-ii_let02021994–families_en.html (accessed February 19, 2008). See also his *On the Family (Familias Consortio): Apostolic Exhortation*, December 15, 1981 (Washington, DC: United States Catholic Conference, 1982), sect. 32, 28–30.

13. M. *Ketubbot* 5:6. For a more thorough description of Jewish norms governing sex, see chap. 3 of my book *Love Your Neighbor and Yourself: A Jewish Approach to Modern Personal Ethics* (Philadelphia: Jewish Publication Society, 2003).

14. I would like to thank professor James Calvin Davis of Middlebury College for the following:

> Regarding our brief conversation on Reformed Christian approaches to sexuality and marriage, the clearest expression

of these "three uses of marriage" I can refer you to is the Westminster Confession, chapter 24, where marriage is described as "ordained for the mutual help of husband and wife; for the increase of mankind with legitimate issue, and of the church with an holy seed; and for preventing of uncleanness." The order there is noteworthy, for what is referred to as the "unitive" function of marriage is listed first, and in my reading the Puritans tended to place much more emphasis on marriage as a social bond of companionship and mutual help than as an order for procreation. John Calvin, in his discussion of the commandment against adultery in the *Institutes of Christian Religion*, talks of marriage as a curb against lust and a commitment to companionship, but in that discussion he never even mentions procreation! Finally, the relative lack of emphasis on procreation is reflected by Cotton Mather's discussion of the grounds of divorce, which include impotence but not infertility. None of this is to say that the Puritans considered childbearing and -rearing unimportant, but it seems clear to me that it was not the chief reason they believed God had ordained marriage for human use.

Here are some references for some of the remarks above:

"The Westminster Confession," in John H. Leith, ed., *Creeds of the Churches: A Reader in Christian Doctrine, from the Bible to the Present* (Richmond, VA: John Knox Press, 1973) chap. 24, 192–230; the source of this reference is on p. 221.

Jean (John) Calvin, *Institutes of the Christian Religion*, John T. McNeill, ed., Ford Lewis Battles, trans. (Philadelphia: Westminster Press, 1960), book II, chap. 8, sect. 41ff., 405ff.

Edmund Morgan, *The Puritan Family* (New York: Harper & Row, 1966), chaps. 2–3.

15. Maimonides's view that marriage serves to curb lust: Maimonides, *Guide for the Perplexed*, part III, chaps. 33 and 49 (Shlomo Pines, trans., Chicago: University of Chicago Press, 1963) 532–34 and 601–13, especially 601–03.

16. These include, for example, the laws defining and banning incest and adultery (Lev. 18, 20), a *kohen* (of the priestly class) from marrying a divorcee (Lev. 21:7), and Jews from marrying non-Jews. On all of this, see Dorff and Rosett, *A Living Tree* (at n.1 above), 469–70, 492–511.

17. *Avot d'Rabbi Natan*, chap. 4; B. *Berakhot* 61a. See pp. 121–122 above.

18. God portrayed as married to the People Israel: Isaiah 54:5; Jeremiah 2:2, 3:20; Hosea 2:21-22. For a discussion of the union of God with the People Israel in Jewish mystical literature, see Norman Lamm, *Faith and Doubt: Studies in Traditional Jewish Thought* (New York: Ktav, 1971), chap. 2 (42–68).

19. National Association of Evangelicals, *For the Health of the Nation: An Evangelical Call to Civic Responsibility* at www.nae.net/images/civic_responsibility2.pdf (accessed October 10, 2007). For some other Protestant voices on marriage, see the websites of most large Protestant denominations and the following:

    James Dobson, *Solid Answers* (Wheaton, IL: Tyndale House Publishers, 1997), especially 479–81, 548.

    Stanley Hauerwas, *A Community of Character: Towards a Constructive Christian Social Ethic* (Notre Dame, IN: University of Notre Dame Press, 1981), especially 168–74.

20. Online at www.usccb.org/seia/marriage.shtml (accessed: February 10, 2008). For further reading of Catholic sources, see the following:

    Catechism of the Catholic Church, nos. 369–73, nos. 1601–1666, and nos. 2331–2400. Washington, DC: United States Conference of Catholic Bishops—Libreria Editrice Vaticana, 2000.

    Congregation for the Doctrine of the Faith. *Considerations Regarding Proposals to Give Legal Recognition to Unions Between Homosexual Persons.* July 2003. Available at www.vatican.va.

    Pope John Paul II. *On the Family (Familiaris Consortio).* Washington, DC: United States Conference of Catholic Bishops, 1982.

    Second Vatican Council. *Pastoral Constitution on the Church in the Modern World (Gaudium et Spes)*, nos. 47–52. December 1965. Available online at www.vatican.va.

    United States Conference of Catholic Bishops. *Follow the Way of Love: A Pastoral Message of the U.S. Catholic Bishops to Families.* Washington, DC: United States Conference of Catholic Bishops, 1993.

    United States Conference of Catholic Bishops. *Faithful Citizenship: A Catholic Call to Political Responsibility.* Washington, DC: United States Conference of Catholic Bishops, 2003.

21. Sylvia Weishaus, Albert R. Marston, and the Bi-Long Shieh, "Long-term Evaluation and Divorce Statistics for *Making Marriage Work*, a

Jewish Marriage Preparation Program," *Journal of Jewish Communal Service,* vol. 70, 2–3 (Winter/Spring 1994), 207–13.

22. National Association of Evangelicals, www.nae.net/index.cfm ?FUSEACTION=editor.page&pageID=47&IDCategory=9 (accessed October 10, 2007).

23. See, for example, *Marriage Encounter,* www.encounter.org/me.htm (accessed December 18, 2007).

24. James Dobson, *What Wives Wish Their Husbands Knew about Women,* quoted in James Dobson, *Solid Answers* (at n. 19), 479–81.

25. B. *Shabbat* 127a.

26. Elliot N. Dorff, *Love Your Neighbor and Yourself: A Jewish Approach to Modern Personal Ethics* (Philadelphia: Jewish Publication Society, 2003), chap. 5.

27. Online at www.faithtrustinstitute.org (accessed March 22, 2008).

6 CHILDREN'S DUTIES TO THEIR PARENTS

1. There is a position in rabbinic literature that restricts the duty to rise before the elderly in Leviticus 19:32 to the learned elderly (B. *Kiddushin* 32b), but the law is that you must rise before anyone who is elderly (defined as age seventy or older), whether learned or not, as long as the person is not a *rasha* (a bad person). This includes non-Jewish elderly, although the honor for them may be through words rather than standing. See B. *Kiddushin* 33a; *M.T. Laws of Study* 6:9; *S.A. Yoreh De'ah* 244:1 (gloss).

2. Pope John Paul II's "Letter to the Elderly, 1999," www.usccb .org/laity/olderpersons.shtml (accessed February 18, 2008).

3. My own book on Jewish medical ethics is entitled *Matters of Life and Death: A Jewish Approach to Modern Medical Ethics* (Philadelphia Jewish Publication Society, 1998). Other American Conservative rabbis who have written books in this field include: David M. Feldman, *Birth Control in Jewish Law* (New York: New York University Press, 1968; republished by Schocken as *Marital Relations, Abortion, and Birth Control in Jewish Law*); David M. Feldman, *Health and Medicine in the Jewish Tradition* (New York: Crossroad, 1986); and Aaron Mackler, *Introduction to Jewish and Catholic Bioethics: A Comparative Analysis* (Washington DC: Georgetown University Press, 2003). Aaron Mackler has also edited the decisions approved by the Conservative movement's Committee on Jewish Law and Standards up to the year 2000 on issues of bioethics in his book *Life*

and Death Responsibilities in Jewish Biomedical Ethics (New York: Jewish Theological Seminary of America, 2000), including responsa by these and other rabbis. These rabbinic rulings can also be accessed at www.rabbinicalassembly.org under "Contemporary Halakhah." In addition, David Golinkin and some other members of the Israeli Masorti *Va'ad Ha-Halakhah* have written responsa on bioethical issues, and they can be found in the collections of the Committee's responsa, published in Hebrew with summaries in English, as well as on the web (in Hebrew only) at www.ResponsaForToday.com or www.schechter.edu.

The books and articles by J. David Bleich, including *Bioethical Dilemmas: A Jewish Perspective* (Jersey City, NJ: Ktav, 1998) and his volumes entitled *Contemporary Halakhic Problems* (Ktav, various dates), Fred Rosner, including *Modern Medicine and Jewish Ethics*, 2nd ed. (Ktav, 1991), and Nisson Shulman, *Jewish Answers to Medical Ethics Questions* (Lanham, MD: Jason Aronson, 1998) are generally good resources for Orthodox positions available in English. Immanuel Jakobovits's book *Jewish Medical Ethics* (Jacksonville, FL: Bloch, 1959, 1975), which began the field of Jewish medical ethics, is still a good statement of an Orthodox perspective as well. The most comprehensive Orthodox treatment of Jewish medical ethics is Avraham Steinberg's *Encyclopedia of Jewish Medical Ethics*, recently translated into English by Fred Rosner (Jerusalem and New York: Feldheim, 2003), 3 vols. Those who read Hebrew might also consult the responsa of Moshe Feinstein and Moshe Tendler and of some of the Israeli Orthodox writers on bioethics, including Abraham Abraham, Simon Glick, Abraham Steinberg, and Eliezer Waldenberg. Some of their writings are now also available in English, as is the Israeli journal of bioethics, *Assia*.

The many books of Reform responsa by Solomon Freehof contain some responsa on bioethics. Other Reform responsa on bioethics can be found in the collections *American Reform Responsa* (New York: CCAR, 1985), *New American Reform Responsa* (CCAR, 1987), and *Questions and Reform Jewish Answers: New American Reform Responsa* (CCAR, 1992), all edited by Walter Jacob. More Reform responsa can be found in the books co-edited by Walter Jacob and Moshe Zemer, including *Death and Euthanasia in Jewish Law: Essays and Responsa* (New York: Freehof Institute of Progressive Halakhah, 1994). The most recent summary statement of Reform positions on this topic is Mark Washofsky's *Jewish Living: A Guide to Contemporary Reform Practice* (New York: UAHC Press, 2001), chap. 6.

4. B. *Bava Metzia* 62a.
5. John Locke affirmed an individual right to property, but Thomas Jefferson, in quoting Locke in the American Declaration of Independence, changed "life, liberty, and property" to "life, liberty, and the pursuit of happiness." See John Locke, *Second Treatise Concerning Civil Government* (1690), chap. 2.
6. Justice Potter Stewart, *Jacobellis v. Ohio*, 878 U.S. 184 (1964). His actual words were:

    I shall not today attempt further to define the kinds of material I understand to be embraced within that shorthand description; and perhaps I could never succeed in intelligibly doing so. But I know it when I see it, and the motion picture involved in this case is not that.
7. Mother Teresa, "Whatever You Did Unto One of the Least, You Did Unto Me," an address at the National Prayer Breakfast sponsored by the U.S. Senate and House of Representatives, February 3, 1994. Her speech can be viewed at www.ewtn.com/New_library/breakfast.htm (accessed November 6, 2007).
8. B. Sanhedrin 74a.
9. Elliot N. Dorff, *Love Your Neighbor and Yourself: A Jewish Approach to Modern Personal Ethics* (Philadelphia: Jewish Publication Society, 2003), chap. 5.

7 PARENTS' DUTIES TO THEIR CHILDREN

1. B. *Kiddushin* 29b.
2. B. *Sotah* 20a, 21b; J *Sotah* 3:1 (16a); *M. T. Laws of Study of Torah* 1:1, 13; *S. A. Yoreh De'ah* 246:6.
3. M. *Ketubbot* 5:5.
4. See, for example, Immanuel Etkes, "Marriage and Torah Study among the *Lomdim* in Lithuania in the Nineteenth Century," in *The Jewish Family: Metaphor and Memory*, David Kraemer, ed. (New York: Oxford University Press, 1989), 164–69.
5. B. *Ketubbot* 49a–49b.
6. M. *Ketubbot* 4:11; B. *Ketubbot* 49b; M.T. *Laws of Marriage* 12:14–15; 13:6; 19:10.
7. T. *Ketubbot* 12:1; B. *Ketubbot* 82b; J. *Ketubbot* 8:11.
8. B. *Ketubbot* 67b; *M. T. Laws of Marriage* 13:1: "He may not give her less than 50 *zuz* [for her clothing]."
9. Leviticus 19:14. In addition to its literal reference to the physically blind, the Rabbis interpret it to demand also that we not mislead

those who lack information or who are intellectually or morally blind by tempting them to do what is improper or a transgression of the law. Thus you violate this law if you lead another person to violate Jewish law in ritual matters (e.g., B. *Pesahim* 22b), personal interactions (e.g., B. *Mo'ed Katan* 17a), or commercial matters (e.g., B. *Bava Metzia* 75b). It also forbids knowingly giving bad advice (e.g, *Sifra Kedoshim* on Leviticus 19:14). The Talmud specifically forbids a father to hit his grown son lest the father violate this law: see B. *Kiddushin* 32a.

10. Roger Simon and Angie Cannon, "An Amazing Journey: The Mirror of the Census Reveals the Character of a Nation," *U.S. News and World Report*, August 6, 2001, 11–18; the statistics on education are on p. 17.

11. Barry A. Kosmin, Sidney Goldstein, Joseph Waksberg, Nava Lerer, Ariella Keysar, and Jeffrey Scheckner, *Highlights of the CJF 1990 National Jewish Population Survey* (New York: Council of Jewish Federations, 1991), 10–11, with comparative figures for the general population listed there from the U.S. Census Report P20 no. 428, table 1, "Years of School Completed by Persons 15 Years Old and Over by Age, Sex, Race, and Hispanic Origin," March 1987. The 1990 CJF Survey breaks this down by Jewish affiliation; I have cited the figures of those born Jewish and affirming Judaism as their religion.

12. *Responsa Rashba attributed to Ramban* (Warsaw: 1883), 272, cited in Basil Herring, *Jewish Ethics and Halakhah for Our Time* (New York: Ktav, 1984), 209. Rashba uses B. *Sotah* 2b, "Forty days prior to the formation of the fetus, a heavenly voice says, 'So-and-so will marry So-and-so,'" to justify his claim that the parents do not have the right to interfere in the natural attraction that God has implanted in this particular man and woman for each other. Rabbi Joseph Colon ("Maharik," 1420–1480) takes the same position on the grounds that the Talmud (B. *Kiddushin* 41a) urges a man to marry a woman to whom he is attracted; see *Responsa Maharik* (Warsaw: 1884), #164:3, 177–78, cited in Herring, *Jewish Ethics and Halakhah for Our Time,* 209.

13. For example, Rabbi Naftali Zvi Judah Berlin ("Netziv," 1817–1893) sees a marriage contrary to parents' wishes as a disgrace to the parents, thus falling under Deuteronomy 27:16, "Cursed be he that dishonors his father and mother" (*Responsa Meshiv Davar* 50). Similarly, Rabbi Abraham Isaiah Karelitz ("Hazon Ish," d. 1953) maintains that the man may marry his beloved only if his parents are not totally opposed (*Novellae of Hazon Ish* to B. *Kiddushin* 30a, p. 287).

14. *S. A. Yoreh De'ah* 240:25, gloss. The age-old practice among Jews of arranged marriages thus assumed that the bride and groom agreed to their parents' choice.
15. B. *Yevamot* 62b: "He who marries off his sons and daughters close to their coming of age [*samukh le-firkan*] is the one of whom it is said, 'And you shall know that your tent is at peace.'" Based on this, a fourteenth-century code of Jewish law, the *Tur*, says, "He who marries early, at age thirteen, is fulfilling the commandment in an exemplary manner" (*Tur, Even Ha'ezer* 1:9). Prior to that, however a person should not marry, according to the *Tur*, because that would be like promiscuity (*zenut*) and wasting of the seed (*hashatat zera*) since the woman could not become pregnant—or so he assumes. Sometimes there were economic reasons for early marriages as well, as the twelfth-century Tosafists make clear: "[The Talmud declares,] 'A man is forbidden to marry off his daughter when she is a minor.' Nevertheless, it is our custom to betroth our daughters even if they are minors because day after day the [oppression of] exile [*galut*] increases, and if a man has the possibility of giving his daughter a dowry now [he betroths her], lest he not have it later on and she will remain an *agunah* forever" (Tosafot, to B. *Kiddushin* 41a). On this, see Rachel Biale, *Women and Jewish Law: An Exploration of Women's Issues in Halakhic Sources* (New York: Schocken, 1984), 65–69. Arthur Green reports that the Hasidic master Rabbi Nahman of Bratzlov (1772–1811) married by age fourteen and had two or three children by the time he was eighteen; see Arthur Green, *Tormented Master: A Life of Rabbi Nahman of Bratslav* (Tuscaloosa, AL: University of Alabama Press, 1979), 34, 43.
16. All of the quotations in this paragraph are from Warren St. John, "Young, Single and Dating at Hyperspeed," *New York Times*, April 21, 2002, sect. 9, 1–2.
17. For the sources of these statistics and much more on how the Jewish tradition applies to issues of infertility, see Elliot N. Dorff, *Matters of Life and Death,* chaps. 3, 4, and 6.
18. "Major Religions of the World Ranked by Number of Adherents," www.adherents.com/Religions_By_Adherents.html (accessed August 7, 2008).
19. Bruce A. Phillips, *Re-Examining Intermarriage: Trends, Textures, Strategies* (Brookline, MA: The Susan and David Wilstein Institute of Jewish Policy Studies at Hebrew College; and New York: The American Jewish Committee, 1997), 77.

20. Grandparents have a duty to educate their grandchildren: B. *Kiddushin* 30a.

8 Elements of the Traditional Jewish Vision of the Ideal World

1. Mark Twain, *Following the Equator and Anti-Imperialist Essays* (New York: Oxford University Press, 1996), chap. 63, p. 623.
2. For example, M. *Avot* 6:4 and Hasidei Ashkenaz, the German Pietists of the fourteenth century.
3. See Elliot N. Dorff, *Matters of Life and Death: A Jewish Approach to Modern Medical Ethics* (Philadelphia: Jewish Publication Society, 1998), 255–264. See pp. 109–116 above.
4. B. *Berakhot* 62b; B. *Yoma* 85b; B. *Sanhedrin* 72a.
5. See Elliot N. Dorff, *To Do the Right and the Good: A Jewish Approach to Modern Social Ethics* (Philadelphia: Jewish Publication Society, 2002), 161–83.

GLOSSARY

This glossary reflects the way that many Jews actually use these words, and not just the technically correct version. When two pronunciations are listed, the first is the way the word is sounded in proper Hebrew and the second is the way it is sometimes heard in common speech, often due to the influence of Yiddish, the folk language of the Jews of northern and eastern Europe. "Kh" is used to represent a guttural sound, similar to the German "ch" (as in *"sprechen"*).

Alenu (ah-LAY-nu): A prayer that first appeared in the fourteenth century as part of the High Holy Day liturgy but has been used since then to end every worship service throughout the Jewish year.

Amidah (ah-mee-DAH or, commonly, ah-MEE-dah): One of the three commonly used titles for the second of the three central units in the worship service, the first being the *Shema* and Its Blessings and the third being the reading of the Torah. It is composed of a series of blessings, many of which are petitionary (except on the Sabbath and holidays, when the petitions are removed out of deference to the holiness of the day). Also called *ha-tefillah* ("the prayer") and *Shemoneh Esrei* ("eighteen"). *Amidah* means "standing," which refers to the fact that the prayer is said standing up.

Amos: One of the biblical prophets; the book in the Bible containing his speeches. Amos lived in the ninth century BCE in northern Israel.

avodah zara (ah-voh-DAH zah-RAH or, commonly, ah-VOH-dah ZAH-rah): Worship of foreign gods, idolatry. Also the name of a tractate of the Mishnah, Tosefta, and Talmud dealing with the laws governing Jews' interactions with idolatry and idolaters.

Babylonian Talmud: See **Talmud**.

berakhah (b'-rah-KHAH); pl. *berakhot* (b'-rah-KHOHT): The Hebrew word for "benediction." *Berakhot* also refers to the very first tractate in the

Mishnah, Tosefta, and Talmud. It deals primarily with Jewish liturgy for each day and for various occasions (e.g., the blessings over various foods).

bet k'nesset (BAIT k'NEH-set): "House of assembly." One of the Hebrew names for a synagogue.

bet midrash (BAIT meed-RASH): "House of study" or "house of interpretation." One of the Hebrew names for a synagogue.

bet tefillah (BAIT teh-fee-LAH): "House of prayer." One of the Hebrew names of a synagogue.

Canaan: The name used in biblical times for what we now call the Land of Israel.

covenant: *Brit,* in Hebrew. Refers to the marriage, as it were, between God and the People Israel, beginning with Abraham and lasting to our own day. The terms of the covenant are spelled out in Jewish law, beginning with the revelation at Mount Sinai, described in chapters 19–24 of the biblical Book of Exodus, and continuing in Jewish legal interpretations and decisions throughout the ages, including contemporary rabbinic rulings. The essence of the covenant is the ongoing relationship between God and the Jewish People, a relationship shaped by Jewish law, prayer, religious thought, questioning God, and other forms of spirituality, including acts of *tikkun olam.*

Ezekiel: One of the biblical prophets, who prophesied to the Jews whom the Babylonians had taken in chains to Babylonia in 586 BCE about their promised return to Israel. His speeches are contained in a biblical book by his name.

gene'vat da'at (g'NAVE-aht DAH-aht): Literally, "stealing a person's mind," that is, deceiving a person.

gittin (GEE-teen): Jewish writs of divorce. Also the name of a tractate in the Mishnah, Tosefta, and Talmud that deals with Jewish laws of divorce.

halakhah (hah-lah-KHAH or, commonly, hah-LAH-khah): The Hebrew word for "Jewish law." Used as an anglicized adjective, *halakhic* (hah-LAH-khic), meaning "legal." From the Hebrew word meaning "to walk" or "to go," so denoting the way in which a person should walk through life.

Hasidic (khah-SIH-dihk): Of the doctrine generally traced to an eighteenth-century Polish Jewish mystic and spiritual leader known as the Ba'al Shem Tov (called also the *BeSHT,* an acronym composed of the initials of his name). Followers are called *Hasidim* (khah-see-DEEM or khah-SIH-dim); sing., *Hasid* (khah-SEED or, commonly, KHAH-sihd) from the Hebrew word *hesed* (KHEH-sed), meaning both loving-kindness and piety.

hesed (KHEH-sed): Literally, "loyalty" (to God and to a fellow human being), with secondary meanings of piety and loving-kindness.

High Holy Days, or **High Holidays:** Rosh Hashanah (the New Year) and Yom Kippur (the Day of Atonement), ten days later. The period between these two days is known as the Ten Days of Repentance. Set by the Jewish lunar calendar, these sacred days usually fall in September but sometimes as late as early October.

Hosea: One of the biblical prophets who lived in the eighth century BCE in the Northern Kingdom of Israel. "Hosea" also refers to a book in the Bible that contains his speeches. Some scholars think that the book consists of the work of two different men named Hosea, one living in the eighth century BCE (chapters 1–3) and the other living in the seventh century BCE (chapters 4–14).

Isaiah: A biblical prophet whose writings are contained in the book by his name. Scholars think that the book actually contains the writings of two different people named Isaiah, one living in the second half of the eighth century BCE and prophesying about events at that time in chapters 1–39 of the book; and the other ("Second Isaiah," or "Isaiah of the Diaspora") living some 150 years later, in the middle of the sixth century BCE and prophesying in chapters 40–66 of the book about the promise that the Jews who had been exiled to Babylonia would return to Israel.

Jeremiah: One of the biblical prophets who prophesied in Judah between 627 and 585 BCE about the imminent destruction of the First Temple due to the Jews' sins. His speeches are contained in a biblical book by his name. He is also assumed to be the author of the biblical Book of Lamentations (*Eikhah* [AY-khah]).

Jerusalem Talmud: See **Talmud**.

Job: A non-Jew who is the protagonist of the biblical Book of Job, which scholars date c. 400 BCE and which raises in stark form the problem of evil, that is, why do the righteous sometimes suffer if there is a just and benign God? The book consists of a folktale—chapters 1 and 2 and the last ten verses of chapter 42—that has a retributive theology (if you sin, you suffer, but if you are righteous, you will ultimately be rewarded), while the middle section openly challenges that thinking and wrestles mightily with a variety of approaches to understanding unjustified suffering.

ketubbot (keh-too-BOAT): Wedding contracts. *Ketubbot* is also the name of the tractate of the Mishnah, Tosefta, and Talmud that deals with Jewish marriage law.

kiddushin (kee-du-SHEEN): Betrothal (literally, "sanctification," or setting aside one person). Also a tractate of the Mishnah, Tosefta, and Talmud developing Jewish laws of betrothal.

lashon ha-ra (lah-SHOWN hah-RAH): Literally, "speaking of bad things," that is, slurs.

Malachi (ma-LA-khee): One of the biblical prophets; also the biblical book containing his speeches, appearing as the last of the prophetic section of the Bible. Scholars believe that he lived around 450 BCE.

Messiah: Literally, "the anointed one." Originally this term is used to designate those authorized to be a king, prophet, or High Priest. In rabbinic times, it designates the one anointed to lead the Israelites in battle against their oppressors, thus ushering in an ideal time.

Micah: One of the biblical prophets; also the book of the Bible containing his speeches. Micah lived in the latter part of the eighth century BCE and was apparently a student of Isaiah.

midrash (meed-RAHSH or, commonly, MID-rahsh); pl. midrashim (mid-rah-SHEEM): From the Hebrew word *darash*, "to seek, search, or demand [meaning from the biblical text]"; also, therefore, a literary genre focused on the explication of the Bible. By extension, midrash refers to a body of rabbinic literature that offers classical interpretations of the Bible.

Midrash Rabbah (meed-RAHSH rab-BAH or, commonly, MID-rahsh RAB-bah): A work made up of ten different midrashic compilations, one of each on the five books of the Torah (*Genesis Rabbah, Exodus Rabbah, Leviticus Rabbah, Numbers Rabbah, Deuteronomy Rabbah*) and the "Five Scrolls" read in the synagogue during the year (namely, Song of Songs, Ruth, Lamentations, Ecclesiastes, and Esther)—for example, *Song of Songs Rabbah, Ruth Rabbah*. These ten independent works were compiled at very different times, most probably between the fifth and thirteenth centuries CE, and in different locales, and they exhibit a variety of midrashic styles. Unlike the Mishnah, they are not a code organized by topic. Instead, their material follows the organization of the different biblical books. *Midrash Rabbah* is the most well known, but it is not the only anthology of classic midrashic texts.

Midrash Tanhuma (meed-RAHSH Tahn-KHU-mah): A midrash on the whole of the Torah, first published in Constantinople in 1522 and frequently republished, containing many sayings and essays attributed to Rabbi Tanhuma, a Palestinian rabbi of the second half of the fourth century CE. It is divided according to the Palestinian triennial cycle of reading the Torah and contains interpretations of the first verse (and sometimes the first two or three verses) of each Torah reading for a given Sabbath according to that cycle. It exists in two primary forms, based on different manuscripts: the Constantinople version and the one published by S. Buber in 1885 based on the Oxford manuscript, which differs from the first version greatly in the first half of the work.

minyan (min-YAN, or, commonly, MIN-yin). A quorum of ten adult Jews, that is, ten Jews beyond their thirteenth birthday. Orthodox and a few Conservative synagogues insist that they be men, but the vast majority of Conservative synagogues and all Reform and Reconstructionist synagogues include women as well, and women may be counted after their bat mitzvah, which may occur as early as age twelve.

Mishnah (meesh-NAH or, commonly, MISH-nah): After the compilations of laws in several sections of the Torah (e.g., Exod. 20–24; Lev. 18–27; Deut. 20–25), the Mishnah is the first written summary of "the Oral Law," that is, the laws and customs communicated through example and speech from generation to generation, from approximately the fifth century BCE to the end of the second century CE. The Mishnah was compiled by Rabbi Judah, the president of the Sanhedrin, in the Land of Israel about the year 200 CE, based on the earlier work of Rabbi Akiva and his students throughout the second century. The Mishnah is divided into six parts, or orders (*sedarim* [say-dah-REEM]; sing. *seder* [SAY-der]), organized by topic. It treats a whole range of legal subjects, including civil law (e.g., contracts, landlord–tenant relationships, property ownership, lost objects), criminal law (e.g., personal injuries, the forms of theft and murder), penalties for infringement of the law, court procedures, family law (e.g., marriage, divorce), agricultural law dealing with the land of Israel, laws governing the ancient Temple's sacrifices, and the first written description of the structure of Jewish prayer.

Mishneh Torah (meesh-NAY toh-RAH or, commonly, MISH-nah TOH-rah): The title of Maimonides's code of Jewish Law, completed in 1180 CE.

mishpat (meesh-PAT); pl. *mishpatim* (meesh-pah-TEEM): Literally, a legal precedent, and, by extension, rules, justice.

mitzvah (meetz-VAH or, commonly, MITZ-vah); pl. *mitzvot* (meetz-VOTE): A Hebrew word used commonly to mean "good deed," but in the more technical sense, denoting any commandment from God, and therefore, by extension, what God wants us to do. Reciting the *Shema* morning and evening, for instance, is a *mitzvah*, and so is helping the poor.

motzi shem ra (moh-TZEE SHAME RAH): Literally, exporting a bad name, that is, slander.

nivvul peh (nee-VOOL PEH): Literally, "befouling one's mouth," referring to foul language.

ona'at d'varim (oh-nah-AHT d'vah-REEM): Literally, "oppression done by means of words," or oppressive speech.

Oral Torah: In Hebrew, *Torah she-B'al Peh* (TOH-rah sheh-bih-ahl-PEH). The commentaries, interpretations, legal writings, and legends that students and teachers have woven around the Written Torah, or *Torah she-Bikhtav* (TOH-rah sheh-BIKH-tahv), that were thought to have been transmitted out loud rather than in writing.

Palestinian Talmud: See **Talmud.**

Pesikta de'Rav Kahana (peh-SEEK-tah d'rahv kah-HAH-nah): A homiletic midrash compiled of sermons that was put together in the late fifth to early sixth century in the Land of Israel, offering biblical interpretations and homilies for the holidays and special Sabbaths.

pidyon ha-ben (peed-YONE hah-BEN): Redemption of the firstborn son from Temple service by giving five *shekels* to a *kohen* (descendant of Aaron). See Numbers 3:44–51. Some parents observe this ceremony today, usually on the thirty-first day after birth.

Rabbi: Literally, "teacher," or "master of the tradition." The first people called by that title lived in the first century CE, and the classical "rabbinic period" lasts from then until the close of the Talmud c. 500 CE. When we speak of "the Rabbis," we are referring to the rabbis of that period, the ones whose interpretations, opinions, and actions are described in the Mishnah, Tosefta, Midrash, and Talmud. The title continues from then to our own day, however, to describe those who are themselves committed to the Jewish tradition in their own lives and have learned the tradition well enough to teach it, having been duly authorized to do so.

rekhilut (reh-khee-LOOT): Gossip, tale-bearing.

Sanhedrin (san-head-REEN or, commonly, san-HEAD-rin): The tractate of the Mishnah and Talmud dealing mainly with legal procedures and the court system. The term is also used for any Jewish court, but especially "*the* Sanhedrin," which was the Supreme Court that existed in Israel from the first century BCE to 361 CE.

Second Isaiah: Also known as "Deutero-Isaiah." Modern scholarship notes a differentiation between chapters 1–39 and 40–55 of the Book of Isaiah, calling them First and Second Isaiah, respectively. There are historical, linguistic, and conceptual differences that separate the two. See **Isaiah**.

Shabbat (shah-BAHT): The Hebrew word for "Sabbath," from a word meaning "to desist [from work]" and thus "to rest." Also the name of the tractate of the Mishnah, Tosefta, and Talmud devoted primarily to the laws of the Sabbath.

sheker (SHEH-ker): Lies, that is, deliberately telling someone something that you know to be false.

Shema (sh'-MAH): The central prayer in the first of the three central units in the worship service, the second being the *Amidah* and the third being the reading of the Torah. The *Shema* is comprised of three citations from the Bible: Deuteronomy 6:4–9, Deuteronomy 11:13–21, and Numbers 15:37–41. The larger liturgical unit in which it is embedded (called the *Shema* and Its Blessings) contains also a formal call to prayer (*Bar'khu*) and a series of blessings on the theological themes that, together with the *Shema*, constitute a liturgical creed of faith. *Shema*, meaning "to hear," is the first word of the first line of the first biblical citation, "Hear O Israel, Adonai is our God, Adonai is One," which is the paradigmatic statement of Jewish faith, the Jews' absolute commitment to the presence of a single and unique God in time and space.

Shemoneh Esrei (sh'-MOH-neh ES-ray): A Hebrew word meaning "eighteen," and therefore a name given to the second of the two main units in the worship service that once had eighteen benedictions in it for the weekday service (it now has nineteen); known also as the *Amidah*.

shevu'ot (sheh-voo-OAT): Oaths; also a tractate of the Mishnah, Tosefta, and Talmud dealing primarily with oaths. Not to be confused with Shavu'ot, the Feast of Weeks.

Shulhan Arukh (Shool-KHAN ah-ROOKH or, commonly, SHOOL-khan AH-rookh): The "Set Table," the title of the code of Jewish law by Joseph Karo, completed in 1563. Shortly thereafter, Moses Isserles added additions ("glosses") to indicate where the practice of northern and eastern European Jews (Ashkenazim) differed from those of Mediterranean Jews

(Sephardim) that Karo had articulated in his code. The code is divided into four parts: *Orah Chayyim* (oh-RAHKH KHAH-yim); *Yoreh De'ah* (YOH-reh DAY-ah); *Even ha-Ezer* (EH-ven hah-AY-zehr); and *Choshen Mishpat* (KHOH-shen mish-PAT).

Sifra (seef-RAH): A midrash on the biblical Book of Leviticus, interpreting and expanding its laws in the order of the verses of Leviticus. Some scholars think that it was created in the school of Rabbi Akiva in the second century, but since it is not mentioned in either of the two Talmuds, it was probably edited and written down not earlier than the end of the fourth century in Israel.

Sifre (Seef-RAY): A book of midrash on the biblical books of Numbers and Deuteronomy, including both their legal and nonlegal sections, organized according to the order of those books. Some scholars think that *Sifre* on Numbers was created in the school of Rabbi Ishmael and that *Sifre* on Deuteronomy was created in the school of Rabbi Akiva, both in the second century, but since the *Sifre* is not mentioned in either of the two Talmuds, it was probably edited and written down not earlier than the end of the fourth century in Israel.

Talmud (tahl-MOOD or, commonly, TAHL-m'd): The name given to each of two great compendia of Jewish law and lore compiled from the first to the sixth centuries CE, and ever since, the literary core of the rabbinic heritage. The *Talmud Yerushalmi* (y'-roo-SHAHL-mee), the "Jerusalem Talmud" or "the Palestinian Talmud," is the earlier one, a product of the Land of Israel generally dated about 400 CE. The better-known *Talmud Bavli* (BAHV-lee), or "Babylonian Talmud," took shape in Babylonia (present-day Iraq), and is traditionally dated about 550 CE. When people say "the Talmud" without specifying which one they mean, they are referring to the Babylonian version. The word "Talmud" comes from the Hebrew root meaning to learn and, in a different form, to teach.

TaNaKh: An acronym derived from the initial letters of the three divisions of the Hebrew Bible: Torah (the Five Books of Moses), *Nevi'im* (Prophets), and *Ketuvim* (Writings).

Temple, First and Second: In ancient times, a central building for the worship of God in Israel. The First Temple was built by Solomon, and its construction is described in the first Book of Kings. In 586 BCE, King Nebuchadnezzar and the Babylonians conquered Judah and destroyed the Temple, sending the Jews into exile in Babylonia. In 538 BCE, the Persians conquered the Babylonians, and a small remnant of the Jews returned to

Palestine. Urged on by Zechariah and Haggai, they rebuilt the Temple and reinstated the sacrificial cult. The Temple was destroyed again by the Romans in 70 CE. The building was razed, but the retaining wall of the Temple mount remains to this day as the Western Wall.

tikkun olam (tee-KOON oh-LAHM): Literally, "repairing the world." Today it is commonly used to characterize Jewish forms of social action.

Torah (TOH-rah): Literally, "instruction," "teaching," or "direction." In its narrowest meaning, Torah refers to the first five books of the Bible, also called the "Five Books of Moses," which is read in the synagogue on Monday, Thursday, the Sabbath, and holidays. In this sense, "the Torah" is sometimes used to refer to the parchment scroll on which these books are written for public reading in the synagogue. "Torah" is used also, by extension, to mean all Jewish sacred literature, including books written in the Middle Ages, the modern period, and even contemporary times, and including not only topics of Jewish law but also Jewish literature, thought, history, and ethics. Thus, in this extended meaning, a person is "studying Torah" when he or she is studying these texts as well as classical Jewish literature (the Bible, Mishnah, Talmud, Midrash).

Tosefta (toe-SEF-tah): Literally, "an addition." The Tosefta is an additional compilation to that of the Mishnah of the Jewish oral tradition of laws and customs to the end of the second century CE. It was compiled in the Land of Israel by Rabbis Hiyyah and Oshayah c. 200 CE. Its authority is secondary to that of the Mishnah. See **Mishnah**.

tractate: The term commonly used for a book of the Mishnah, Tosefta, or Talmud, so called because each tractate is a treatise on a specific area of Jewish law.

tzedek (TZEH-dek), **tzedakah** (tzeh-dah-KAH or, commonly, tzeh-DAH-kah): Justice, with a secondary meaning of acts of supporting the poor or other worthy causes, such as schools.

Zechariah: One of the twelve minor prophetic books of the Bible dated from the sixth century BCE, though there is disagreement as to dating. Zechariah was one of the three prophets to accompany the exiled Jews who returned from Babylon to Jerusalem in 538 BCE. He prophesied, together with Haggai and Malachi, in the second year of the reign of King Darius of Persia.

SUGGESTIONS FOR FURTHER READING

These suggested references are divided into the various aspects of *tikkun olam* that each chapter covers. A given entry may be repeated if it is relevant to the topics of more than one chapter. These are clearly *selected* references; on many of these topics, tens, if not hundreds, of books have been written. Because the goal of this volume is to introduce Jewish thought on these matters to Christians, along with some comparative Christian thought, these suggestions focus on Jewish writings.

1 THE MEANING AND SIGNIFICANCE OF *TIKKUN OLAM*

Agus, Jacob B. *The Vision and the Way: An Interpretation of Jewish Ethics*. New York: Frederick Ungar Publishing Company, 1966.

Berkovits, Eliezer. *Not in Heaven: The Nature and Function of Halakha*. New York: Ktav, 1983.

Borowitz, Eugene. *The Jewish Moral Virtues*. Philadelphia: Jewish Publication Society, 1999.

————, ed. *Reform Jewish Ethics & the Halakhah: An Experiment in Decision Making*. West Orange, NJ: Behrman House, 1988.

Cohen, A. *Everyman's Talmud*. New York: E. P. Dutton & Co., 1949, chaps. 3 ("The Doctrine of Man") and 6 ("Social Life").

Dorff, Elliot N. *To Do the Right and the Good: A Jewish Approach to Modern Social Ethics*. Philadelphia: Jewish Publication Society, 2002.

————. *The Way Into Tikkun Olam* (Repairing the World). Woodstock, VT: Jewish Lights Publishing, 2007.

Freund, Richard A. *Understanding Jewish Ethics*. San Francisco: EMText, 1990.

Friedman, Shalom. *Small Acts of Kindness: Striving for Derech Eretz in Everyday Life*. Jerusalem and New York: Urim, 2004.

Jacobs, Louis. *Jewish Personal and Social Ethics*. West Orange, NJ: Behrman House, 1990.

Kaplan, Mordecai M. *The Future of the American Jew*. New York: Macmillan, 1948 (repr. by New York: Reconstructionist Press, 1967), especially chap. 15 ("Basic Values in Jewish Religion").

Novak, David. *Jewish Social Ethics*. New York: Oxford University Press, 1992.

Rose, Or N., Jo Ellen Green Kaiser and Margie Klein, eds. *Righteous Indignation: A Jewish Call for Justice*. Woodstock, VT: Jewish Lights Publishing, 2008.

Schulweis, Harold M. *Conscience: The Duty to Obey and the Duty to Disobey*. Woodstock, VT: Jewish Lights Publishing, 2008.

Schwarz, Sidney. *Judaism and Justice: The Jewish Passion to Repair the World*. Woodstock, VT: Jewish Lights Publishing, 2008.

Shatz, David, Chaim I. Waxman, and Nathan J. Diament, eds. *Tikkun Olam: Social Responsibility in Jewish Thought and Law*. Northvale, NJ: Jason Aronson, 1997.

Sherwin, Byron L. *In Partnership with God: Contemporary Jewish Law and Ethics*. Syracuse, NY: Syracuse University Press, 1990.

———. *Jewish Ethics for the Twenty-First Century*. Syracuse, NY: Syracuse University Press, 2000.

Sherwin, Byron L. and Seymour J. Cohen. *Creating an Ethical Jewish Life: A Practical Introduction to Classic Teachings on How to Be a Jew*. Woodstock, VT: Jewish Lights Publishing, 2001.

Sidorsky, David, ed. *Essays on Human Rights: Contemporary Issues and Jewish Perspectives*. Philadelphia: Jewish Publication Society, 1979.

Vorspan, Albert, and David Saperstein. *Jewish Dimensions of Social Justice: Tough Moral Choices in a New Millenium*. New York: Union of American Hebrew Congregations Press, 1998.

Weiss, Avraham. *Spiritual Activism: A Jewish Guide to Leadership and Repairing the World.* Woodstock, VT: Jewish Lights Publishing, 2008.

2 WHY SHOULD I CARE: THE EXAMPLE OF CARING FOR THE POOR

Jewish materials on why we should care:

Dorff, Elliot N. *Mitzvah Means Commandment.* New York: United Synagogue of America, 1989 (on the motivations delineated in the Bible and rabbinic literature to live by Jewish law, including the laws that demand that we care for the poor).

————. *For the Love of God and People: A Philosophy of Jewish Law.* Philadelphia: Jewish Publication Society, 2007, chap. 4 (a more concise exposition than *Mitzvah Means Commandment* on the motivations to live by Jewish law, including the laws that demand that we care for the poor).

Jewish materials on poverty:

Bonner, Michael David. *Poverty and Charity in Middle Eastern Contexts.* Albany: State University of New York Press, 2003.

Cottle, Thomas. *Hidden Survivors: Portraits of Poor Jews in America.* Englewood Cliffs, NJ: Prentice-Hall, 1980.

Dorff, Elliot N. *To Do the Right and the Good: A Jewish Approach to Modern Social Ethics.* Philadelphia: Jewish Publication Society, 2002, chap. 6 ("Substantive Justice: A Jewish Approach to Poverty").

Gamaron, Hillel, ed. *Jewish Law Association Studies XIV: The Jerusalem 2002 Conference Volume.* Binghamton, NY: Global Academic Publishers, Binghamton University, 2002.

Hirsch, Richard. *There Shall Be No Poor.* New York: Union of American Hebrew Congregations, Commission on Social Action of Reform Judaism, 1965.

Neusner, Jacob. *Tzedakah: Can Jewish Philanthropy Buy Jewish Survival?* Chappaqua, NY: Rossel Books, 1982.

The Poor Among Us: Jewish Tradition and Social Policy. New York: American Jewish Committee, 1986.

3 The Power of Words

Dorff, Elliot N. *Matters of Life and Death: A Jewish Approach to Modern Medical Ethics.* Philadelphia: Jewish Publication Society, 1998, especially 255–64.

Grinald, Ze'ev. *Ta'haras Halashon: A Guide to the Laws of Lashon Hara and Rechilus.* New York and Jerusalem: Feldheim, 1994.

Pliskin, Zelig. *Guard Your Tongue: A Practical Guide to the Laws of Loshon Hora Based on Chofetz Chayim.* Brooklyn: Pliskin, 1975.

Potok, Chaim. *The Ethics of Language.* New York: Leaders Training Fellowship of the Jewish Theological Seminary of America, 1964.

Telushkin, Joseph. *Words That Hurt, Words That Heal: How to Choose Words Wisely and Well.* New York: William Morrow, 1996.

4 The Ministry of Presence

Cohen, A. *Everyman's Talmud.* New York: E. P. Dutton & Co., 1949, chap. 8 ("The Physical Life").

Dorff, Elliot N. *Matters of Life and Death: A Jewish Approach to Modern Medical Ethics.* Philadelphia: Jewish Publication Society, 1998. See especially pp. 255–264.

Mackler, Aaron, ed. *Introduction to Jewish and Catholic Bioethics: A Comparative Analysis.* Washington, DC: Georgetown University Press, 2003.

———. *Life and Death Responsibilities in Jewish Biomedical Ethics.* New York: Jewish Theological Seminary of America, 2000.

Steinberg, Avraham. *Encyclopedia of Jewish Medical Ethics.* Fred Rosner, trans. Jerusalem and New York: Feldheim Publishers, 2003, 3 vols.

Teutsch, David. *Bioethics: Reinvigorating the Practice of Contemporary Jewish Ethics.* Wyncote, PA: Reconstructionist Rabbinical College, 2005.

5,6,7 Duties of Spouses to Each Other, Children's Duties to Their Parents, and Parent's Duties to Their Children

Biale, Rachel. *Women & Jewish Law: An Exploration of Women's Issues in Halakhic Sources.* New York: Schocken, 1984.

Blidstein, Gerald. *Honor Thy Father and Mother.* New York: Ktav, 1975.

Cohen, A. *Everyman's Talmud.* New York: E. P. Dutton & Co., 1949, chap. 5 ("Domestic Life").

Dorff, Elliot N. *Love Your Neighbor and Yourself: A Jewish Approach to Modern Personal Ethics.* Philadelphia: Jewish Publication Society, 2003, chaps. 3 ("Sex and the Family"), 4 ("Parents and Children"), and 5 ("Family Violence").

Gratz, Naomi. *Silence Is Deadly: Judaism Confronts Wifebeating.* Northvale, NJ: Jason Aronson, 1998.

Hauptman, Judith. *Rereading the Rabbis: A Woman's Voice.* Boulder, CO: Westview, 1998.

Isaacs, Leora W. *Jewish Family Matters: A Leader's Guide.* New York: United Synagogue of Conservative Judaism, Commission on Jewish Education, 1994.

Isaacs, Ronald H. *Every Person's Guide to Jewish Sexuality.* Northvale, NJ: Jason Aronson, 2000.

Kramer, David, ed. *The Jewish Family: Metaphor and Memory.* New York: Oxford University Press, 1989.

Lev, Rachel. *Shine the Light: Sexual Abuse and Healing in the Jewish Community.* Boston: Northeastern University Press, 2003.

Spirituality/Lawrence Kushner

Filling Words with Light: Hasidic and Mystical Reflections on Jewish Prayer
By Lawrence Kushner and Nehemia Polen
5½ x 8½, 176 pp, Quality PB, 978-1-58023-238-8 **$16.99**; HC, 978-1-58023-216-6 **$21.99**

The Book of Letters: A Mystical Hebrew Alphabet
Popular HC Edition, 6 x 9, 80 pp, 2-color text, 978-1-879045-00-2 **$24.95**
Collector's Limited Edition, 9 x 12, 80 pp, gold foil embossed pages, w/limited edition silkscreened
print, 978-1-879045-04-0 **$349.00**

The Book of Miracles: A Young Person's Guide to Jewish Spiritual Awareness
6 x 9, 96 pp, 2-color illus., HC, 978-1-879045-78-1 **$16.95** For ages 9 and up

The Book of Words: Talking Spiritual Life, Living Spiritual Talk
6 x 9, 160 pp, Quality PB, 978-1-58023-020-9 **$16.95**

Eyes Remade for Wonder: A Lawrence Kushner Reader Introduction by Thomas Moore
6 x 9, 240 pp, Quality PB, 978-1-58023-042-1 **$18.95**

God Was in This Place & I, i Did Not Know: Finding Self, Spirituality and
Ultimate Meaning 6 x 9, 192 pp, Quality PB, 978-1-879045-33-0 **$16.95**

Honey from the Rock: An Introduction to Jewish Mysticism
6 x 9, 176 pp, Quality PB, 978-1-58023-073-5 **$16.95**

Invisible Lines of Connection: Sacred Stories of the Ordinary
5½ x 8½, 160 pp, Quality PB, 978-1-879045-98-9 **$15.95**

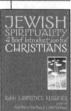

Jewish Spirituality—A Brief Introduction for Christians
5½ x 8½, 112 pp, Quality PB, 978-1-58023-150-3 **$12.95**

The River of Light: Jewish Mystical Awareness
6 x 9, 192 pp, Quality PB, 978-1-58023-096-4 **$16.95**

The Way Into Jewish Mystical Tradition
6 x 9, 224 pp, Quality PB, 978-1-58023-200-5 **$18.99**; HC, 978-1-58023-029-2 **$21.95**

Spirituality / Crafts

(from SkyLight Paths, our sister imprint)

The Knitting Way: A Guide to Spiritual Self-Discovery
by Linda Skolnik and Janice MacDaniels
Examines how you can explore and strengthen your spiritual life
through knitting.
7 x 9, 240 pp, Quality PB, b/w photographs, 978-1-59473-079-5 **$16.99**

The Scrapbooking Journey: A Hands-On Guide to Spiritual
Discovery by Cory Richardson-Lauve; Foreword by Stacy Julian
Reveals how this craft can become a practice used to deepen and shape
your life.
7 x 9, 176 pp, Quality PB, 8-page full-color insert, plus b/w photographs
978-1-59473-216-4 **$18.99**

The Painting Path: Embodying Spiritual Discovery through Yoga,
Brush and Color by Linda Novick; Foreword by Richard Segalman
Explores the divine connection you can experience through creativity.
7 x 9, 208 pp, 8-page full-color insert, plus b/w photographs
Quality PB, 978-1-59473-226-3 **$18.99**

The Quilting Path: A Guide to Spiritual Discovery through Fabric,
Thread and Kabbalah by Louise Silk
Explores how to cultivate personal growth through quilt making.
7 x 9, 192 pp, Quality PB, b/w photographs and illustrations, 978-1-59473-206-5 **$16.99**

Contemplative Crochet
A Hands-On Guide for Interlocking Faith and Craft
by Cindy Crandall-Frazier; Foreword by Linda Skolnik
Illuminates the spiritual lessons you can learn through crocheting.
7 x 9, 208 pp, b/w photographs, Quality PB, 978-1-59473-238-6 **$16.99**

Inspiration

Happiness and the Human Spirit: The Spirituality of Becoming the Best You Can Be *By Abraham J. Twerski, MD*
Shows you that true happiness is attainable once you stop looking outside yourself for the source. 6 x 9, 176 pp, HC, 978-1-58023-343-9 **$19.99**

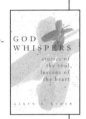

The Bridge to Forgiveness: Stories and Prayers for Finding God and Restoring Wholeness *By Rabbi Karyn D. Kedar*
Examines how forgiveness can be the bridge that connects us to wholeness and peace.
6 x 9, 176 pp, HC, 978-1-58023-324-8 **$19.99**

God's To-Do List: 103 Ways to Be an Angel and Do God's Work on Earth
By Dr. Ron Wolfson 6 x 9, 150 pp, Quality PB, 978-1-58023-301-9 **$16.99**

God in All Moments: Mystical & Practical Spiritual Wisdom from Hasidic Masters
Edited and translated by Or N. Rose with Ebn D. Leader
5½ x 8½, 192 pp, Quality PB, 978-1-58023-186-2 **$16.95**

Our Dance with God: Finding Prayer, Perspective and Meaning in the Stories of Our Lives *By Karyn D. Kedar* 6 x 9, 176 pp, Quality PB, 978-1-58023-202-9 **$16.99**
Also Available: **The Dance of the Dolphin** (HC edition of *Our Dance with God*)
6 x 9, 176 pp, HC, 978-1-58023-154-1 **$19.95**

The Empty Chair: Finding Hope and Joy—Timeless Wisdom from a Hasidic Master, Rebbe Nachman of Breslov *Adapted by Moshe Mykoff and the Breslov Research Institute*
4 x 6, 128 pp, 2-color text, Deluxe PB w/flaps, 978-1-879045-67-5 **$9.99**

The Gentle Weapon: Prayers for Everyday and Not-So-Everyday Moments—
Timeless Wisdom from the Teachings of the Hasidic Master, Rebbe Nachman of Breslov
Adapted by Moshe Mykoff and S. C. Mizrahi, together with the Breslov Research Institute
4 x 6, 144 pp, 2-color text, Deluxe PB w/flaps, 978-1-58023-022-3 **$9.99**

God Whispers: Stories of the Soul, Lessons of the Heart *By Karyn D. Kedar*
6 x 9, 176 pp, Quality PB, 978-1-58023-088-9 **$15.95**

Restful Reflections: Nighttime Inspiration to Calm the Soul, Based on Jewish Wisdom
By Rabbi Kerry M. Olitzky & Rabbi Lori Forman 4½ x 6½, 448 pp, Quality PB, 978-1-58023-091-9 **$15.95**

Sacred Intentions: Daily Inspiration to Strengthen the Spirit, Based on Jewish Wisdom
By Rabbi Kerry M. Olitzky and Rabbi Lori Forman 4½ x 6½, 448 pp, Quality PB, 978-1-58023-061-2 **$15.95**

Kabbalah/Mysticism/Enneagram

Awakening to Kabbalah: The Guiding Light of Spiritual Fulfillment
By Rav Michael Laitman, PhD 6 x 9, 192 pp, HC, 978-1-58023-264-7 **$21.99**

Seek My Face: A Jewish Mystical Theology *By Arthur Green*
6 x 9, 304 pp, Quality PB, 978-1-58023-130-5 **$19.95**

Zohar: Annotated & Explained
Translation and annotation by Daniel C. Matt; Foreword by Andrew Harvey
5½ x 8½, 176 pp, Quality PB, 978-1-893361-51-5 **$15.99** *(A SkyLight Paths book)*

Ehyeh: A Kabbalah for Tomorrow
By Arthur Green 6 x 9, 224 pp, Quality PB, 978-1-58023-213-5 **$16.99**

The Flame of the Heart: Prayers of a Chasidic Mystic *By Reb Noson of Breslov. Translated by David Sears with the Breslov Research Institute* 5 x 7¼, 160 pp, Quality PB, 978-1-58023-246-3 **$15.99**

The Gift of Kabbalah: Discovering the Secrets of Heaven, Renewing Your Life on Earth
By Tamar Frankiel, PhD 6 x 9, 256 pp, Quality PB, 978-1-58023-141-1 **$16.95;**
HC, 978-1-58023-108-4 **$21.95**

Kabbalah: A Brief Introduction for Christians
By Tamar Frankiel, PhD 5½ x 8½, 208 pp, Quality PB, 978-1-58023-303-3 **$16.99**

The Lost Princess and Other Kabbalistic Tales of Rebbe Nachman of Breslov
The Seven Beggars and Other Kabbalistic Tales of Rebbe Nachman of Breslov
Translated by Rabbi Aryeh Kaplan; Preface by Rabbi Chaim Kramer
Lost Princess: 6 x 9, 400 pp, Quality PB, 978-1-58023-217-3 **$18.99**
Seven Beggars: 6 x 9, 192 pp, Quality PB, 978-1-58023-250-0 **$16.99**

See also *The Way Into Jewish Mystical Tradition* in Spirituality / The Way Into... Series

Spirituality

Journeys to a Jewish Life: Inspiring Stories from the Spiritual Journeys of American Jews *By Paula Amann*
Examines the soul treks of Jews lost and found. 6 x 9, 208 pp, HC, 978-1-58023-317-0 **$19.99**

The Adventures of Rabbi Harvey: A Graphic Novel of Jewish Wisdom and Wit in the Wild West *By Steve Sheinkin*
Jewish and American folktales combine in this witty and original graphic novel collection. Creatively retold and set on the western frontier of the 1870s.
6 x 9, 144 pp, Full-color illus., Quality PB, 978-1-58023-310-1 **$16.99**
Also Available: **The Adventures of Rabbi Harvey Teacher's Guide**
8½ x 11, 32 pp, PB, 978-1-58023-326-2 **$8.99**

Ethics of the Sages: Pirke Avot—Annotated & Explained
Translation and Annotation by Rabbi Rami Shapiro
5½ x 8½, 192 pp, Quality PB, 978-1-59473-207-2 **$16.99** *(A SkyLight Paths book)*

A Book of Life: Embracing Judaism as a Spiritual Practice
By Michael Strassfeld 6 x 9, 528 pp, Quality PB, 978-1-58023-247-0 **$19.99**

Meaning and Mitzvah: Daily Practices for Reclaiming Judaism through Prayer, God, Torah, Hebrew, Mitzvot and Peoplehood *By Rabbi Goldie Milgram*
7 x 9, 336 pp, Quality PB, 978-1-58023-256-2 **$19.99**

The Soul of the Story: Meetings with Remarkable People
By Rabbi David Zeller 6 x 9, 288 pp, HC, 978-1-58023-272-2 **$21.99**

Aleph-Bet Yoga: Embodying the Hebrew Letters for Physical and Spiritual Well-Being
By Steven A. Rapp. Foreword by Tamar Frankiel, PhD and Judy Greenfeld. Preface by Hart Lazer.
7 x 10, 128 pp, b/w photos, Quality PB, Layflat binding, 978-1-58023-162-6 **$16.95**

Does the Soul Survive? A Jewish Journey to Belief in Afterlife, Past Lives & Living with Purpose *By Rabbi Elie Kaplan Spitz; Foreword by Brian L. Weiss, MD*
6 x 9, 288 pp, Quality PB, 978-1-58023-165-7 **$16.99**

First Steps to a New Jewish Spirit: Reb Zalman's Guide to Recapturing the Intimacy & Ecstasy in Your Relationship with God *By Rabbi Zalman M. Schachter-Shalomi with Donald Gropman* 6 x 9, 144 pp, Quality PB, 978-1-58023-182-4 **$16.95**

God in Our Relationships: Spirituality between People from the Teachings of Martin Buber *By Rabbi Dennis S. Ross* 5½ x 8½, 160 pp, Quality PB, 978-1-58023-147-3 **$16.95**

Judaism, Physics and God: Searching for Sacred Metaphors in a Post-Einstein World
By Rabbi David W. Nelson 6 x 9, 368 pp, Quality PB, inc. reader's discussion guide, 978-1-58023-306-4 **$18.99**;
HC, 352 pp, 978-1-58023-252-4 **$24.99**

The Jewish Lights Spirituality Handbook: A Guide to Understanding, Exploring & Living a Spiritual Life *Edited by Stuart M. Matlins*
What exactly is "Jewish" about spirituality? How do I make it a part of my life? Fifty of today's foremost spiritual leaders share their ideas and experience with us.
6 x 9, 456 pp, Quality PB, 978-1-58023-093-3 **$19.99**

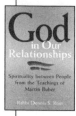

Bringing the Psalms to Life: How to Understand and Use the Book of Psalms
By Daniel F. Polish 6 x 9, 208 pp, Quality PB, 978-1-58023-157-2 **$16.95**;
HC, 978-1-58023-077-3 **$21.95**

God & the Big Bang: Discovering Harmony between Science & Spirituality
By Daniel C. Matt 6 x 9, 216 pp, Quality PB, 978-1-879045-89-7 **$16.99**

Minding the Temple of the Soul: Balancing Body, Mind, and Spirit through Traditional Jewish Prayer, Movement, and Meditation *By Tamar Frankiel, PhD, and Judy Greenfeld*
7 x 10, 184 pp, illus., Quality PB, 978-1-879045-64-4 **$16.95**
Audiotape of the Blessings and Meditations: 60 min. **$9.95**
Videotape of the Movements and Meditations: 46 min. **$20.00**

One God Clapping: The Spiritual Path of a Zen Rabbi *By Alan Lew with Sherril Jaffe*
5½ x 8½, 336 pp, Quality PB, 978-1-58023-115-2 **$16.95**

There Is No Messiah ... and You're It: The Stunning Transformation of Judaism's Most Provocative Idea *By Rabbi Robert N. Levine, DD*
6 x 9, 192 pp, Quality PB, 978-1-58023-255-5 **$16.95**

These Are the Words: A Vocabulary of Jewish Spiritual Life
By Arthur Green 6 x 9, 304 pp, Quality PB, 978-1-58023-107-7 **$18.95**

Theology/Philosophy/The Way Into... Series

The Way Into... series offers an accessible and highly usable "guided tour" of the Jewish faith, people, history and beliefs—in total, an introduction to Judaism that will enable you to understand and interact with the sacred texts of the Jewish tradition. Each volume is written by a leading contemporary scholar and teacher, and explores one key aspect of Judaism. *The Way Into...* series enables all readers to achieve a real sense of Jewish cultural literacy through guided study.

The Way Into Encountering God in Judaism

By Neil Gillman
For everyone who wants to understand how Jews have encountered God throughout history and today.
6 x 9, 240 pp, Quality PB, 978-1-58023-199-2 **$18.99**; HC, 978-1-58023-025-4 **$21.95**

Also Available: **The Jewish Approach to God:** A Brief Introduction for Christians
By Neil Gillman
5½ x 8½, 192 pp, Quality PB, 978-1-58023-190-9 **$16.95**

The Way Into Jewish Mystical Tradition

By Lawrence Kushner
Allows readers to interact directly with the sacred mystical text of the Jewish tradition. An accessible introduction to the concepts of Jewish mysticism, their religious and spiritual significance and how they relate to life today.
6 x 9, 224 pp, Quality PB, 978-1-58023-200-5 **$18.99**; HC, 978-1-58023-029-2 **$21.95**

The Way Into Jewish Prayer

By Lawrence A. Hoffman
Opens the door to 3,000 years of Jewish prayer, making available all anyone needs to feel at home in the Jewish way of communicating with God.
6 x 9, 208 pp, Quality PB, 978-1-58023-201-2 **$18.99**

Also Available: **The Way Into Jewish Prayer Teacher's Guide**
By Rabbi Jennifer Ossakow Goldsmith
8½ x 11, 42 pp, PB, 978-1-58023-345-3 **$8.99**
Visit our website to download a free copy.

The Way Into Judaism and the Environment

By Jeremy Benstein
Explores the ways in which Judaism contributes to contemporary social-environmental issues, the extent to which Judaism is part of the problem and how it can be part of the solution.
6 x 9, 288 pp, HC, 978-1-58023-268-5 **$24.99**

The Way Into *Tikkun Olam* (Repairing the World)

By Elliot N. Dorff
An accessible introduction to the Jewish concept of the individual's responsibility to care for others and repair the world.
6 x 9, 320 pp, HC, 978-1-58023-269-2 **$24.99**; 304 pp, Quality PB, 978-1-58023-328-6 **$18.99**

The Way Into Torah

By Norman J. Cohen
Helps guide in the exploration of the origins and development of Torah, explains why it should be studied and how to do it.
6 x 9, 176 pp, Quality PB, 978-1-58023-198-5 **$16.99**

The Way Into the Varieties of Jewishness

By Sylvia Barack Fishman, PhD
Explores the religious and historical understanding of what it has meant to be Jewish from ancient times to the present controversy over "Who is a Jew?"
6 x 9, 288 pp, HC, 978-1-58023-030-8 **$24.99**

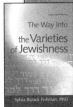

Theology/Philosophy

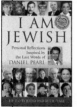

I Am Jewish
Personal Reflections Inspired by the Last Words of Daniel Pearl
Almost 150 Jews—both famous and not—from all walks of life, from all around the world, write about many aspects of their Judaism.
Edited by Judea and Ruth Pearl
6 x 9, 304 pp, Deluxe PB w/flaps, 978-1-58023-259-3 **$18.99**
Download a free copy of the *I Am Jewish Teacher's Guide* at our website:
www.jewishlights.com

A Touch of the Sacred: A Theologian's Informal Guide to Jewish Belief
By Dr. Eugene B. Borowitz and Frances W. Schwartz Explores the musings from the leading theologian of liberal Judaism. 6 x 9, 256 pp, HC, 978-1-58023-337-8 **$21.99**

Talking about God: Exploring the Meaning of Religious Life with Kierkegaard, Buber, Tillich and Heschel *By Daniel F. Polish, PhD*
Examines the meaning of the human religious experience with the greatest theologians of modern times. 6 x 9, 160 pp, HC, 978-1-59473-230-0 **$21.99** *(A SkyLight Paths book)*

Jews & Judaism in the 21st Century: Human Responsibility, the Presence of God, and the Future of the Covenant
Edited by Rabbi Edward Feinstein; Foreword by Paula E. Hyman
Five celebrated leaders in Judaism examine contemporary Jewish life.
6 x 9, 192 pp, HC, 978-1-58023-315-6 **$24.99**

The Death of Death: Resurrection and Immortality in Jewish Thought
By Neil Gillman 6 x 9, 336 pp, Quality PB, 978-1-58023-081-0 **$18.95**

Ethics of the Sages: Pirke Avot—Annotated & Explained
Translation & Annotation by Rabbi Rami Shapiro
5½ x 8½, 208 pp, Quality PB, 978-1-59473-207-2 **$16.99** *(A SkyLight Paths book)*

Hasidic Tales: Annotated & Explained
By Rabbi Rami Shapiro; Foreword by Andrew Harvey
5½ x 8½, 240 pp, Quality PB, 978-1-893361-86-7 **$16.95** *(A SkyLight Paths Book)*

A Heart of Many Rooms: Celebrating the Many Voices within Judaism
By David Hartman 6 x 9, 352 pp, Quality PB, 978-1-58023-156-5 **$19.95**

The Hebrew Prophets: Selections Annotated & Explained
Translation & Annotation by Rabbi Rami Shapiro; Foreword by Zalman M. Schachter-Shalomi
5½ x 8½, 224 pp, Quality PB, 978-1-59473-037-5 **$16.99** *(A SkyLight Paths book)*

Keeping Faith with the Psalms: Deepen Your Relationship with God Using the Book of Psalms *By Daniel F. Polish* 6 x 9, 320 pp, Quality PB, 978-1-58023-300-2 **$18.99**

A Living Covenant: The Innovative Spirit in Traditional Judaism
By David Hartman 6 x 9, 368 pp, Quality PB, 978-1-58023-011-7 **$20.00**

Love and Terror in the God Encounter
The Theological Legacy of Rabbi Joseph B. Soloveitchik
By David Hartman 6 x 9, 240 pp, Quality PB, 978-1-58023-176-3 **$19.95**

The Personhood of God: Biblical Theology, Human Faith and the Divine Image
By Dr. Yochanan Muffs; Foreword by Dr. David Hartman 6 x 9, 240 pp, HC, 978-1-58023-265-4 **$24.99**

Traces of God: Seeing God in Torah, History and Everyday Life
By Neil Gillman 6 x 9, 240 pp, HC, 978-1-58023-249-4 **$21.99**

Your Word Is Fire: The Hasidic Masters on Contemplative Prayer
Edited and translated by Arthur Green and Barry W. Holtz
6 x 9, 160 pp, Quality PB, 978-1-879045-25-5 **$15.95**

Travel

Israel—A Spiritual Travel Guide, 2nd Edition
A Companion for the Modern Jewish Pilgrim
By Rabbi Lawrence A. Hoffman 4¾ x 10, 256 pp, Quality PB, illus., 978-1-58023-261-6 **$18.99**
Also Available: **The Israel Mission Leader's Guide** 978-1-58023-085-8 **$4.95**